Money Matters
Personal Giving in American Churches

DEAN R. HOGE
CHARLES E. ZECH
PATRICK H. MCNAMARA
MICHAEL J. DONAHUE

Westminster John Knox Press
Louisville, Kentucky

Book design by Jennifer K. Cox
Cover design by Kevin Darst

First edition

Published by Westminster John Knox Press
Louisville, Kentucky

This book is printed on acid free paper that meets the American National Standards Institute Z39.48 standard. ∞

PRINTED IN THE UNITED STATES OF AMERICA

96 97 98 99 00 01 02 03 04 05 — 10 9 8 7 6 5 4 3 2 1

Library of Congress Cataloging-in-Publication Data

Money Matters : personal giving in American churches / Dean R. Hoge
. . . [et al.} . . . —1st ed.
          p.   cm.
    Includes bibliographical references and index.
    ISBN 0-664-25687-2 (alk. paper)
    1. Christian giving.   2. Christian giving—Case studies.   3. United States—
Religious life and customs.   I. Hoge. Dean R. date.
BV772.M527   1996
248'.6'0973—dc20   96-22896

Money Matters

The authors would like to thank their wives—
Josephine, Ann, Joan, and Joanne—for all of their support and advice.

———⋅✦⋅———

They made everything better and easier.

Contents

Tables and Figures

TABLES

FIGURES

Introduction

The phrase "give generously" is a reminder most American church-goers have always heeded well. Full collection plates and baskets traditionally testified to a sense of loyalty toward one's church, matched by few other institutions in society. This was the situation throughout much of American history, from frontier settlements to established urban neighborhoods.

Today, however, things seem to be changing. At a time when baby boomers are assuming leadership within churches, studies tell us that young adults are less loyal to their denominations than their parents were. Baby boomers switch churches more frequently than any previous group, and as members, they want more control than ever over how their contributions are spent. The era when people gave large sums to denominational leaders with implicit trust is fading fast. Generous giving can no longer be taken for granted.

Yet some denominations and local churches seem quite unaffected by these trends. The Assemblies of God and the Southern Baptist Convention, as we shall see, successfully maintain the ideal of tithing for many of their members. Some mainline congregations are flourishing as well. But many are not. We have much more to say about these trends in this book.

STUDYING CONGREGATIONAL GIVING

Research requires funding. The Lilly Endowment is one of the few large foundations to have as a part of its mission "to support the causes of religion, education and community development."[1] In recent years the endowment has sought to assist church leaders in adjusting to a changing financial climate. In 1990 it announced research grants to investigate trends in church finances. The authors of this book proposed to the endowment an interdenominational study that would examine the factors that influence the levels of religious giving, and in 1992 the endowment awarded us a grant. The study we proposed was the most extensive ever done on this topic.

Designing any research study requires a series of decisions and judgment calls. In this study, four major decisions were made early in the process. First, we were aware that current trends in church finances reflect two factors: (1) a shift in the levels of individual and household giving and (2) a shift in congregational decisions about allocation of the money that comes in. The latter trend seemed to us more difficult to research and also less urgent, so we limited ourselves to the former and gave our attention entirely to identifying factors that encourage or discourage individual giving. Therefore our research investigates what factors influence church members in their decision to make contributions to the church; it does not investigate how churches allocate and spend the money that comes in.

Second, we chose to focus on interdenominational comparisons. This was partly because levels of giving differ from one denomination to another and partly because each denomination would benefit by seeing itself in comparison with others. Which denominations? How many? Some of our advisers argued for a large number, to make the study more comprehensive; others favored a cost-conscious approach, pointing out that an eight-denomination study would cost twice as much as a four-denomination one but would not be twice as valuable. In addition, some denominations—such as The Church of Jesus Christ of Latter-day Saints (Mormons)—have church polity and practice that are so distinct that to include them would not be instructive to other denominations. After much discussion, we settled on five denominations: the Assemblies of God, the Southern Baptist Convention, the Roman Catholic Church, the Evangelical Lutheran Church in America (ELCA), and the Presbyterian Church (U.S.A). The Presbyterians and Lutherans represent mainline Protestant denominations that are experiencing financial changes. The Baptists and Assemblies of God are two conservative Protestant denominations with strong giving patterns. The Catholic Church is important because of its size, unique congregational polity, and low level of giving.

Third, we discussed how to gather new data. We decided on a nationwide study in which data were gathered from nine sampling areas, one for each U.S. Census region. We concluded that either we or trained field workers would have to visit each congregation or parish, and we would have to conduct small surveys of members in each congregation. In the summer of 1992, we pretested methods of gathering congregational information and of surveying laypersons, by both mail and phone. For the lay survey we chose a mailed questionnaire, using machine-readable forms.

When we approached the denominations concerning their level of participation, we did, however, encounter some resistance. In our attempts to ask some sensitive questions about finances, as well as about congregational and denominational leadership, it became clear to us that we would have to ensure confidentiality to all levels of church governance and polity, as well as to all participants. We did so. The names of all individuals, churches, pastors, and towns involved in our research are confidential and have been changed for this book.

Fourth, gathering data directly from church members by mailed questionnaires is probably the best available method, but it is not free from error. Large biases may sneak in. As an alternative source of information, and also as a "validity check" on our survey of church members, we commissioned a nationally representative Gallup poll. It interviewed one thousand persons by telephone who described themselves as members of the three largest denominations in our study—Baptist, Catholic, and Lutheran. The poll included many of the same questions we asked in the church-member questionnaire and thus gave us a check on the biases in our lay survey.

But nationwide telephone surveys are also not free from bias and have their limitations. Random-digit dialing typically yields about sixty to seventy completed interviews for every one hundred eligible persons reached, and it entirely omits persons who do not have phones. Yet the shortcomings of phone surveys are of a different sort from those of mailed surveys, and each of the methods of data collection provides a useful check on the other.

SAMPLING THE CONGREGATIONS AND GATHERING THE DATA

We developed and pretested a nine-page Congregation Profile Booklet (see Appendix B), which asked each congregation questions regarding its size, location, organized groups and programs, receipts and expenditures in the previous year, stewardship programs, debts, endowments, theological teachings, and so on. We also developed a four-page questionnaire to be mailed to a random sample of members in each congregation. It included fifty-six questions about the congregation, the denomination, stewardship, leadership, attitudes regarding giving, and so on. It asked information on the member's church involvement, financial giving, and level of satisfaction with the congregation. It did not, however, ask the respondent's name.

By late summer of 1992, we had done enough pretesting to be confident with the research methods. Deciding to study 125 congregations per denomination, we randomly selected one sampling area in each of the nine U.S. Census regions. We calculated the proportion of each denomination's churches located in each sampling area.

Between January and July 1993, we traveled to all of the sampling areas, met with leaders of the denominations, selected a random sample of congregations for the study, hired and trained field workers, and, in some instances, met with groups of pastors to explain the study. The field workers contacted the pastors and tried to secure their cooperation. We succeeded in including 84.8 percent of the churches that were in our initial sample lists. Any church that refused to participate was replaced by another that matched, as closely as possible, the initial church's location and size.

The field workers visited the churches that had agreed to cooperate, and working together, the field workers and pastors completed the Congregation Profile Booklets, which we had sent to the pastors earlier. Then the field workers gathered a random sample of thirty members from the church rolls. To these members we then mailed the lay questionnaire. We received a return rate of 61.2 percent, which is somewhat higher than typical for this kind of research study. Data collection was finished by early 1994.

Between late 1993 and early 1995 we studied twelve congregations in depth. We selected congregations nominated by denominational officers as being successful and exemplary. Each of us chose different churches and visited them repeatedly, gathering documents and interviewing the pastor and numerous parishioners.

SCOPE OF THE STUDY

Formulating the questionnaires themselves called for decision making about various kinds of giving. Should we include religious giving outside of congregations and parishes, for example, money sent directly to Maryknoll Missions or to Church World Service? Should we include giving to projects that are more humanitarian than purely religious, such as Habitat for Humanity? Should we include the annual diocesan appeal, found in most Catholic dioceses, or Peter's Pence, the annual appeal for funds going directly to the Vatican? Religious appeals today come in all shapes and sizes, as anyone will see when his or her name gets onto computerized mailing lists. For example, a gift of a few dollars to one Catholic mission program will open one's mailbox to dozens of appeals from other Catholic causes in the next year. We found it was easy to include all these forms of giving in our lay questionnaire, so we did so. But we decided against a serious study of the receipts and practices of these organizations. Our information is solely from our surveys of laypersons and pastors.

Capital campaigns were another issue that demanded a decision about inclusion in our research. Most churches engage in capital campaigns at some time or other, usually when putting up a church building or an addition. Capital campaigns usually collect pledges for specific projects, normally to be paid over a three-year period. They are clearly distinguishable from ongoing giving, yet they interested us enough that we asked pastors about them and also asked lay members about contributions to them.

It is important to mention here that a profession has arisen in the United States that helps organizations with capital campaigns. In the last half-century, the profession of fund-raisers (sometimes called "development professionals") has arisen and now employs about twenty thousand to forty thousand professionals, plus support staff. It has its own professional organizations, journals, and conventions.[2] The fund-raising profession serves all sorts of organizations, not just religious ones. Every university, hospital, health organization, and museum has a development staff.

Early in our work we discovered that this profession bases its practices and theories on experience, not on a corpus of social-scientific research. This surprised us. There is little research on voluntary giving and fund-raising decisions. Yet the profession of fund-raising thrives, and numerous how-to books on fund-raising campaigns, management of development offices, and public relations are being sold. Do their assertions and rules apply to churches? The answer is unclear, because churches are different from secular organizations. Surely, one cannot "market" religion as one markets soap. We return to these questions below, but let us state our conclusions here: (1) churches *are* basically different from secular organizations, and (2) ongoing giving *is* different from short-term capital campaigns in churches.

ASSUMPTIONS ABOUT ETHICS

A fundamental question we faced was whether or not we should investigate the ethics of present-day practices. Should we assume a posture that religious giving is good, or should we define and distinguish what is good and what is bad? Anyone who reads the newspaper knows that financial practices of religious organizations contain both good and bad and that some pastors behave in a manner unworthy of their calling. Ethical problems seem greatest in entrepreneurial religious movements and churches working outside the established denominations. Yet indefensible practices can be found everywhere.

Overall, however, we decided that an analysis of the ethics of fund-raising and religious giving was beyond our scope. This has become a field in itself. The fund-raising profession has made good progress in policing itself. For example, charitable organizations, such as the American Heart

Association, must now disclose what percentage of the money collected is spent for the fund-raising process itself. Moreover, fund-raisers are prohibited from entering into contracts with organizations in which they get a percentage of the take.

The posture guiding our research shortcuts this issue. We assume that religious giving is generally a good thing and that most churches are ethical and responsible. In effect, we bracket off the range of ethical issues from our project, one complicated enough as it is.

THEOLOGICAL DEFINITIONS

Researchers in this field cannot avoid theological assumptions, since everyone holds them. An investigator asking about church finances is immediately in a tangle of conflicting realities. The problem is the same that any sociologist or anthropologist faces when studying a religious group closely—the negotiation of realities. What is true? What is real and what is illusory? Religious beliefs matter, since behavior flows from them. As the social theorist W. I. Thomas demonstrated, "If men define situations as real, they are real in their consequences."[3] That is, if anything is believed as true, it will have consequences as if it were true. Religious giving is a clear example of a consequence.

The negotiating of beliefs often causes anxiety. An interviewee will feel the need to know: "Are you one of us or not?" "Are you committed to our beliefs and way of life or not?" "Do you believe what I say or not?" If the answers are no, other questions arise: "Are you against us?" "Will you injure or criticize us?" "Can we trust you enough to be honest with you?" When the discussion turns to matters of faith, the interviewees will want to know whether or not they are talking to a fellow believer.

Often, when studying individual churches, we found ourselves in groups that were advocating political or social causes with which we might agree or disagree. For example, one of us sat in several Sunday school classes that were planning to lobby against open homosexual behavior and a gay-oriented newspaper in the county. Another witnessed a church's attempt to influence a local school board election. In such settings we kept our feelings to ourselves and repeated over and over that we were just trying to learn about the particular church.

Any sociologist knows that his or her identity needs to be presented and negotiated, and it needs to be defined in a way most beneficial to the study itself. The four researchers in this study openly explained that we are all committed Christians and church attenders, but we are both Protestant and Catholic, and we are working together to achieve a broad picture.

SENSITIVE ISSUES

Religious giving is an especially difficult and sensitive topic, inviting cynicism and suspicion from some observers. Any preacher who claims that he or she is totally committed to the Lord and cares little about salary is open to suspicion, as is anyone who says that he or she is giving money to the church solely for the glory of God, without any thought of self. Though religious giving seems largely altruistic, many people today doubt the very existence of altruism or selflessness and conclude that the real motive for all giving is personal gain, increasing personal stature or reputation, or something else.

A second difficulty is conflicted feelings about finances. Some church members have had their fill of religious appeals that make them feel guilty. Preachers know that parishioners would avoid stewardship sermons if they could. Many clergy loathe stewardship sermons, since they feel an inherent conflict between their sincere personal ministry to parishioners and the necessity to ask the same people for money. A researcher who shows up and tells someone he is interested in religious giving will often observe a mildly startled reaction, as though an inner voice were saying, "Oh no—not that sensitive topic."

A third difficulty is the level of secrecy about financial matters in all churches. Norms about how much secrecy is needed vary from congregation to congregation and denomination to denomination. In no church did we find information available to the membership showing the amount of giving by each family; this is always confidential. In no church were the sizes of pledges made public—though the finance committee often knew and sometimes the pastor knew. Salaries of clergy and other employees are secret in some denominations but openly available in others. Total giving in any congregation or parish is sometimes a semiguarded secret, sometimes entirely secret. Little financial information is published in the Catholic Church. For our project, we had to use whatever summary data we could gather.

USES OF THE BOOK

The research study was designed to be practical and useful to church leaders. This book was written for the same purpose. We use plain, low-tech talk to tell the findings of our surveys and state our conclusions. We wanted to produce a book that would be useful to pastors and church leaders who wish to understand the basics of church giving and how it might be improved. The book is not a theological treatise or a pitch for any stewardship programs. It is a serious sociological and psychological treatise by a team of academics determined to get some clarity on a bewildering subject.

The science of data analysis has its own jargon, which we tried to eliminate from this book. Yet we could not remove it entirely. We retained two technical terms commonplace to social researchers but not to most people. Readers of the book need not know what they mean in any depth.

The first term is *correlation*. It is a statistic that tells the degree to which one variable can be predicted from another. If the prediction is quite accurate, the correlation is high; if not, the correlation is low. For example, if IQ and grades in a sample of high school students are highly associated so that IQ scores strongly predict grades, the correlation will be strong.

Correlations range from −1.0 to +1.0, and the midpoint (0) indicates a total lack of association between the two variables. The plus or minus sign of a correlation says nothing about the strength of the relationship; it indicates direction only. For example, if per-member giving in a congregation increases as congregation size increases, the correlation between the two is positive. But if giving increases as size decreases, the correlation would be reversed, that is, negative.

A correlation of +.50 and a correlation of −.50 are equally strong in terms of predicting one variable from the other. The only difference is that with a positive association, one variable increases as the other increases, whereas with a negative association, one variable decreases as the other increases. In the social sciences, correlations of .20 or stronger are generally considered moderate, those over .30 are considered strong, and those over .40 quite strong.

The second term is *significant*. This is a statistic that tells if differences between numbers are great enough that the differences are not merely the result of random chance. When we say a difference between two groups is "significant at .05," we mean there is a 95 percent probability that the difference is real and not just the result of random fluctuations. Researchers have confidence in the reality of significant findings.

Readers who find these terms unfamiliar should relax. This book is written so that both statisticians and nonstatisticians can get the story. When we include data tables in the book, we describe the findings in the text so that table-averse readers can learn easily what the table shows.

OUTLINE OF THE CHAPTERS

Chapter 1 reviews the organization and practices of each of the five denominations. In chapter 2, we review our research findings about congregations and individuals within them. Chapter 3 reveals the individual factors, and chapter 4 the congregational factors, that affect religious giving. Chapters 5 and 6 discuss findings from the case studies of individual churches, and chapter 7 states our conclusions.

Appendix A provides details of the 1993 nationwide study, along with information about the long, technical *Research Report on the American Congregational Giving Study* (finished in 1995) and the set of data, both of which are available to researchers. Appendix B contains the Congregation Profile Booklet, and Appendix C gives the lay questionnaire.

ACKNOWLEDGMENTS

We wish to thank the numerous persons who helped us carry out this study: Douglas Griffin, graduate student at the Catholic University of America, who contributed to an extensive literature review and then carried out most of the pretesting; D. Paul Sullins, also a Catholic University graduate student, who supervised much of the mailing of lay questionnaires; Peter Zaleski of Villanova University and Fenggang Yang of Catholic University who helped with data analysis; and Robert Wilson of the Institute for Social Research, University of New Mexico, who helped in many ways. Research assistants at Villanova University were Farnia Maghsoudlov, Katherine Dews, David Supplee, and Fan Levin; at the University of New Mexico, Kristine Johnson. Deborah Chard-Wieschem did yeoman's work on the two midwestern sites, and Richard J. Gordon of Search Institute in Minneapolis applied his skills to managing our data sets. Statistical advice was given to us by Seymour Sudman, David Baker, and Peter Zaleski.

We thank the liaison persons from the five denominations for giving us direction and facilitating data collection: the Reverend Clyde L. Hawkins, the Reverend James L. Powell, Francis X. Doyle, Kenneth Inskeep, and Keith Wulff. Other denominational leaders who helped us include Robert Dale, Robert Rhoden, and Kirk Hadaway.

Special thanks go to the church members and clergy of the congregations we visited to compile our case studies. It was a wonderful experience for us.

Over a hundred people helped us gather data in the nine sampling areas in different parts of the nation. Their names are listed in the *Research Report*, together with our thanks.

The writing and editing process was greatly aided by Eugene Roehlkepartain, Loren Mead, and Thomas Sweetser, S.J. We are indebted to our editor, Stephanie Egnotovich of Westminster John Knox Press, for expert editorial advice.

Nothing would have been possible without financial support from the Lilly Endowment, Inc. We especially thank Fred Hofheinz, program officer for religion, who gave us unceasing support and encouragement.

Dean Hoge, Charles Zech,
Patrick McNamara, Michael Donahue

1

An Overview
of Church Giving

We begin this chapter with a consideration of some basic concepts regarding philanthropy—both in general and with regard to church giving. We then turn to brief "state-of-the-church" examinations of giving in each of the five denominations discussed in this book.

PHILANTHROPIC GIVING
AND CHURCH GIVING

There are five basic facts about philanthropic giving and church giving in the United States.

1. The majority of all philanthropic giving in the United States goes to churches: 63 percent, according to one recent estimate based on nationwide polling.[1] This figure has been quite stable over time. The preponderance of this particular form of giving indicates that religious giving is unique, different from other philanthropy.

2. The increase in religious giving over a recent twenty-five-year period was somewhat lower than the rate of inflation. The total amount increases each year, but not quite as fast as the increase in family incomes. As John and Sylvia Ronsvalle of empty tomb, inc., have found in their trend studies, the percentage of household income given by American Protestants has fallen gradually, from 3.1 percent in 1968 to 2.5 percent in 1992.[2]

3. The level of giving to churches varies greatly, depending on the denomination. Members of some denominations give five times as much as members of others, in terms of percentage of household income. Why the immense differences? Certainly the religious needs of people do not vary that much from denomination to denomination, and human nature is not that different. We can only conclude that the explanation is to be found in how religious groups differ from one another, both theologically and organizationally. Figure 1–1 presents the mean percentage of income contributed for each of twenty-three denominations. Latter-day Saints (Mormons) head the list with over 7 percent. Unitarian-Universalists give the least (less than 1 percent). Almost half of the denominations range from 2 to 3 percent.

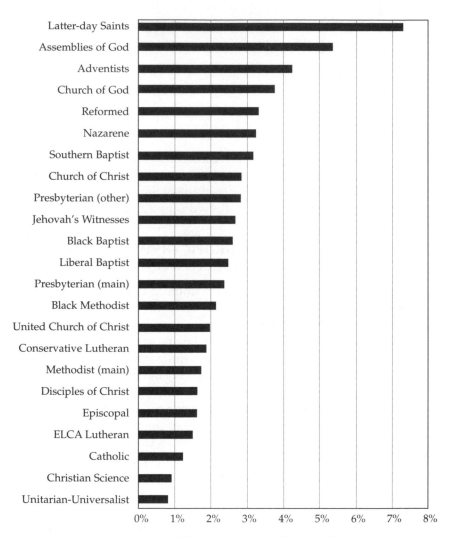

FIGURE 1–1.
GIVING AS A PERCENTAGE OF INCOME
BY DENOMINATION, 1987–1989
Data is based on responses by persons who atte. d services at least yearly.
Data from General Social Survey, 1987–1989.

Denominations in the United States can be classified in five categories in terms of giving: conservative Protestant, black Protestant, mainline Protestant, Catholic, and other. Conservative Protestants give the most—over 3 percent of their household income. Black Protestants give about 2.5 percent, and mainline Protestants follow at about 2 percent. Catholic giving is lower, at less than 1.5 percent. At the very bottom are smaller and newer religious groups—the Christian Scientists and the Unitarian-Universalists. In general, the more sectlike the denomination (that is, the more it maintains a clear distinctiveness from the prevailing culture), the higher the percentage given. This has been a constant finding in all research.

4. The amounts given by church members in any congregation vary widely. All research shows that a minority of members give the most money. As a rule of thumb, 75 percent of the money in a typical church is given by 25 percent of the people. Sometimes the ratios are closer to 80:20. Figure 1–2 shows the amounts given by people who identified themselves as Catholics, mainline Protestants, and "other Protestants" (mainly conservatives and evangelicals).

To make Figure 1–2, we took survey data from Catholics, mainline Protestants, and other Protestants, and we organized them in terms of how much they gave to their churches in the previous year, from low givers to high givers. Then we cut each denominational group into five equal-sized parts, called quintiles. They are represented by the five vertical bars. Note that the bottom one-fifth of all three groups did not give anything to their churches, and the second one-fifth gave an average of only $22 to $26 per year. Most of the money in each group is given by the top quintile, that is, the top 20 percent of the people. The overall pattern is the same for Catholics, mainline Protestants, and other Protestants, except that the rate of increase in the top two-fifths is fastest for the conservative Protestants and slowest for the Catholics. The main denominational differences occur in only the top quintile.

Why is giving so uneven? Family incomes in a typical church do not vary by such extremes. Strength of faith probably does not vary that much either, although this is difficult to know. From other research we know that the amount of "skew" (lopsidedness) in religious giving is similar to that in nonreligious member organizations. That is, both in churches and in nonreligious organizations, 75 percent of the money is given by 25 percent of the members. This fact suggests that the pattern has something to do with the way people behave in organizations or groups generally, rather than being something unique to religion. One explanation we have heard is that a core leadership group sometimes develops in churches and other organizations, and its members are motivated to high giving while

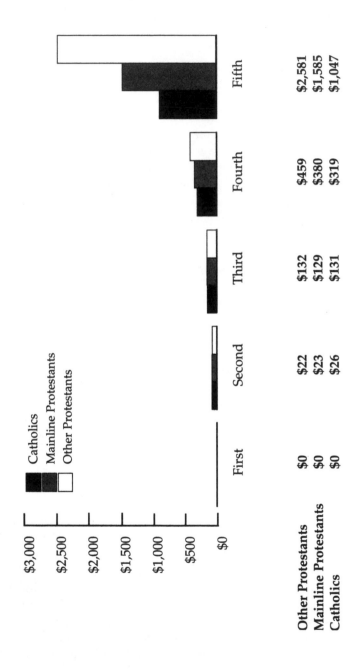

FIGURE 1–2.
ANNUAL FAMILY CONTRIBUTIONS BY QUINTILES
Data from General Social Survey, combined 1987, 1988, and 1989.

other members feel excluded from leadership and thus give less. Whether this explanation is important is unclear.

5. Two trends are occurring in church giving. First, since the 1950s, Protestant churches have spent increasing proportions of their money on local operations and programs and decreasing proportions on missions and denominational causes. In the mid-1990s, an average of 10 to 15 percent of all contributions are being spent on missions outside the local church, whereas in the 1950s, the figure was roughly twice as high.[3] The percentage going to missions continues to decline. Why? Possible explanations offered by analysts include greater competition among congregations locally, which leads each to spend more on its own programs; the higher salaries of clergy and lay staff; the loss of volunteer time to local churches as increasing numbers of women enter the workforce; and the greater consumer orientation of young adults. The importance of these possible factors is unknown.

The second trend in some denominations (Lutheran, Congregationalist, Presbyterian, among others) is that local churches are sending a decreasing percentage of their mission moneys to denominational programs. More and more money is being given to mission efforts, local and worldwide, that are independent of the denominations.[4]

Jointly, these two trends in giving result in a long-term decline in funds available to the national denominations for their programs and compel a downsizing of programs and staff. This problem is a major preoccupation of denominational leaders today. People are asking if the denominational structures as we now know them can survive.[5]

With these facts as a backdrop, we now turn to a few words of explanation about the denominations we studied. We proceed alphabetically—Assemblies of God, Baptist, Catholic, Lutheran, and Presbyterian.[6]

THE FIVE DENOMINATIONS

Assemblies of God

The Assemblies of God is unique in several ways among the five denominations we studied. It is the most recently founded denomination, having been established in 1914 in Hot Springs, Arkansas. It is a Pentecostal denomination, based in the gift of speaking in tongues ("baptism in the Spirit"), belief in the life of the spirit, literal biblicism, and emotional fervor. Worship services include speaking in tongues, enthusiastic singing, and, usually, altar calls. The level of church giving in the Assemblies of God is high relative to other Protestant denominations.

The Assemblies of God is a product of the Holiness movement, and its theology includes conversion and personal holiness, such as abstinence from drinking, smoking, drugs, nonmarital sex, ostentation, and gambling. After 1914 it grew rapidly, at first mainly in the American South and West. Most of the early members were white, but recently many Hispanics have joined and are now estimated at 15 percent of the total membership.[7] In 1994 the Assemblies of God reported 11,823 congregations in the United States, with about 2.3 million members and adherents. In its statistical summaries the denomination stresses attendance more than membership. Attendance in the United States grew 33 percent from 1978 to 1994, but in the last decade attendance grew only 6 percent.[8]

Churches tend to be smaller than in mainline Protestantism; many have fewer than 100 members and adherents. Average weekly attendance at Assemblies of God churches in 1994 was about 130 to 140; average number of members was 114; average of members plus adherents was 197.

Worldwide, the Assemblies of God has about 23 to 25 million members and adherents in 140 countries. This growth is the product of a remarkably large missionary program, coordinated from the world headquarters in Springfield, Missouri. The fastest growth has been in Brazil, Korea, and the Philippines.

In the beginning, the Assemblies of God members tended to be poor urbanites, including many recent arrivals from rural areas. These members felt the power of the movement, which clearly exhibited the gifts of the Spirit—healing, empowerment, and changed lives. The early preachers stressed the need to be clearly removed from the mainstream of American life. Early lists of "social sins" included tobacco in all its forms, secret societies, life insurance, doctors, liquor, dance halls, theaters, movies, Coca-Cola, public swimming, beauty parlors, and jewelry. But over the years these views have eased, so that any mention of Coca-Cola, life insurance, and doctors has disappeared from discussion of sins. While in a survey in the 1960s, 91 percent of members said they disapproved of dancing and 98 percent disapproved of gambling, in a 1983 survey only two-thirds of the respondents disapproved of each.[9] In short, the denomination has accommodated itself to the mainstream society. In urban areas its style has moved closer to evangelicalism and has sometimes tried to constrain public display of gifts of the spirit, which might put off city folk. As Margaret Poloma, author of a leading book on the Assemblies, put it, the Assemblies of God has "crossed the tracks."[10]

The Assemblies of God has always been structured as a franchise of preachers. Since its 1914 founding, it has consistently felt that the Assemblies of God should not be allowed to evolve into a denomination like the others. It is still officially called a "movement" or a "cooperative fellowship." It takes pride in avoiding central authority and standardization and in giving preachers wide latitude to be entrepreneurial. Preachers are not required to have seminary training for certification, but they are required to have received the gift of tongues. This freedom from strictures has probably led to the dynamism in evangelism; at the same time, it has opened the door to scandals. Two famous Assemblies of God evangelists, Jim Bakker and Jimmy Swaggart, were ousted after widely publicized sexual and financial misdeeds in the 1980s.

Preachers clearly have the power at all levels in the movement—local, district, and national. Local churches vote for lay leaders, but the clergy have their say as to which laypersons are nominated for election, and everyone acknowledges that clergy run the church. The denominational financial structure is unique in that local ministers—not congregations—are required to pay a tithe to the district office for the annual renewal of their credentials. (The exact definition of the word *tithe* in each district varies between 5 percent of total income and 10 percent of total income.) Congregations have no obligation to pay anything. Local churches are autonomous. Each owns its own property (except for new home mission churches) and selects its own pastor when there is a vacancy.

The mission program is kept separate from denominational budgets. All financial support for missionary efforts is voluntary, not obligatory, and missions support is not in the local congregation's budget. Church members are asked annually to make one-year pledges for specific missionaries. Mission money is given by individual members, not by churches. Total giving to U.S. congregations in 1994 was approximately $1.41 billion, and total giving to foreign missions was $109 million.

Unlike most denominations, the Assemblies of God puts little emphasis on membership. Membership carries with it the obligations of regular participation, agreement with doctrines, and tithing. (The requirements are not stressed equally in all local churches.) A large percentage of churchgoers are deterred by these requirements and thus do not become members, despite many years of attendance. Nonmembers who attend the churches are entitled to all ministerial services, such as marrying, burying, and counseling, but they are not eligible for leadership offices.

Past research into different denominations in the United States has seldom included the Assemblies of God. For years, the leadership had little contact with other denominations. Our 1993 study is one of the first we know of to look at the Assemblies of God in comparison with other denominations.

The Southern Baptist Convention

The Southern Baptist Convention nationally includes 39,910 local churches, with 57 percent of these located in "the old South" below the Mason-Dixon Line and east of the Mississippi River. Another 21 percent are located in the Southwest. The churches vary widely in size, but the majority are small: 21 percent have fewer than 100 members, 22 percent have between 100 and 200 members, 32 percent have between 200 and 500 members, 14 percent have between 500 and 1,000, and 11 percent exceed 1,000. Roughly 100 churches in large cities have over 5,000 members. The mean church size is 391 members; the median is 233.[11] Membership data on Southern Baptist churches is not precise, since the reported numbers include "nonresidential members" who live some distance away from the churches, and these make up 29 percent of the total. The total number of "resident members" reported in 1994 was 11,094,044, an approximation of the number who were at least mininally active in church life. Southern Baptists practice adult baptism by immersion. No infants are baptized, and no small children are members. Most baptisms are of persons eight to twenty years old.

Eighty-nine percent of the churches have pastors, either full time or part time. Half of the pastors work in the church part time and make their principal living in other occupations. Local autonomy and authority are highly valued. Most local churches have their own constitutions and by-laws, but not all; some merely follow local traditions. A typical church has an elected clerk, treasurer, moderator, trustees, and deacons. A church has congregational business meetings monthly or quarterly, during which budgets, salaries, and all other topics are decided by a vote of members present. Pastors are also chosen by a vote of the members. Most salaries of clergy and lay staff are public knowledge, but in some large churches individual salaries are not shown but are reported only in group salary totals.

The clergy/laity distinction is a small one. Clergy have few, if any, powers or privileges that are not also given to laity. Clergy are ordained by local churches. Pastors are normally hired for an indefinite period of time; they may continue as long as both they and the members wish. There is no obligation that a pastor be a seminary graduate; at present, about one-half of the pastors of Southern Baptist churches are seminary graduates. The local church may hire whomever it wishes, even non-Baptist pastors.

The local churches voluntarily join larger groups, which exist on three levels. Churches usually take part in all three. The first level is the association, usually encompassing one or several counties. For a church to be a member, it must apply, demonstrate acceptable doctrine, and contribute financially to the association's programs. Local churches may be expelled from the association if they violate rules approved by the body or (on rare occasions) if they have practices offensive to other churches.

The second level is the state convention, comprising one or more states. There are thirty-nine conventions in all. Membership of a church in a state convention is voluntary, and every member church is strongly urged to contribute to the state convention programs to be in good standing.

The third level is national—the Southern Baptist Convention—where the same rules apply as with the state convention. All three levels are autonomous in relation to one another.

Local churches own their own property. Church governance is seen as preeminently a local affair, except for programs that require broader cooperation—mainly mission efforts, Sunday school curricula, colleges, and universities.

The larger churches have an annual "call for giving," usually in connection with the adoption of the annual budget. Both clergy and lay leaders ask members to give, and stewardship promotion materials are mailed to church members. A limited number of churches have phone canvasses or personal visitations. Smaller churches operate more informally.

Pledge cards with members' names and signatures are used mainly in large churches, but they are not used in the majority of churches, since many members dislike them. (The Baptist name for these is "commitment cards.") An estimated one-fourth of the churches use them. Recently, some churches, however, have begun to ask members for an estimate of their giving in the coming year. Amounts of annual pledges are always kept confidential. Pew envelopes are used in over 90 percent of all Southern Baptist churches, but most churches do not keep records of individuals' giving, and in only a minority of churches are reports sent monthly or quarterly to members, indicating how much an individual or family has given.

Per capita giving in 1994 was $502 (based on resident membership). Assuming two members per family, this is approximately 2.9 percent of family income.[12] Per capita giving increased somewhat faster than inflation during the 1980s. As a percentage of total church expenditures, mission expenditures remained at approximately 17 percent from 1970 to 1994.

The national convention and the state conventions have a Cooperative Program of giving to support Baptist causes and missions. The percentage going to each cause or mission is fixed by vote of delegates—"messengers"—attending the annual meeting. When a local church gives to this program, it sends a monthly check to the state convention, which in turn sends a percentage to the national office. Not all mission giving goes through the state or national Cooperative Program, but most of it does. The percentage is gradually declining, however. In 1960, the Cooperative Program received 10.1 percent of total church giving; in 1980 the amount was 9 percent, and by 1994 it had decreased to 7 percent. Other mission giving is expended by local churches to whatever program they prefer.

In most states, three special offerings are taken each year. One is in December, to support foreign missions, and another is at Easter, to support home missions. Both are very large. The Easter offering totaled $37.2 million nationally in 1994, and the December offering reached $85.9 million. These offerings are promoted widely, and givers are assured that 100 percent of the money goes directly to mission programs. The third special offering is for state mission programs and is normally taken in September. Local churches may take other special offerings as they desire.

The Roman Catholic Church

The U.S. Roman Catholic Church has an estimated sixty million members. It has 19,723 parishes and 3,370 mission parishes, organized into 163 dioceses and 36 archdioceses.

Catholic parishes are different from the congregations in all the other denominations in one respect: size. A nationwide study done at the University of Notre Dame in the mid-1980s found an average of 2,300 persons residing within parish boundaries, making Catholic parishes over eight times as large, on average, as Protestant churches.[13] Parish sizes varied widely: 16 percent had more than 5,000 members; at the other extreme, 18 percent had fewer than 500. Large parishes are found in major cities with predominantly Catholic neighborhoods, for example, New York City or Los Angeles. Small parishes are mainly in rural areas.

The number of active Catholics in a parish is smaller than the total membership number would indicate. Parishes rarely have up-to-date census lists, but they have registry lists composed of all families and individuals who signed up voluntarily to be members of that parish or who have enrolled their children in parochial schools or religious education. Two recent studies estimated that about three out of four baptized Catholics in the United States are on a parish registry list.[14] The registry list is a rough analogue to a Protestant church membership list.

By canon law, all parishes are managed by ordained priests, who are directly responsible to diocesan bishops. All priests are appointed to parishes by the bishops, sometimes in consultation with lay leaders from the parishes involved. Large parishes formerly had two or three priests, but because of the shortage of priests, this is less common today. Instead, parishes are hiring lay ministers and pastoral coordinators to provide religious education, music, liturgy, and other ministries.

The new code of canon law mandates that all parishes form councils with advisory roles to help the pastor manage the financial and ministerial affairs of the parish. In some parishes, financial decisions are made as part of the duties of the parish council in an advisory role. In other parishes, the finance council is separate from the parish council. Parish councils are functioning in about three-fourths of American parishes.

In all research, Catholic giving has consistently been found to be well below that of Protestant churchgoers. Why? Catholic historians such as Jay Dolan point to the poor immigrant backgrounds of the bulk of American Catholics.[15] We have found little systematic research on the question. The 1983 Notre Dame parish study surveyed registered members of a representative sample of parishes and found that the mean self-reported, per-family contribution to the parish was $559 (the median was $332). These figures are biased upward because of the greater willingness of committed members to cooperate in surveys.

Forty-five percent of all parishes in the Notre Dame study had schools (usually elementary), virtually all of which received direct subsidies from parish offerings. The amount of the subsidy varied widely. In some dioceses it averaged 10 to 25 percent of parish offerings, in others close to 50 percent. Recent research has found that in 1992, school subsidies averaged 30 percent of parish income in those parishes having schools. This percentage is gradually moving downward.[16]

All parishes are required to pay an assessment to their diocese, based either on a percentage of the offerings or on a formula related to parish income and the number of parishioners. Typically, the assessment is about 8 to 12 percent of total parish income. Diocesan and national programs, including missions and social service, are supported from this assessment. In addition, parishes are asked to participate in special collections for diocesan and national causes—a total of about ten to twelve offerings a year. Most parishes do not participate in all of these offerings. Except for saying yes or no to these special offerings, the pastor and parish council have little to do with allocating mission funds.

Catholic giving from the early 1960s through 1984 was analyzed in the widely read *Catholic Contributions: Sociology and Policy* by sociologist Andrew Greeley and retired Catholic bishop William McManus. Greeley and McManus said that in the early 1960s, both Catholics and Protestants gave an average of 2.2 percent of income to their churches. By the mid-1970s, while Protestant contributions remained at 2.2 percent, Catholic contributions had dropped to 1.6 percent, and by 1984, to 1.1 percent.[17] Greeley believed that dissatisfaction with church authority and sexual teaching accounted for much of the "alienation" that lowered giving levels. Other factors, he asserted, were also in play: "terrible sermons; inept counseling; arbitrary rules and regulations . . . little regard for the rights and dignity of women."[18]

Later, questions about religious giving were asked in the nationwide General Social Survey, conducted by the National Opinion Research

Center, from 1987 through 1989. Catholic giving lagged behind Protestant and Jewish giving (e.g., in 1989, the average Catholic contribution to religion was $308, compared with $653 for Protestants).[19] Joseph Claude Harris, a church finance expert, commented that if Catholics gave to all charities, both religious and secular, at the average level of giving for all American households, "the Sunday collection in the U.S. Catholic Church would increase by $1.963 billion, a gain of 36 percent over the present level of the Sunday offering total."[20]

Harris carried out a study in 1992 that involved a stratified random sample of 714 parishes. The average yearly household contribution for all parishes was $280, but within parishes, the amounts given varied widely. He found "an enormous difference in the extent of giving among households in a parish. On average, a small group of 13.2 percent of registered households gave 58.6 percent of the parish revenue."[21]

Explanations for the long-term Catholic decline in giving, as well as indications of what factors might increase giving, have appeared in several studies since the Greeley and McManus study of 1987. Both the Harris 1992 study and research by economists Peter A. Zaleski and Charles E. Zech indicate that reducing parish size would increase household giving. Harris points out that "the smallest parishes had 15.3 percent more participating households per thousand than the largest parishes. The average household gift changed in a similar fashion."[22] Zaleski and Zech are more tentative, remarking that "even if Catholic congregational economics, parish size, and attitudes all changed to more closely resemble that of Protestants, Catholic contributions would still fall short of those of Protestants."[23]

In a 1992 study of parishes in the Archdiocese of Cincinnati, diocesan researchers Jeff Rexhausen and Michael Cieslak found that two factors together explained just over half of Sunday giving. The more important factor (particularly in parishes in large cities) was the percentage of members who attend mass regularly. The second factor was the presence of a giving program in the parish.[24] In smaller parishes, these two factors were joined by household income and the number of households in the parish. Parish size was inversely related to giving: the larger the parish, the lower the per capita giving.

The most exhaustive list of factors that probably affect Catholic giving was compiled by church consultant Thomas Sweetser and his associates. They suggested nineteen factors. Most important are the perception that the church is rich and can survive without the individual's contribution; members being at odds with certain church teachings, such as birth control, abortion, and divorce and remarriage; members not being asked to contribute; poor fiscal management; the lack of a giving tradition in American Catholicism; sharp increases in school tuition; congregations that are too big; outdated theology; poor leadership; and poor communication.[25]

Scattered indications in today's Catholic Church point to stewardship and sacrificial giving programs as capable of raising giving levels within a parish. Though no nationwide, systematic program surveys have yet been made, individual dioceses and parishes report upturns in Sunday giving in parishes that use stewardship programs. Successful pastors stress that years of "reflecting, preaching, and organizing" are required before substantial results are visible.[26]

The Evangelical
Lutheran Church in America

The Evangelical Lutheran Church in America (ELCA) has 10,892 congregations. In 1994 the median congregational size was 323 baptized members and the mean size was 477. Twenty percent of ELCA congregations had more than 687 members, and 20 percent had fewer than 147. The ELCA is organized into sixty-five geographical synods, whose practices and policies vary.

Each synod is headed by a bishop, who is elected for a four-year term by clergy and laity. Clergy are hired by joint action of bishops and parish leadership. When there is a pastoral vacancy in a congregation, the synod bishop consults with the parish lay leaders and then submits several names. A parish committee reviews the materials, meets the candidates, and invites their choice to an interview and a meeting with congregation members. Then the congregation votes on the pastoral candidate.

In each congregation, financial decisions are made by the members. The members elect congregation councils composed of twelve to twenty-one members, each for a three-year term; one-third are elected each year at annual congregational meetings. Congregation councils make decisions between annual meetings. They prepare a budget and submit it for approval at the annual congregational meeting, where a vote is taken.

The budget includes a proposed financial commitment to synodical and national programs, called "mission support." The size of this share is proposed annually by synod leaders to each congregation, based on a formula; it is commonly from 10 percent to 20 percent of the expected congregational offerings. The congregation is not required to pay this amount, though there is some pressure on the clergy to do so. In actual practice, almost all congregations make some payment. If a church cannot pay, there is no penalty.

Parish leaders make final decisions about other financial matters, such as local capital campaigns, participation in synod or churchwide special appeals, and support for other benevolence and mission programs. Synod leaders request that all congregations take part in synod and churchwide special appeals, and the majority do so. Most congregations give some financial support to missionaries and service projects not in the synodical requests.

In 1994, total annual giving per confirmed communing member to the congregation was $508. This amount has been growing gradually each year; in 1987, it was $355.

The term *benevolences* refers to all money spent for mission and service outside the congregation itself. In 1994, ELCA benevolences totaled $187 million, or 13.2 percent of total congregational disbursements. Of this amount, 63 percent was paid for mission support and another 20 percent was sent to synodical and churchwide mission and service programs. The remaining 17 percent was spent on mission and service projects selected by the individual congregations.

Almost 70 percent of ELCA congregations report having a financial stewardship emphasis, 56 percent use a system of written financial commitments (pledges), and 64 percent ask their members to consider tithing. Almost all use weekly envelopes. In recent years, increasing numbers of Lutheran members have made out checks once a month instead of using the weekly envelopes. Most congregations send members quarterly or annual statements reporting the amount those members have given. No congregations make public a report of how much each family gives.

Kenneth Inskeep, director of ELCA's Department for Research and Evaluation, points out that ELCA per capita giving increased 27 percent from 1979 to 1989.[27] Yet total giving to ELCA synods and the churchwide organization declined 4.4 percent between 1979 and 1991, largely due to membership losses. There is little evidence that whatever clergy disenchantment may exist concerning synods and the worldwide church "spills over" onto the laity. The organizational financial problem is more disinterest than unhappiness with denominational leadership. According to Inskeep, "distance and disinterest" of the laity "may make allocation of funds beyond the congregation especially vulnerable to the pressure of rising local congregational expenses." He concludes that although asking ELCA congregational members to pledge does increase the amount given, weakened denominational loyalty and diminished ethnic identity are partially responsible for reduced giving to synodical and worldwide programs.

ELCA leadership, anticipating "a relatively flat level of financial support in the near future" and "costs that are rising faster than income," with a consequent "cycle of reduced mission capabilities," have recently recommended strategies for financial stewardship. These must involve more than fund-raising; ELCA members must be helped "to develop faith-filled lives." In addition, the story of ELCA's mission must be made more compelling and lay leaders "equipped and nurtured" so that they will "guide this church as it funds its mission activities." New methods of financial support are to be coordinated and developed. Organizational reform proposals include reducing the number of synods and exploring ways of meeting rising costs in pension payments and medical benefits.[28]

The Presbyterian Church (U.S.A.)

The Presbyterian Church (U.S.A.) has 2.7 million members and 11,400 congregations whose average membership in 1994 was 237; the median membership was 130. Not many congregations are large: only 11 percent have over 500 members and 3 percent have more than 1,000. About 41 percent have 100 or fewer members.[29]

The local churches are governed by a *Book of Order* that specifies rules of decision making. The highest authority in a Presbyterian church is the "session," composed of lay members elected by the membership for three-year terms. Typically, sessions are composed of eight to twenty-five persons (about fifteen members is common). The session must have the senior ordained clergyperson as its moderator, and all session meetings must have a clergy member in charge. All decisions are by majority vote, and all decisions, except for a few specified in the *Book of Order*, are final when voted on by the local session. Only decisions about hiring and firing ordained clergy, buying and selling real estate, and undertaking building projects large enough to involve mortgages need to be ratified by the presbytery.

The presbytery is a regional body governing local churches, typically including forty to one hundred churches. Depending on its size, each local church may have one or two clergy voting delegates and one or two session-member voting delegates at presbytery meetings; others are welcome as observers.

As specified by the *Book of Order*, the annual budget of a local church is voted on by the session on the basis of recommendations from its finance committee. But the "term of call" (one-year employment contract) with each ordained clergyperson must be voted on annually in a meeting of all members. At that time, all financial arrangements and job descriptions of clergy are reviewed and approved. Also at the annual meeting, everyone is given a detailed report of finances in the past year and the proposed budget for the coming year. Discussion is invited. All staff salaries are public knowledge.

About two-thirds of Presbyterian churches hold an annual stewardship drive in the fall of the year; all large churches do but not all small ones. Only a small number are able to mount a personal visitation campaign each year, during which lay members visit other members to ask for pledges. More commonly, the pledge drive is done by mail. Several letters are sent to all members, telling of the coming year's budget, the needs of the church, and the importance of stewardship as a part of Christian life. During this two- to four-week pledge drive, sermons are typically on stewardship themes. Sometimes clergy are the key spokespersons to ask for pledges during the worship services, and sometimes lay leaders; it depends on local preferences.

The church treasurer keeps a tally of how much each pledging member gives and sends a report to the person every three months. At the end of the calendar year, the treasurer sends a final report, which also serves as a receipt for tax purposes. Envelopes are generally used. The amount any head of household pledges to the church is, in most churches (but not all), a secret, known only to the treasurer and secretary.

The total regular offering in the denomination came to about $1.49 billion in 1994, or $553 per member. An additional two-thirds billion came in through wills, bequests, investment income, and occasional local capital campaigns.

The national denomination sponsors four special offerings each year: at Easter, used for hunger, meeting human needs, and furthering self-development; at Christmas, used for minority education and clergy pensions; in the fall, used for peacemaking programs; and in the late spring, pledged to global missions and new church development. Local churches are not required to participate, but one denominational officer estimated that one-half of the churches collect all four offerings. The total amount collected in these offerings totaled about $15 million in 1994, or about $5.53 per member. (Besides these four annual offerings, Presbyterians in 1994 gave $5 million to special offerings for hunger, disaster relief, and seminaries.) Local churches are under no obligation to participate in these offerings, but there is some pressure on clergy to do so. The Presbyterian Church (U.S.A.) national research office recently inquired into attitudes about these special offerings, and the prevailing sentiment is that "we don't want any more than four."

To remain in good standing, each local church must pay an "apportionment," which is a tax to denominational offices. (A few temporary exceptions are made.) The money is split between the presbytery, synod, and national levels. The amount varies from presbytery to presbytery but averaged about $16 to $24 per member in 1994. Any other payments to higher denominational offices are optional; they are comprised of the special offerings, noted above, and gifts to denominational missions.

Today, the denominational mission offerings comprise 8.6 percent of the total money that members give to local churches; nondenominational missions comprise another 5 to 7 percent. Typically, this figure is higher for larger churches than for smaller ones. Overall, it has been gradually moving downward over the past two decades as local churches increasingly select their own mission causes. To illustrate, revenues sent to General Assembly programs, after adjustment for inflation, fell by more than 50 percent in the period from 1973 to 1988.[30] Denominational leaders have developed "designated giving" for specific programs, if local churches desire, in hopes of increasing the total amounts given. Nevertheless, the money given for denominational mission continues to decline. "Unified giving" to the denominational mission boards has been shrinking faster than the overall amount.

Also, all churches expend some amounts for local mission and social outreach, in addition to the 8.6 percent mentioned above. These monies add up to about $50 million per year and go to what is called "local mission." In general, the larger and more affluent the church, the more money per person is spent on mission, either local or denominational.

Other fund-raising activities in Presbyterian churches are relatively small. The largest is undertaken by the nationwide Presbyterian women's organization, which takes offerings and sponsors projects for its favorite missions; the organization raised $6 million in 1994. Local youth groups often have fund-raisers to support their activities, trips, and camps. Women's organizations sometimes have bazaars or dinners. There are no raffles or games of chance, since Presbyterians are opposed to these activities.

One denominational leader told us that, as a rule of thumb, Presbyterians give $500 per member. Churches of one hundred members typically have budgets of $50,000, and churches of two hundred members have budgets of about $100,000. The giving average increases only in large, affluent churches. In a typical church, over half of the budget goes for staff salaries. Normally, the church size is indirectly proportional to the percentage of the budget going for staff: the smaller church, the higher the percentage.

These five denominations represent a wide range of American Protestantism, as well as the Roman Catholic Church. We will now turn to the findings of our 1993 study. Chapters 2, 3, and 4 give the results and test hypotheses about levels of giving. The findings are depicted so that readers can look at each denomination separately or the five collectively.

2

Congregations
and Laity: Profiles

The nationwide data we gathered in 1993 are the basis for this book. We have two sources of information about the 625 congregations we studied: (1) the nine-page Congregation Profile Booklet on each congregation, filled out in most cases by pastors; and (2) the 10,902 mail questionnaires from laity.

This chapter describes the congregations and lay members in the five denominations. It depicts the findings in data tables and discusses what we think is important. First is the information on congregations, taken from the Congregation Profile Booklet.

THE CONGREGATIONS

Size and Age

We asked each church three questions about size. The first question was about the number of resident members (youth or older). For Lutherans, this meant "confirmed communing members," and for Catholics, this meant the number listed in the parish registry. Since the Assemblies of God has a more restricted meaning of "member," the closest analogue to other denominations was the total number of members plus frequent attenders on the denomination's mailing list. At least one-fourth of the Assemblies' congregations on the denominational lists had fewer than fifty members and frequent attenders and had to be excluded from the study; this was much less often the case in the other Protestant denominations.

As additional measures of size, we asked how many households were registered or represented in the congregation and how many people attended worship on a typical weekend (see Table 2–1; please note that all table percentages may not add up to exactly 100 percent because of rounding).

TABLE 2–1.
CONGREGATION SIZE AND AGE

	Assemblies of God	Baptist	Catholic	Lutheran	Presbyterian
Average number of members*	266	318	2,723	319	303
Average number of households	105	167	1,041	183	173
Average worship attendance on a typical weekend in all worship services	168	161	1,255	146	155
When was the congregation founded?					
Percent before 1900	0	33	36	47	57
Percent 1900–1949	36	26	33	15	21
Percent 1950–1979	36	29	29	36	19
Percent 1980 or later	28	12	2	3	3

*For Assemblies of God, the number includes members plus frequent attenders on the mailing list.
Based on Congregation Profile Booklet questions 2, 4, 5, and 6.

We learned during the data collection that the pastors' reports on the size of their churches were imprecise. Some pastors reported inflated numbers of members, and some used different definitions of "member," even though we clearly specified what we wanted. As a result, after studying the information, we believe that the reported figures for some Assemblies of God and Baptist churches are too high. Actual membership sizes are probably a bit smaller, but we had no reliable way to correct the data. If the figures are truly too high, as we believe they are, the per-member contributions shown below are underestimates.

The Protestant congregations are small and roughly similar in size, while Catholic parishes vary widely in size (see Figure 2–1). Catholic parishes are more than eight times as large as Protestant congregations, with 18 percent having more than five thousand members. Also, Assemblies of God congregations are much younger (years since founding) than the others. The Presbyterian congregations are the oldest.

Race, Education,
and Income of Members

We asked the pastors to estimate several characteristics of their members. Although not very reliable, the estimates are worth looking at. (See Table A–3.) Briefly, the Assemblies of God pastors reported slightly younger members and a higher percentage of minorities than did the other pastors. In terms of education and income, the Presbyterians were the highest and the Assemblies of God the lowest. The estimated percentages of

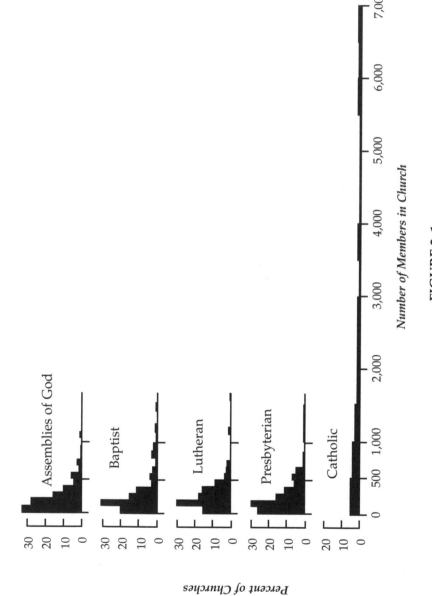

FIGURE 2–1.

SIZES OF CHURCHES IN THE FIVE DENOMINATIONS

members with a college degree were: Assemblies, 19 percent; Baptists, 26 percent; Catholics, 29 percent; Lutherans, 28 percent; and Presbyterians, 45 percent.

Levels of Giving

Each congregation reported its receipts in the last fiscal year in eight categories: (1) regular offerings or pledges; (2) special offerings, denominational or diocesan appeals, and other special appeals (including capital campaigns); (3) special fund-raisers (fairs, bingo, bake sales, and the like); (4) wills, bequests, and special gifts; (5) investments; (6) rents and fees; (7) judicatory subsidies (synod, diocese, conference, presbytery); (8) other. (See Table A–4.) Table 2–2 shows overall average receipts.

TABLE 2–2.
AVERAGE ANNUAL RECEIPTS
AND GIVING IN THE MOST RECENT YEAR*

	Assemblies of God	Baptist	Catholic	Lutheran	Presbyterian
Total receipts	$165.8	181.5	374.8	143.8	230.5
Receipts from regular offerings, special offerings, and appeals	$155.2	174.9	320.7	125.5	191.5

*Dollar amounts indicate thousands.
Based on Congregation Profile Booklet question 21. For exact wording, see Appendix B. Data are mostly for fiscal year 1992.

In all five denominations, the majority of receipts came from regular offerings and special offerings. Fund-raisers accounted for surprisingly little, even in Catholic parishes, which often have a tradition of bingo and games of chance.

Table 2–2 indicates that Catholic parishes operate at a much lower per-member cost than do Protestant congregations. Whereas Catholic churches are, on average, more than eight times as large as Protestant churches, the annual income in Catholic parishes is only twice as high.

How much does the average member or attender contribute to the parish? We divided total giving ("regular offerings or pledges" and "special offerings, denominational or diocesan appeals, and other special appeals") by the number of members, households, and attenders.[1] The results are shown in Table 2–3.

TABLE 2–3.
AVERAGE ANNUAL CONTRIBUTIONS

	Assemblies of God	Baptist	Catholic	Lutheran	Presbyterian
Per member	$628	550	160	415	611
Per household	$1,696	1,154	386	746	1,085
Per attender	$877	952	283	824	1,106

The comparisons of the five denominations differ slightly depending on which of the three measures of giving we use. If we look at contributions per member or household, we find Assemblies of God highest, followed by the Presbyterians and Baptists. But if we look at contributions per average attendee, the Presbyterians are highest; the Baptists, second; and the Assemblies of God, third. On all measures, the Catholics are lowest.[2]

Capital Campaigns, Endowments, Debts

How many congregations are in the midst of capital campaigns, and how many have endowments or mortgage debts? We asked, "Was your congregation involved in a capital campaign last year for enlarged facilities, new equipment, other capital improvements, or debt relief?" "Does your congregation have an endowment?" and "Last year, did your congregation have a mortgage debt?" See Table 2–4.

TABLE 2–4.
CONGREGATIONS HAVING CAPITAL CAMPAIGNS, ENDOWMENTS, AND MORTGAGE DEBTS*

	Assemblies of God	Baptist	Catholic	Lutheran	Presbyterian
Involved in a capital campaign	25	26	22	29	36
With an endowment of $100K or more	1	3	10	12	18
With a mortgage debt	62	46	32	37	23

*In percentages.
Based on Congregation Profile Booklet questions 22, 23, and 25.

From Table 2–4, we see that roughly one-fourth or more of all the congregations in any given denomination are now in a capital campaign.

(Capital campaigns normally last about three years, including the payoff period.) Only a few congregations have large endowments; those that do are principally found in the mainline Protestant denominations. The majority of the Assemblies of God churches have mortgage debts, but in the other denominations the percentage of churches with debts is lower.

Parochial Schools,
Day-Care Centers, and Latchkey Programs

Parochial schools are found mostly in Catholic parishes, with a few also in Assemblies of God congregations (See Table 2–5). Day-care centers, preschool programs, and latchkey programs are most common in Catholic parishes and less so in Assemblies of God and Baptist congregations than elsewhere.

TABLE 2–5.
CONGREGATIONS HAVING FIVE TYPES OF PROGRAMS*

	Assemblies of God	Baptist	Catholic	Lutheran	Presbyterian
The congregation sponsors					
A parochial five-day-a-week school	8	0	39	2	1
A parochial school, together with other congregations	2	0	30	0	0
A day-care center or preschool	9	10	35	18	30
A before- or after-school "latchkey" program	5	3	21	6	9

*In percentages.
Based on Congregation Profile Booklet questions 15, 16, 17, and 18.

Are these programs costly to operate? We asked the parishes sponsoring parochial schools to report where the funds came from to operate them. The average figures reported for the Catholic schools were $225,900 from tuition; $138,700 from direct parish subsidy; $6,300 from indirect parish subsidy, in such items as janitorial service or utilities; $29,700 from fund-raising programs; and $5,800 from other sources, for a total of $406,500 per year. We have no information on the sizes of the schools.

The figures reported by the Assemblies of God congregations with five-day-a-week schools were lower, averaging $148,000 per year to run the school. We do not know the schools' sizes.

Thirty percent of the Catholic parishes cosponsor a parochial school with other parishes. Usually these are elementary schools, but a few are high schools. In cosponsorship cases, the costs to the parish are much lower. The average direct parish subsidy to the school was approximately $83,800, and the average indirect parish subsidy was approximately $12,600. Tuition scholarships paid by the parish averaged $1,800. The total cost to the parish was thus approximately $98,200. A few Catholic parishes had both their own (elementary) school and a cosponsored (secondary) school.

Day-care, preschool, and latchkey programs are not a serious drain on church resources, because most are self-supporting, paid for by user fees.

Congregational Expenditures

We asked each congregation about its expenditures in the previous year, in four categories: (1) congregational operations, programs, and ministry (including all staff salaries and benefits, as well as money put into reserve); (2) subsidies to school, day-care, or latchkey programs; (3) denominational mission work and programs; and (4) other mission work and programs. (See Table A–5.) Categories 3 and 4 combined are the total expenditures sent out of the congregation for mission work, diocesan offices, denominational offices, and social programs (see Table 2–6).

TABLE 2–6.
AVERAGE CONGREGATIONAL EXPENDITURES IN PREVIOUS YEAR*

	Assemblies of God	Baptist	Catholic	Lutheran	Presbyterian
Total expenditures	$164.7	179.9	388.5	148.6	229.7
1. Congregational programs and operations	$144.1	149.4	266.5	128.6	195.8
2. Subsidies to schools and programs	$1.3	.1	80.3	1.1	.7
3. Denominational missions	$16.3	25.8	34.5	15.2	19.3
4. Other missions	$2.4	2.4	7.1	3.3	13.9
Parts 3 + 4 as percentage of total expenditures	11.4	15.7	10.7	12.5	14.4

*Dollar amounts indicate thousands.
Figures do not add up exactly, due to rounding.

The proportion of total expenditures going for mission work and programs is quite uniform across the denominations, ranging from 10.7 percent (Catholics) to 15.7 percent (Baptists). Our Catholic advisers argued that the Catholic percentage is too low to be representative, since in most dioceses a parish is obligated to pay 10 to 12 percent of all contributions to the diocesan office, and in addition, there are special mission offerings. In reality, probably the number is higher than the 10.7 percent given in Table 2–6.

The Presbyterians have the highest proportion of money directed to mission programs other than those of the denomination—42 percent (that is, roughly $13,900 out of a total of $33,200). This finding surprised us. It seems that the Presbyterians send their mission money to a variety of programs and projects.

Financial Decision Making

Do these denominations differ in how they make decisions about their annual budgets? We asked each congregation to tell us (1) who was involved in the preparation of the budget and (2) who had the *final* say in approving it (see Table 2–7).

TABLE 2–7.
THE BUDGET PROCESS*

	Assemblies of God	Baptist	Catholic	Lutheran	Presbyterian
Who is involved in preparing the budget? (percent checking each)					
Pastor(s)	77	82	94	82	82
Paid staff	20	39	52	18	24
Governing board, pastoral council, or committees	80	41	34	89	92
Finance committee	31	94	83	64	87
Congregation members via other channels	10	46	9	26	28
Who has *final* say in approving the budget?					
Pastor(s)	16	0	69	0	0
Governing board or pastoral council	43	0	8	0	91
Finance committee	0	0	11	0	1
Congregation members	25	98	0	100	6
Pastor and governing board	11	0	2	0	0
Pastor and finance committee	0	0	6	0	0
Pastor, governing board, and finance committee	2	0	2	0	0
Other, or other combination	3	2	1	0	2

*In percentages.
Based on Congregation Profile Booklet questions 26 and 27.

In all denominations, many persons—pastors, staff, and committee members—are involved in preparing the congregation's budget. When it comes to having the final say in setting budgets, however, the denominations differ widely. The Baptist and Lutheran churches are clear and uniform: The congregation votes on all budgets. The Presbyterians have a constitutional rule that the governing board (the session) must vote on budgets, but actual practices vary slightly. Catholic budgets are usually given final approval by the pastor, though in about 30 percent of the parishes, lay councils or finance committees share in the final decision making. The Catholic Church is consistently the least democratic in budget setting.

The Assemblies of God congregations seem to vary widely. In some, the pastor makes the final decision; in others, the lay board makes the decision or the congregation votes.

It is worth noting that we originally offered only the first four choices—pastors, governing board, finance committee, and congregation members—for replies to the question about final say in the budget. But a number of pastors insisted that final say was shared in their congregations, so for these instances, we coded their answers in the last four categories.

Stewardship Programs

How many of these churches emphasize the importance of tithing or of giving a certain proportion of one's income? In gathering the data, we needed to define *tithing* and *stewardship* carefully. The word *tithing* is often used today in a loose sense meaning "giving a large amount" or "giving a proportion of income," rather than in the strict sense of giving one-tenth of one's income. Therefore, when asking about tithing, we defined it in its strict sense.

The concept of *stewardship* is also imprecise. We used the phrase "biblical concept of stewardship of God's gifts" in the Congregation Profile Booklet to indicate to pastors that we meant the specific New Testament theology of stewardship, as opposed to appeals for funds or requests for resources in general. The questions in Table 2–8 were answered by the pastors.

The Assemblies of God churches are almost unanimous in teaching that tithing is obligatory and that God expects it. Giving a tithe is understood to ensure God's favor and spiritual protection. The Baptists stress this also, but not quite unanimously. The Catholics, Lutherans, and Presbyterians stress that tithing is not obligatory; however, a good Christian should make a plan to give a definite *proportion* of his or her income to the church. Catholic parishes stress tithing the least of the five denominations: 20 percent of Catholic parishes stress neither tithing nor proportionate giving.

TABLE 2–8.
TEACHINGS ABOUT TITHING AND GIVING*

	Assemblies of God	Baptist	Catholic	Lutheran	Presbyterian
Congregation's teaching emphasis with regard to tithing (i.e., giving at least 10 percent of income)					
1. The tithe belongs to God and is due to God. Christians should give additional offerings as they are able.	99	81	5	2	14
2. The tithe is an ideal but not obligatory.	2	9	17	34	32
3. Giving a *proportion* of one's income, not tithing, is emphasized.	0	7	58	58	42
4. Proportionate giving is not emphasized.	0	3	20	6	12
What emphasis do you give to the biblical concept of stewardship of God's gifts?					
1. Year-round emphasis	55	36	16	27	23
2. Occasional emphasis	45	58	44	64	66
3. Emphasized once per year	0	4	19	5	9
4. None	1	2	21	4	2
In your program to encourage giving, which had the greater emphasis?					
1. Giving a certain percentage of income	66	45	19	40	23
2. Supporting the programs of the church	11	20	47	30	41
3. 1 and 2 equally	15	25	19	24	29
4. No such program	8	10	16	6	8

*In percentages.
Based on Congregation Profile Booklet questions 32, 37, and 29. For exact wording, see Appendix B.

All the Protestants emphasized the biblical concept of stewardship, but the Catholic parishes did so less; 21 percent of the Catholic parishes did not accentuate it at all. The percentages of churches within each denomination stressing stewardship year-round or occasionally were as follows: Assemblies of God, 100 percent; Baptist, 94 percent; Catholic, 60 percent; Lutheran, 91 percent; and Presbyterian, 89 percent.

Questions 2 and 3 in Table 2–8 show that churches varied in stressing stewardship of God's gifts versus supporting the programs of the church.

The Catholics and Presbyterians were the most likely to stress church programs as a motivation for giving, while the Assemblies of God were quite clear in not doing this.

Table 2–9 summarizes the methods by which the churches promote stewardship, defined broadly.

TABLE 2–9.
PROGRAMS PROMOTING STEWARDSHIP*

	Assemblies of God	Baptist	Catholic	Lutheran	Presbyterian
The congregation uses					
Pledge cards or commitment cards	43	18	46	59	89
Numbered envelopes	19	65	94	93	87
Monthly or quarterly receipts	23	39	16	72	68
Annual receipts	77	61	50	67	68
Strategies used to encourage giving to support the congregation's budget include					
Sermons on stewardship	90	88	74	91	93
Appeals or testimonies during worship services	86	77	70	71	87
Distribution of promotional material	59	77	74	92	93
Canvassing every member by phone	8	3	3	5	9
Canvassing every member in person	11	4	1	18	20
Canvassing some members by phone	13	7	18	19	35
Canvassing some members in person	14	12	15	22	30
How is stewardship emphasized?					
Sermons	96	94	70	91	92
Lay testimonials	66	59	28	51	65
Bible study or Sunday school classes	75	72	9	55	44
Articles in the church newsletter	51	56	65	89	87

*In percentages.
Based on Congregation Profile Booklet questions 30, 28, and 38.

All the denominations emphasized stewardship in various ways, the Catholics less so than the others. The use of pledge cards was least common among Baptists; only 18 percent of the Baptist congregations reported using them.

To encourage giving, most congregations used sermons, appeals, testimonials, and promotional material. Not many canvassed members. The Presbyterians did the most canvassing—65 percent of the churches canvassed some members by phone or in person. The Baptists did the least—19 percent canvassed at least some members. The Assemblies of God and Baptists stressed stewardship regularly in Bible studies and Sunday school classes; the Lutherans and Presbyterians did this a bit less, and only 9 percent of the Catholics did it.

Theological Teachings on Christian Life and the Church

Some sociologists stress the importance of evangelical theology, personal piety, and maintaining a high commitment to specific Christian values (called "high demand" in sociological theory) in understanding levels of religious giving.[3] We asked three questions related to these issues (see Table 2–10).

The differences among denominations are dramatic. On the first question, the five denominations differ on the priorities of church life. The questionnaire offered four responses, and the majority of Assemblies of God and Baptist pastors chose "Helping others to commit their lives to Christ," while the majority of the pastors in the other denominations chose an emphasis on spiritual growth and personal fulfillment. Very few in any denomination chose the response about the remediation of unjust social structures.

In response to question 2, the denominations divide clearly into two groups with regard to the validity of various interpretations of Christian faith. The Assemblies of God, Catholics, and Baptists are clear in teaching that their own interpretation of Christianity is the valid one, while the Lutherans and Presbyterians tend to teach that there may be many valid interpretations.

On the third question, regarding Christian abstinences, the Assemblies of God and Baptists were clearly higher than the other three denominations. We should explain why we asked the pastors about abstinences. They are one aspect of life that sets committed church members off from the other people in town. Traditionally, abstinence from alcohol and gambling has been important in Christian life. But abstinences are not the only form of committed Christian living; there are others, and we could have asked, for example, about service to the poor or political action to reform society. These are also channels of Christian commitment. We probably should have asked more about other channels, at least to clarify that there are different modes of counterculturalism in Christian life today.

TABLE 2–10.
THEOLOGICAL TEACHINGS*

	Assemblies of God	Baptist	Catholic	Lutheran	Presbyterian
Which is emphasized most strongly in your congregation?					
1. Helping others to commit their lives to Christ.	50	54	5	10	21
2. Helping to change unjust and oppressive social structures or to alleviate human misery.	0	1	3	2	8
3. Following the life and teachings of Jesus as the basis for spiritual growth and personal fulfillment.	50	45	62	63	67
4. Faithfully participating in the tradition and sacraments of the church; maintaining the historical integrity of the faith.	0	0	30	25	3
What is your congregation's approach to interpreting the biblical meaning of Christian faith and the church?					
1. There is one best or true interpretation, and our congregation comes *closest* to teaching it.	79	65	83	24	7
2. There is one best or true interpretation, but no church can legitimately claim to be closer to it than another.	12	24	1	25	27
3. There are probably many valid interpretations, so many churches may be correctly teaching Christian faith.	9	11	16	51	66
Does your congregation teach abstinence from—? (percentage replying "yes")					
Certain kinds of food	7	5	13	0	0
Alcohol and/or tobacco	94	85	4	4	5
Gambling	90	81	2	2	6
Certain amusements, such as movies, nightclubs, or dancing	90	59	10	1	2
Other (primarily nonmarital sex)	25	31	37	8	18

*In percentages.
Based on Congregation Profile Booklet questions 33, 34, and 35.

ATTITUDES AND
BEHAVIORS OF LAITY

Our second set of information came from the 10,902 lay questionnaires. During data analysis, we quickly discovered that the lay respondents were not a random sample of laity. Biases entering during the sampling process and from the 61 percent response rate produced a sample of disproportionately loyal and active members. The bias is clearly visible when we compare the sample with the Gallup poll. The laity in our sample are also older and more affluent than average. As far as we can tell, the bias is similar in all five denominations. The lay questionnaire data *cannot be used* as an accurate description of average laity in any denomination. Its value is mainly in making denominational comparisons and especially in further analysis that relates lay characteristics to levels of giving.

The percentages of persons in the sample who were over sixty years of age were as follows: Assemblies of God, 22 percent; Baptists, 37 percent; Catholics, 38 percent; Lutherans, 37 percent; and Presbyterians, 43 percent. Approximate average family incomes were: Assemblies of God, $39,000; Baptists, $43,000; Catholics, $46,000; Lutherans, $44,000; and Presbyterians, $54,000. (See Table A–6.) Members of the Assemblies of God were the youngest and least affluent, the Presbyterians the oldest and most affluent.

Frequency of churchgoing, as reported in the lay survey, varied widely from denomination to denomination. The Assemblies of God and Baptist respondents go very often—66 percent of the former and 51 percent of the latter reported going more than once a week, compared with 20 percent of the Catholics, 4 percent of the Lutherans, and 7 percent of the Presbyterians.

Attitudes about
the Local Congregation

Table 2–11 shows that Catholic laity are somewhat unique in being more dissatisfied than others. They are the least likely to say that typical church members have enough influence in decisions about church money (48 percent, with the next lowest the Assemblies of God, at 67 percent); that church members have enough information about church funds (53 percent, with the next lowest the Assemblies of God, at 71 percent); that church decisions are made after open discussion with members (47 percent, with the next lowest the Assemblies of God, at 72 percent); and that congregation budget priorities are appropriate (53 percent, with the next lowest the Lutherans, at 69 percent).

Catholic lay attitudes about decision-making processes in their congregations are more in line with those of other denominations. Although they

TABLE 2–11.
ATTITUDES ABOUT THE LOCAL CONGREGATION*

	Assemblies of God	Baptist	Catholic	Lutheran	Presbyterian
How much enthusiasm do you feel about the work and programs of your congregation?					
Very high	33	26	17	16	22
Moderately high	49	52	51	55	56
Moderately low	12	16	18	19	16
Very low, or generally opposed	3	4	6	5	4
Do typical members of your congregation have enough influence in decisions about church money?					
Yes	67	79	48	69	70
Do you have enough information about the handling of funds by leaders of your congregation?					
Yes	71	81	53	73	76
Does your congregation have serious financial needs?					
Yes, very serious	11	6	6	9	8
Yes, somewhat serious	29	31	33	38	32
No, only routine	42	50	38	40	45
No, it is financially well off	6	6	6	4	5
Don't know	12	6	18	10	9
Who should handle financial matters in your congregation?					
I prefer clergy	3	1	9	1	1
I prefer a combination of clergy and lay	82	65	78	68	68
I prefer lay leaders	9	28	4	23	27
I have no preference	7	6	9	8	5

(table continues)

are the lowest in approving these processes, they are not so different from others (72 percent, with the next lowest the Lutherans, at 81 percent). It may seem inconsistent that Catholics report the least lay involvement in decision making yet a fairly high approval of present-day processes. Yet it fits with our experiences in the case studies, as we report later.

Overall enthusiasm for the congregation's work and programs is lower for Catholics and Lutherans than for the others, but the differences are not very great.

Table 2–11 *(continued).*

	Assemblies of God	Baptist	Catholic	Lutheran	Presbyterian
Strongly or Moderately Agree					
If I had to change the congregation I attend, I would feel a great sense of loss.	79	79	65	67	71
Opportunities to serve in lay leadership in my congregation are available, if one is willing to make the commitment.	89	91	85	88	91
Important decisions in my congregation are made with open discussion by leaders and members.	72	87	47	77	74
Overall, I approve of the decision-making processes in my congregation.	84	87	72	81	85
The budget priorities of my congregation are appropriate.	74	81	53	69	72
Pledge Cards					
Did you or someone else in your family fill out a pledge card for the year?					
Yes	31	29	52	60	79
Do you approve of using pledge cards?					
Yes	37	41	48	58	78

*In percentages.
Based on Lay Questionnaire questions 6, 4, 3, 2, 9, 21, 22, 23, 31, 24, 7, and 8. For exact wording, see Appendix C.

When asked whether they preferred clergy or laity to handle financial matters in their congregation, the Assemblies of God and Catholic members favored clergy more than did the other three denominations. Yet the preponderant view in all denominations is that both clergy and lay leaders should participate jointly.

The last two questions in Table 2–11 report on pledge cards. Use of pledge cards is by far the most common among Presbyterians, least common among Baptists and Assemblies of God. The Presbyterians are by far the most accepting of the use of pledge cards, and the Assemblies of God members are the least.

Theological Attitudes

We never doubted that theological attitudes were important in understanding church contributions. The research task was to identify the particular theological attitudes that are crucial to this understanding and to ask laity about them in a way that was clear and reliable. We asked several questions about theological topics, and two that turned out to be important are in Table 2–12.

TABLE 2–12.
THEOLOGICAL ATTITUDES OF LAITY*

	Assemblies of God	Baptist	Catholic	Lutheran	Presbyterian
Do you agree or disagree with the following statement?					
Only followers of Jesus Christ can be saved.					
Strongly agree or moderately agree	86	83	35	52	49
What do you believe the *primary* duty of Christians is?					
Helping others to commit their lives to Christ.	60	56	6	14	16
Helping to change unjust social structures.	0	1	6	4	6
Following the teachings of Jesus as the basis for spiritual growth.	38	41	60	63	66
Faithfully participating in the tradition and sacraments of the church.	0	1	22	11	5
Cannot choose or don't know.	2	2	6	7	7

*In percentages.
Based on Lay Questionnaire questions 20 and 33.

The first statement in the table is a measure of how distinctive and exclusive the people see Christian teachings as being. The Assemblies of God and Baptists are by far the highest in saying that only followers of Jesus Christ can be saved; the mainline denominations are in the middle, and the Catholics are lowest. We expected the conservative groups to be highest, but the low Catholic score was a surprise. Of the five denominations, Catholics appear to be the most tolerant and open to other religions.

The second question in the table shows lay attitudes about the primary duty of Christians. The major finding is that Assemblies of God and Baptists are far ahead of the others in stressing evangelism (the wording is "Helping others to commit their lives to Christ") as the primary Christian responsibility. The mainline denominations give greater emphasis to spiritual growth and (to a very limited extent) changing unjust social structures and participating in the tradition and sacraments. The Catholics are unique in that they stress tradition and sacraments more than the other denominations.

Attitudes about the Denomination

Table 2–13 reports lay attitudes toward their denominations and denominational leaders. When we asked laity about their level of enthusiasm for denominational work and programs, members of the Assemblies

TABLE 2–13.
LAY MEMBERS' ATTITUDES ABOUT THE DENOMINATION*

	Assemblies of God	Baptist	Catholic	Lutheran	Presbyterian
How much enthusiasm do you feel about the work and programs of your denomination?					
Very high	34	18	14	10	10
Moderately high	47	51	50	47	47
Moderately low	10	18	19	23	24
Very low or generally opposed	2	6	6	7	9
Do lay members have sufficient influence on the decision making in your denomination?					
Yes	66	68	49	66	69
Do you have enough information about the handling of funds by the leaders of your denomination?					
Yes	54	51	34	46	46
Overall, I approve of the decision-making processes in my denomination.					
Strongly agree or moderately agree	70	51	54	54	49

(table continues)

Table 2–13 *(continued)*.

	Assemblies of God	Baptist	Catholic	Lutheran	Presbyterian
Do you read denominational magazines, newspapers, or newsletters?					
Yes, regularly	40	45	36	34	24
Yes, occasionally	40	34	36	38	38
Rarely or never	20	21	28	28	38
Does your denomination as a whole have serious financial needs?					
Yes, very serious needs	4	9	13	7	10
Yes, somewhat serious needs	18	33	38	35	34
No, only routine needs	38	31	23	23	22
No, it is financially well off	3	2	7	2	2
Don't know	38	25	20	33	32
Mission Funding					
Do you prefer that the denomination select and fund mission projects, or do you prefer to select them?					
I prefer that the denomination select	19	35	23	23	20
I prefer giving to those I select	25	16	31	20	25
I prefer a combination of both	51	43	36	46	49
No opinion	5	6	10	11	6
Would you prefer that congregations make more decisions about missions and outreach programs, rather than having denominational leaders decide?					
Prefer more local decision-making	36	50	44	50	56
I like the situation now	48	37	33	29	29
Prefer more denominational decision making	3	4	4	3	3
No opinion	13	10	20	18	12

*In percentages.
Based on Lay Questionnaire questions 18, 12, 14, 32, 17, 13, 16, and 19. For exact wording, see Appendix C.

of God reported the most enthusiasm and the Lutherans and Presbyterians the least.

Do laity feel that they have enough influence on denominational decision making and enough information about denominational finances? Catholic laity are the most unhappy in both respects (shown in the second and third questions in the table). The Presbyterians are the least in contact with their national denomination, as evidenced by the fact that they read denominational periodicals less than members of the other faiths do.

Some observers have hypothesized that Catholics give less to their church because they are less convinced that their parish and denomination have serious needs. This hypothesis is false at both the level of the parish and the level of the denomination. Catholics are no different from members of other denominations in their perceptions of local congregational needs (see also Table 2–11). At the level of the denomination, Catholics are a bit *more* convinced than the others that it has serious needs (Table 2–13, question 6). In spite of what some people say about the pomp, glitter, and ceremony of the Vatican in Rome, it does not seem to have made Catholics believe that the worldwide Catholic Church is wealthy.

Of the five denominations, the Assemblies of God members are least likely to believe that their denomination has serious needs—and yet they are the biggest contributors of the five. Clearly, the perception of denominational needs is not crucial in influencing giving.

Would laity prefer more local decision making, as opposed to denominational decision making, about missions and outreach? Yes. These feelings are especially strong among Presbyterian and Lutheran laity and weakest in the Assemblies of God.

Ratings of Leaders

As expected, all laypersons rated their local leaders higher than their denominational leaders in trustworthiness, accountability, and overall leadership (see Table 2–14). It was surprising to us how low the levels of trust in denominational leaders were. The ratings of denominational leaders were lowest of all by the Presbyterian laity, highest by the Assemblies of God laity.

Another important finding was the low Catholic rating of financial accountability of local parish leaders; Catholic laity rated their parish leaders nineteen percentage points lower than ratings by any other denomination's laity.

Level of Giving

In the lay questionnaire, we asked the church members how they decide on how much money to give, and we also asked them to report on their giving in the previous year (see Table 2–15).

The first question shows that the Assemblies of God and Baptist laity are by far the most likely to tithe, and Presbyterians are the most likely to decide on an annual dollar amount of giving. Catholics are the most likely to decide week by week.

TABLE 2–14.
RATING CONGREGATIONAL AND DENOMINATIONAL LEADERS*

	Assemblies of God	Baptist	Catholic	Lutheran	Presbyterian
How much do you trust the handling and allocation of funds by the leaders of your congregation?					
High level of trust†	81	81	66	69	73
How much do you trust the handling and allocation of funds by the leaders of your denomination?					
High level of trust	68	43	46	47	43
The leaders of my congregation are sufficiently accountable to members regarding how church contributions are used.					
Strongly agree or moderately agree	80	87	61	81	81
The leaders of my denomination are sufficiently accountable to members regarding how church contributions are used.					
Strongly agree or moderately agree	61	56	44	49	44
Overall, the pastor of my congregation is doing a good job.					
Strongly agree or moderately agree	93	89	87	87	87
Overall, the leadership of my denomination is doing a good job.					
Strongly agree or moderately agree	82	60	71	66	54

*In percentages.
†On the first question, the response choices were "High level of trust," "Medium level of trust," "Low level of trust," and "No opinion."
Based on Lay Questionnaire questions 5, 15, 27, 28, 29, and 30.

The second question tells us that most church members perceive their congregations as promoting a "stewardship approach" to the giving of time, talent, and money. This has a positive effect on some members, no effect on others. Very seldom does it produce a negative effect. Note that one-quarter of the Catholic respondents were not sure whether or not their parish had a stewardship emphasis.

TABLE 2–15.
LEVELS OF GIVING AND ATTITUDES TOWARD GIVING

	Assemblies of God	Baptist	Catholic	Lutheran	Presbyterian
How do you decide how much money to contribute to your congregation?*					
I give 10 percent or more of my income.	73	44	4	7	9
I decide on a percentage of my income annually.	3	7	6	8	9
I decide on an annual dollar amount.	2	9	14	22	41
I decide on a weekly dollar amount.	8	19	39	38	25
I give what I can afford each week.	15	22	37	26	15
Has your congregation actively promoted a "stewardship approach" to the giving of time, talent, and money, which teaches the spiritual meaning of how we use God's gifts?*					
Yes, and therefore I am likely to give more.	42	34	20	28	35
Yes, but it has no effect on my giving.	30	38	44	53	51
Yes, and therefore I am likely to give less.	0	0	1	1	1
No	15	17	10	8	6
Don't know	13	11	25	10	7
Average Household Contributions Last Year					
To your church in regular offerings, not including a capital campaign	$2,985	2,479	819	1,196	1,635
To your church for a special capital campaign	$308	371	239	310	452
To groups or causes in your denomination other than the local congregation	$270	201	203	127	156
To all religious groups or causes outside your denomination	$305	194	129	138	259
To nonreligious charities, community organizations, or social causes	$141	220	244	261	401

(table continues)

Table 2–15 *(continued)*.

	Assemblies of God	Baptist	Catholic	Lutheran	Presbyterian
Total contributions to the congregation	$3,254	2,810	1,032	1,471	2,036
Total religious giving	$3,820	3,194	1,346	1,727	2,443
Contributions to the congregation as a percent of household income	8.3	6.9	2.9	3.7	3.9
Total religious giving as a percent of household income	9.9	7.8	3.7	4.4	4.8

*Responses indicated in percentages.
Based on Lay Questionnaire questions 11, 10, 37, 38, 39, 40, and 41. For exact wording, see Appendix C.

The lower half of the table summarizes self-reported giving. The levels of giving in each denomination are shown in Figure 2–2. (For more detail, see Table A–7.) The levels of giving in the table are higher than we have seen in any other research, indicating that our sample is biased toward people strongly committed to their churches.[4] Again, we caution the reader that the laypersons in our survey are not a random sample.[5]

Self-reported levels of religious giving are clearly highest for the Assemblies of God, with Baptists second. Catholics are by far the lowest. Only 19 percent of the Catholics contributed $1,001 last year, compared with 72 percent of the Assemblies of God members, 56 percent of the Baptists, 39 percent of the Lutherans, and 46 percent of the Presbyterians. The relative levels of giving are the same as reported in the Congregation Profile Booklet (Table 2–3), making us believe that the biases are somewhat the same in each denomination.

Giving to secular causes is low, compared with giving to one's congregation or parish; the Presbyterian laity give the most to secular causes, and the Assemblies of God give the least.[6] Clearly, differences in congregational giving in the five denominations cannot be explained by countervailing levels of religious giving outside the congregation or by levels of secular giving. We have frequently heard it argued that Catholic giving to the parish is low because Catholics are giving so much to other Catholic causes. This argument is false.

Are there patterns for *where* church members decide to give their money? Are certain types of people more inclined to give to nonreligious charities than other types? We checked whether family income, education, or frequency of church attendance was related to decisions about

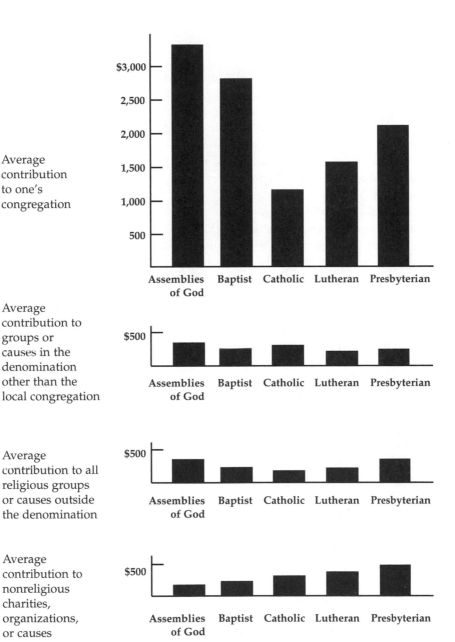

Average
contribution
to one's
congregation

Average
contribution to
groups or
causes in the
denomination
other than the
local congregation

Average
contribution to all
religious groups
or causes outside
the denomination

Average
contribution to
nonreligious
charities,
organizations,
or causes

**FIGURE 2–2.
LEVELS OF SELF-REPORTED
HOUSEHOLD GIVING**

where to send money among members of each of the five denominations.

First, we looked at what might influence the percentage of religious giving going outside the local congregation. We found that members who attend regularly tend to give a lower percentage of their religious giving to such causes, compared with people who attend less frequently. The pattern is fairly strong among Assemblies of God and Baptist members but weaker in the other denominations. We found that level of income and level of education were not predictors of religious giving outside the congregation.

How about giving to nonreligious charities and causes? Here we found definite patterns, as shown in Figure 2–3. Family income is one factor; except for Assemblies of God and Baptist members, the higher the family income, the higher the percentage of total giving that goes to nonreligious charities (top of Figure 2–3). An even stronger factor is the rate of church attendance, shown in the bottom of Figure 2–3. People who attend church regularly direct a much lower percentage of their total giving to nonreligious causes, while infrequent attenders give higher percentages. The relationship between level of education and percentage of nonreligious giving was also moderately strong, with the more educated members in each denomination giving a higher percentage to nonreligious causes.

We can summarize: People heavily involved in the life of their congregation give a higher percentage of their total philanthropic giving to their congregation.

All past research has found that giving to congregations is very unequal, with a few members giving most of the funds and many other members giving little or nothing. This seems to happen in all denominations and even in most nonreligious philanthropic organizations. We found the same pattern, best illustrated by our Gallup poll findings (see Figure 2–4). The figure divides Baptists, Catholics, and Lutherans into quintiles, that is, five equal-sized groups. Then it lines up the five from the lowest giving to the highest giving and depicts the average giving in each group. The top of Figure 2–4 shows giving to one's congregation, and the bottom shows all other religious giving. About half of the total giving is done by the fifth quintile (the upper 20 percent), and the greatest denominational differences occur in the fourth and fifth quintiles (the upper 40 percent). We believe that the refusal of some Gallup respondents to report their giving reduced the extremeness of the skew; other evidence indicates that people who refused to report their giving gave little, so if everyone had answered the questions, the five quintiles would have been even more unequal.

FAMILY INCOME

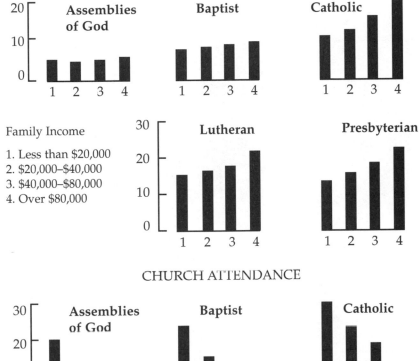

Family Income

1. Less than $20,000
2. $20,000–$40,000
3. $40,000–$80,000
4. Over $80,000

CHURCH ATTENDANCE

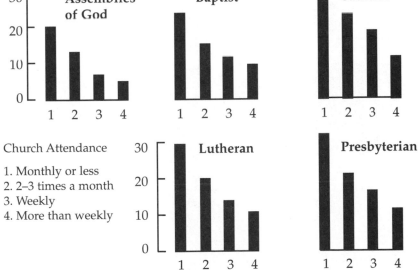

Church Attendance

1. Monthly or less
2. 2–3 times a month
3. Weekly
4. More than weekly

FIGURE 2–3.
PERCENT OF TOTAL GIVING
GOING TO NONRELIGIOUS CHARITIES BY LEVELS
OF FAMILY INCOME AND CHURCH ATTENDANCE

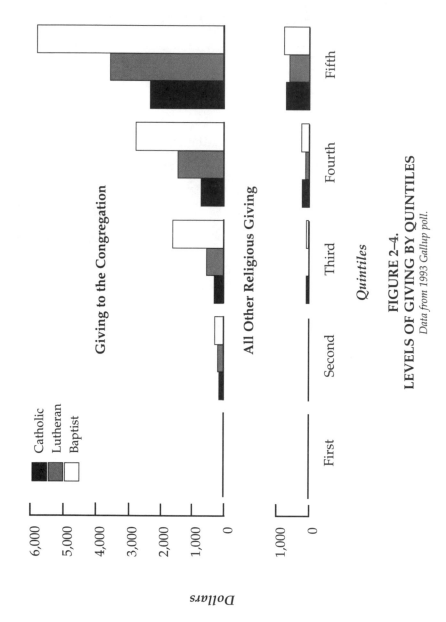

FIGURE 2–4.
LEVELS OF GIVING BY QUINTILES
Data from 1993 Gallup poll.

Volunteering

We asked about the amount of volunteering the members do in their churches. The hours of volunteering were highest for the Assemblies of God and Baptist laity, lowest for the Catholic laity. The average hours the members volunteered for church tasks in the last month were 5.3 for Assemblies of God, 5.6 for Baptists, 2.2 for Catholics, 3.1 for Lutherans, and 3.6 for Presbyterians. Thus the amount of time donated by members in the five denominations is proportional to the amount of money they give. In further analysis, we again found that people who give more money also tend to volunteer more hours to their congregations.

SUMMARY

In this chapter we have described the five denominations so that the reader can see how they compare on various measures: congregation size, levels of giving, and constitutional procedures. These denominations are also clearly different in their teachings about the truth of various Christian interpretations, the importance of tithing and certain abstinences in everyday living, and the primary duties of Christians. This sort of comparative information is helpful, but it does not tell us *which* factors account for the variations in giving. To know that, we need to relate these measures to the levels of giving, to see which factors are associated and which are plausibly influential. This is the task described in chapters 3 and 4.

3
Individual Factors
Influencing Giving

From other research on religious giving, we compiled twenty-two hypotheses about why church members give large amounts or small amounts to their churches. Thirteen hypotheses were about characteristics of individual church members, and we examine these hypotheses in this chapter. The other nine hypotheses were about the congregation as an institution. They are discussed in chapter 4. But before we can discuss individual giving, we must explain several technical issues and terms.

AVAILABLE MEASURES OF GIVING

The first part of our analysis is about individual church members. It asks which of their attitudes or personal characteristics predict high or low giving. In the lay questionnaire, we asked each respondent his or her level of household giving to the congregation and also his or her annual family income. The Gallup poll had parallel questions.

The second part of our analysis (see chapter 4) is at the level of the congregation. It asks which characteristics of congregations predict high or low giving. Some traits of congregations are institutional (for example, size), and some are really a matter of the characteristics of individual members (for example, overall attitudes and levels of enthusiasm). Analysis at the level of the congregation needs to utilize both elements. The most reliable method of doing this is to combine lay attitudes within each congregation into a single score, then to relate that score to other characteristics of the congregation. We did this for all 625 congregations.

We had two measures of giving to congregations. The first was the congregation's total giving in the previous year, as reported by pastors in the Congregation Profile Booklets, divided by the number of members. This ratio is per-member giving. But as mentioned earlier, we have some doubts about the accuracy of the membership figures given to us. This would be a major problem when comparing denominations but is far less so for analyses within each denomination. To estimate the percentage of household income given in each congregation, we divided the total amount given to the church by the estimated total income of the member families, based on the responses in the Congregation Profile Booklets.

The second measure of congregational giving was derived from the lay questionnaires. The measure was the average amount given (regular giving and giving to special campaigns) by the households of the laypersons in each congregation's sample. This measure has a weakness in that it depends on a limited sample of parishioners. But it is based on actual reports of giving and family incomes, not estimates made by someone else. As we show, this second measure proved the more useful of the two in the hypothesis testing.[1]

Technical Details about the Data

Three technical details need to be explained. The first has to do with the number of lay questionnaires in each congregation. On average, we received 17.4 lay questionnaires per congregation in response to the 30 that were sent, but for some congregations the number was much lower. We needed a minimum number returned per congregation for inclusion in the analysis, and after some experimentation we chose 10 as the lower limit. All congregations with fewer than 10 lay questionnaires returned were removed from the analysis. This reduced the number of congregations to 103 for Assemblies, 97 for Baptists, 119 for Catholics, 123 for Lutherans, and 122 for Presbyterians, for a total of 564. It raised the average number of questionnaires per congregation to 18.5.

Second, correlations involving religious giving are artificially weakened by skewness in the data; that is, most church members give little, but a few give large amounts. This introduces a statistical weakness in that skewness unduly depresses correlations.[2] With financial data of the type we have, it is common procedure for researchers to transform the amount of money given by taking the square root; this strengthens correlations and brings them closer to their true level. We took the square root of the money given in all the correlational analysis. But in the discussion and data here, all reports of dollar amounts or percentages are in actual dollars, untransformed.

Third, a few lay respondents reported extremely high levels of giving to their congregations. We were puzzled by this. Not many people can afford to give $40,000, $50,000, or more to their congregations in one year, but 12 of the 10,902 lay respondents reported giving $40,000 or more. We checked for errors in the data entry, but we found none. We suspect that these were one-time gifts, not annual gifts. These 12 outliers reduced the value of the correlations, so we deleted them in all the correlation analysis.

HYPOTHESES ABOUT INDIVIDUALS
WHO GIVE TO CHURCHES

The following hypotheses look at the influence of characteristics of individuals. In some of the hypotheses, we have grouped several specific characteristics together, for the sake of simplicity, because they are related.

Hypothesis 1: **Individual background factors influence giving. Specifically, persons of higher income, higher education, and fewer dependent children give more. Older persons give more. Race, urban versus rural residence, and geographical region influence giving.**

This is a family of hypotheses that are conveniently discussed together.

Income

All past research has demonstrated that level of family income greatly influences giving to the congregation, and we found the same here. The self-reported levels of giving to the congregation (regular plus special giving) by different income categories are shown in Figure 3–1. In all denominations, members with low-income levels give at similar (low) rates; but as incomes increase, the lines diverge, with Assemblies and Baptist members giving far higher percentages of their income than the others. The Catholic trend line is remarkably flat for persons with incomes below $80,000.

The percentage of household income given to the church varies inversely with income, so that high-income households tend to give a lower percentage. All past research has found this same pattern. Figure 3–2 shows the relationships; both giving and household income were self-reported. All five lines slope downward to the right, and the lines level out for the higher-income families.

Education

As we might expect, religious giving increases as the level of education increases, much as it increases as family income rises. Figure 3–3 shows self-reported household giving to the congregation by respondents at four educational levels. It has the expected pattern, except for Catholics. Catholics' level of giving is essentially unrelated to their education.

Dependent Children

Do households with more dependent children under eighteen years of age give more or less than other households? No. At the individual level,

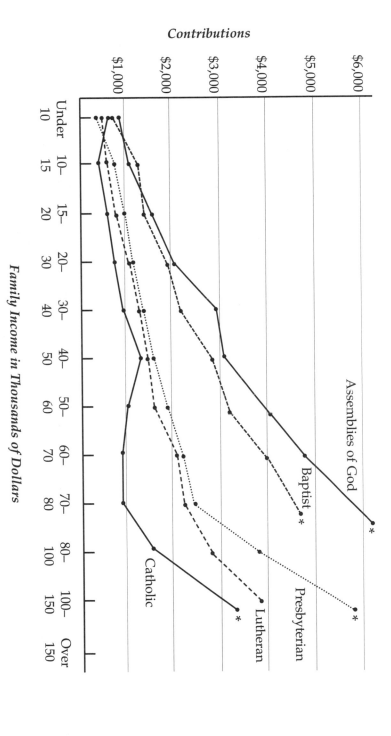

FIGURE 3–1.
CONGREGATIONAL GIVING BY FAMILY INCOME
Final point is average of two categories, due to unstable data at the high end of each distribution. Groups with less than fifty cases are not shown.

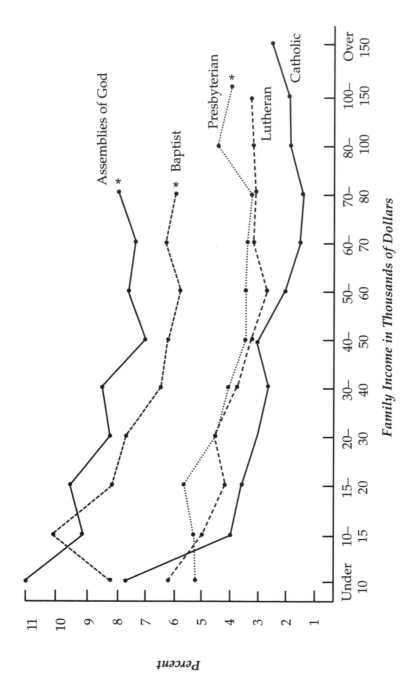

FIGURE 3–2.

PERCENT OF FAMILY INCOME CONTRIBUTED TO THE CONGREGATION

*Final point is average of two categories, due to erratic data. Groups with less than fifty cases are not shown.

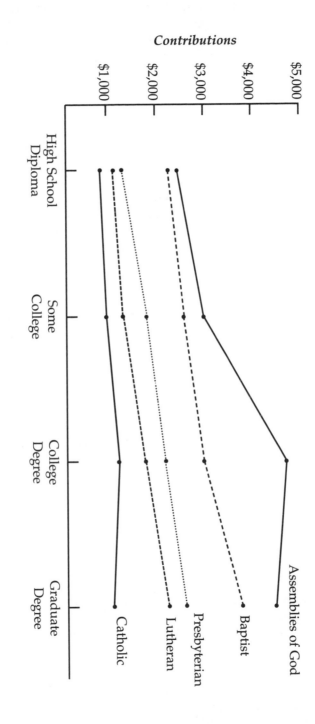

FIGURE 3–3.
CONGREGATIONAL GIVING BY LEVEL OF EDUCATION

when we related the total number of dependent children to self-reported amount contributed, we found no associations. We controlled for age by computing these correlations solely for persons fifty years of age or younger and again found nothing. The number of dependent children in a household is unrelated to church giving.

Age

Past research has consistently found that religious giving varies by age, with the highest giving done by people fifty to sixty-five years old. After age 65, giving decreases because household income often decreases. Figure 3–4 shows levels of self-reported giving by age in our study. The highest levels of giving are by persons between forty-five and seventy-five years of age. The lines for Assemblies of God and Baptists dip sharply in the older ages, unlike the lines for the other denominations, which change little for older members. This decline may be related to the greater numbers of church members in these two denominations who tithe.

Age relates more strongly to the percentage of household income given to the congregation, as Figure 3–5 shows. Older persons tend to give higher percentages of their income. This probably has to do with how much income people of various ages consider to be "disposable."

Race

We asked all the laypersons about their racial group, and when we compared the groups' levels of giving, only one pattern was significant: Among Assemblies of God laity, whites gave more than did Hispanics. Whites reported giving an average of $3,246, while Hispanics reported $2,821. This reflects their relative incomes—white Assemblies of God laity averaged $41,105 in family income, while Hispanics averaged $32,939. In the other denominations, no patterns with regard to whites and Hispanics appeared. Comparisons of whites and African Americans were not possible, due to the small number of African Americans in the sample.

Urban versus Rural

In the Congregation Profile Booklet, we requested that each church identify itself by location in one of eight community types, ranging from large city (population over 250,000) to rural area. Three denominations had significant differences in amounts given in urban and rural churches—Baptists, Lutherans, and Presbyterians. Baptist churches in urban areas (cities and suburbs) clearly had a higher per-membership contribution and a higher percentage of family income contributed. Contributions in Baptist

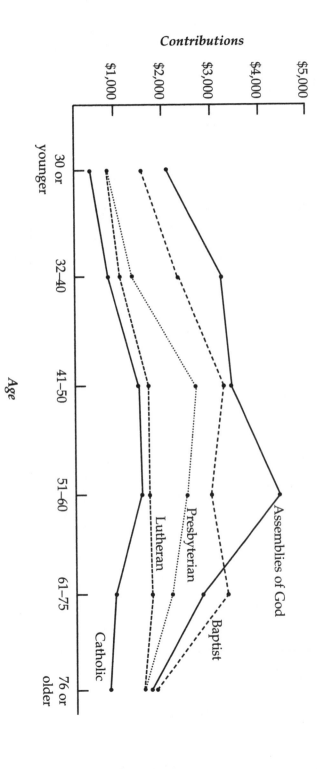

FIGURE 3–4.
CONGREGATIONAL GIVING BY AGE

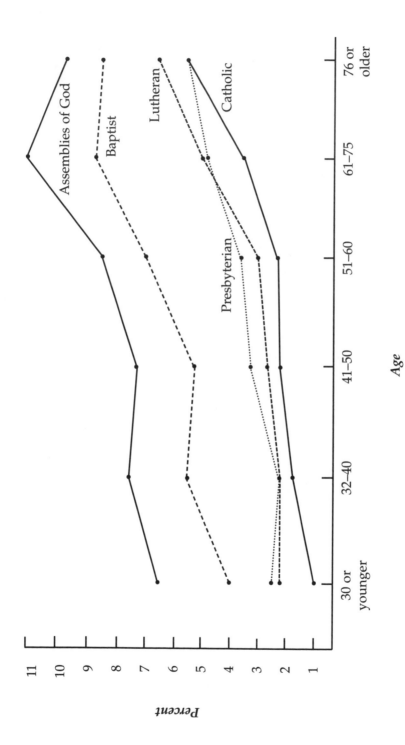

FIGURE 3–5.
PERCENT OF INCOME CONTRIBUTED BY AGE

churches in village and rural churches were lower. Lutheran churches had the same pattern, though less striking. Lutheran churches in medium-sized cities and their suburbs had higher levels of giving than did churches in other areas. Highest levels were in churches in the suburbs of medium-sized cities, where giving averaged $595 per member; second highest were in churches in medium-sized cities, where giving averaged $571 per member. The same pattern occurred with percentage of family income contributed.

The Presbyterian pattern was somewhat erratic, but the village and rural churches were clearly the lowest in giving.

Region of the Nation

We compared four regions of the nation—Northeast, Midwest, South, and West. Baptist and Presbyterian giving was significantly higher in the West, while Catholic and Lutheran giving was highest in the South.[3] These patterns are not very reliable, since our study was not designed to produce precise data on regional differences.

Hypothesis 2: Married members give more than single or widowed members, and married members whose spouses attend the same church give more.

True. We asked about marital status and whether the respondent's spouse attends the same church. The results were clear: Married members give far more than those who are single, divorced, or widowed. Moreover, in four of the denominations, people who are married give far more if their partner attends the same congregation as they do. But Catholics are an exception; married Catholics whose spouses do not attend the same parish give slightly more. This may be because Catholics married to Protestant spouses are influenced by an example of higher giving by their spouses, but we do not know; this is speculation. (For the data, see Table A–8.)

Hypothesis 3: Members whose children attend five-day-a-week religious schools give less to the congregation or parish.

False. This hypothesis refers mainly to Assemblies of God members and Catholics. Eleven percent of Assemblies members and 13 percent of Catholics have children in such schools. It has been argued that parents of children in religious schools have less money left for giving to their churches, and hence they give less. But the statement is untrue. We had several ways to test it, and none of the tests supported it. In fact, among both Assemblies of God and Catholic members, those with children in religious schools give more, not less, to their churches. Average giving per Assemblies household with children in religious school was $4,270; in those without, it was $3,125. For Catholics with children in religious schools, average giving per household was $1,528; for those without, it was $960. The Gallup poll had data on this topic also but indicated no difference in giving between Catholics with and without children in religious schools.

Are there overall differences in giving between Catholic parishes with schools and without schools? No. We compared average giving in parishes with a parish school, parishes cosponsoring a school, and parishes with no school. The differences in giving were small and unreliable. (For the data see Table A–9.) Apparently, parents of parochial school students are more involved in the parish and hence give more.

In sum: Although the data are not entirely consistent, no analyses show that parents with children in five-day-a-week religious schools give *less* to the parish. They give at roughly the same rate as other people their age, possibly at a higher rate. This conclusion agrees with the 1994 study by Educational Testing Service (see note 3, above).

Hypothesis 4: Members who perceive more democratic decision making regarding use of church funds give more.

Since this was an important hypothesis guiding our study, we asked numerous questions to test it. In the lay questionnaires we included six questions about parish decision making, and in the Gallup poll we included three. We expected to find support for the hypothesis, but to our surprise, we found little. Yet one specific aspect of it was supported.

In the analysis, we first correlated attitudes of individuals with self-reported giving. There were no relationships. Next we looked at the congregation level, correlating average attitudes with average self-reported giving in each congregation. The results showed some support for the hypothesis. (For the data, see Tables A–10 and A–11.) The clearest support was on the statement "Opportunities to serve in lay leadership in my congregation are available, if one is willing to make the commitment." In all denominations, agreement with this statement was associated with higher giving. The reason is possibly that church members who feel excluded from opportunities for lay leadership feel disesteemed and hence give less.

In summary, feelings about democratic decision making are only a secondary factor in religious giving, not a primary one. These feelings seem to be important in at least one respect: People who feel that democratic processes in the church are being blocked or subverted will tend to give less. That is, *blockages* of democratic decision making are apparently more consequential than the actual constitutional processes, whatever they may be. Dissatisfaction is the main factor, not the nature of the constitutional process.

One statement in the lay questionnaire turned out to be important: "Overall, I approve of the decision-making processes in my *denomination.*" Among Catholics, agreement with this statement was associated with higher giving. Among Assemblies of God and Lutheran members, agreement with this statement had no association with giving. But among Southern Baptists and Presbyterians, agreement was associated with *lower* giving. (See Table A–10.) That is, Southern Baptist and Presbyterian parishioners who disapprove of denominational decision making tend to give *more* to their congregations.

Reform-minded Catholics often argue that more democratic decision making at all levels of the church would enhance the level of giving. To them we reply that the decision-making procedures in themselves have no measurable effect. Only insofar as the procedures are able to reduce the *dissatisfaction* among laity will they have an influence on the level of giving. The level of dissatisfaction is the key thing.

Hypothesis 5: **Members give more when they perceive adequate accountability by congregational and denominational leaders regarding use of funds.**

To our surprise, the findings to support this hypothesis were weak. In the lay members' questionnaire we included four questions about accountability of leaders. Three of the questions were included in the Gallup poll.

In the Gallup poll, only one pattern occurred: Baptists and Lutherans who feel they have enough information about the handling of funds in their congregation gave a higher percent of their income. For Baptists the correlation was .29; for Lutherans, .23. Both are fairly weak.[4] For Catholics, there was no association.

In the lay questionnaire, however, a few patterns appeared (see Table 3–1). The clearest pattern is that laity who feel they have sufficient information on *congregational* finances tend to give more; this is the case in all denominations. Having enough information on *denominational* finances is associated with higher giving only among Catholics.

The feeling that *congregational* leaders are sufficiently accountable is associated with higher giving among Baptists, Catholics, and Lutherans. The feeling that *denominational* leaders are sufficiently accountable is

TABLE 3–1.
SELF-REPORTED GIVING BY ATTITUDES ON ACCOUNTABILITY

	Assemblies of God	Baptist	Catholic	Lutheran	Presbyterian
Do you have enough information about the handling of funds by the leaders of your congregation?					
Yes	$3,461*	2,996*	1,221*	1,583*	2,129*
No	3,123	2,450	875	1,383	2,040
Do you have enough information about the handling of funds by the leaders of your denomination?					
Yes	$3,322	2,835*	1,313*	1,583	1,942*
No	3,461	3,073	941	1,586	2,424
The leaders of my *congregation* are sufficiently accountable regarding how contributions are used.					
Strongly agree	$3,501*	3,121*	1,267*	1,666*	2,193
Moderately agree	3,154	2,486	997	1,492	1,937
Neither agree nor disagree	2,285	1,488	816	903	1,618
Moderately disagree	3,141	—	1,248	1,272	2,341
Strongly disagree	—	—	730	—	—
The leaders of my *denomination* are sufficiently accountable regarding how contributions are used.					
Strongly agree	$3,616	2,795	1,483*	1,811*	2,000*
Moderately agree	2,953	2,796	884	1,513	1,824
Neither agree nor disagree	3,009	2,564	880	1,246	1,772
Moderately disagree	3,407	3,435	1,273	1,609	2,822
Strongly disagree	3,548	3,012	809	1,608	2,718

*Significant at .05. Groups with fewer than fifty persons are not shown.
Based on Lay Questionnaire items 3, 14, 27, and 28. For exact wording, see Appendix C.

associated with higher giving for Catholics but lower giving for Presbyterians. Apparently, some Presbyterians feel alienated from the denomination. For Assemblies of God, Baptists, and Lutherans, the patterns are mixed and unclear.

We found stronger patterns when we looked at average attitudes at the congregational level. Within each denomination, the associations between these attitudes and church giving were mixed, but when we combined all five denominations, the correlations became stronger: Feelings that congregational and denominational leaders are sufficiently accountable are associated with higher giving. Put simply, denominations whose members feel higher accountability of leaders also have higher giving.

In summary, the hypothesis finds some support, but it is not equally important in all denominations. In all of them, members' attitudes that they have enough information about local finances are associated with higher giving. In three denominations—Baptists, Catholics, and Lutherans—the belief that congregational leaders are sufficiently accountable is associated with higher giving. Feelings about accountability of denominational leaders have weak and mixed associations with giving. If we look at the pooled data of all five denominations, the patterns are stronger.

Hypothesis 6: Members who have doubts about honesty and openness in the handling of church funds give less.

The lay questionnaire included two questions: "How much do you trust the handling and allocation of funds by the leaders of your congregation?" (question 5) and "How much do you trust the handling and allocation of funds by the leaders of your denomination?" (question 15). At the level of individuals, we correlated the responses to these items with self-reported giving and found no associations. The Gallup poll had one question about trust, but it also had no association with giving.

At the congregational level, the correlations with both questions were noteworthy only when we pooled all five denominations; within each denomination, the correlations were weak. We conclude that although doubts about honesty and openness in handling church funds do exist, they are generally unimportant in affecting levels of giving.

Is the lack of support for this hypothesis because the levels of trust are so high that doubts (even though they might affect giving) are too infrequent to have a measurable effect? At the congregational level, yes. The laity reported strong trust in congregational leaders. The percentages of laity saying they have a "high level of trust" were Assemblies of God, 81 percent; Baptists, 81 percent; Catholics, 66 percent; Lutherans, 69 percent; and Presbyterians, 73 percent. Almost no one said they had a "low level of trust" at the congregational level. But at the denominational level, infrequent doubts resulting from strong trust are not the explanation, since the levels of trust were lower. The percentages of laity saying they have a "high level of trust" in denominational leaders were Assemblies of God, 68 percent; Baptists, 43 percent; Catholics, 46 percent; Lutherans, 47 percent; and Presbyterians, 43 percent. We can only conclude that doubts about denominational leadership have little effect on local church giving.

Hypothesis 7: **Members who are actively involved
   in congregational life give more.**

This hypothesis has been proven repeatedly in past research, and our
project provided more proof. Our data are shown in Table A–12. Clearly,
church attendance and hours spent volunteering for church work are
highly predictive of giving. All research studies agree.

Do people who have been members a longer time tend to give more
than others, if all else is equal? Yes, in all five denominations, though the
overall differences are small.

Hypothesis 8: **Members who feel they have adequate
   communications with congregational and denominational leaders and who are more enthusiastic
   about them give more.**

We found modest support. This hypothesis has two levels: congregation and denomination. Since church members give directly to the congregation and—for the most part—indirectly to the denomination, we expected the factors concerning the congregation to have greater impact. We
look first at the congregational level.

Feelings about the Congregation

Of the four questions in the lay questionnaire that asked for respondents'
feelings about the congregation, one proved to have no association at all
with levels of giving, despite multiple tests. This question stated, "Overall,
the pastor of my *congregation* is doing a good job." Responses to it are not
related to level of giving, largely because pastors received uniformly high
ratings. Apparently feelings of support or alienation regarding the pastor
are not important *in general* in influencing members' giving. In spite of the
numerous stories we have heard from individuals about how they
stopped giving due to the uninspiring leadership of their pastor, such feelings are apparently not decisive in general.

This surprising finding could have occurred because our lay samples
did not include many inactive or alienated members, due to our research
method. But this possibility is remote, because in the Gallup poll we asked
the identical question and had identical results.

The other three questions about the congregation and their correlations with giving are shown in Table A–13. At the level of individuals, all
findings were too weak to show. When average attitudes in each congregation are correlated with average giving, moderately strong associations
appeared *across* denominations, but seldom within denominations. For

example, if we combine the denominations and look at the statement "If I had to change the congregation I attend, I would feel a great sense of loss," average attitudes correlated with levels of giving at .26 and with the percent of income contributed at .36. Yet the corresponding correlations *within* each denomination are never this strong. This tells us that denominations with parishioners who are relatively more attached to their churches have higher levels of giving, while variation in attachment to churches within each denomination has less impact.

The Gallup poll asked four questions about congregations: "How much enthusiasm do you feel, in general, about the work and programs of your congregation?"; "If I had to change the congregation I attend, I would feel a great sense of loss"; "The budget priorities of my congregation are appropriate"; and "Overall, the pastor of my *congregation* is doing a good job." Only the second of these items had noteworthy correlations with religious giving. Its correlations with the percent of family income given were .28 for Baptists, .20 for Catholics, and .12 for Lutherans. These associations are modest, yet strong enough to take note of. It seems that feelings of love and attachment for the congregation are more important than ratings of the congregation's leadership and programs.

Feelings about the Denomination

To our surprise, attitudes about the denomination had as strong an impact on level of giving as attitudes about the congregation. Though the patterns were weak and mixed, some strong correlations occurred for the Baptists and Catholics. (See Table A–14.) Among Catholics, communication with the larger church structures seems to affect giving; responses to the question "Do you read any magazines, newspapers, or newsletters published by your denomination?" correlated quite strongly with giving among Catholics.

Two of the lay questionnaire items—those asking about level of enthusiasm for the denomination and whether denominational leaders were doing a good job—were included in the Gallup poll. Neither related to giving.

In summary, the hypothesis has modest support. Feelings of attachment to one's congregation predict a somewhat higher percentage of income given in all denominations except the Assemblies of God. Having enthusiasm for congregational programs predicted higher giving among Baptists and Lutherans but not among the others. Feelings about one's denomination also affect levels of giving, especially reports of how much the layperson reads denominational materials; people who read denominational magazines and newsletters give a bit more than others.

Hypothesis 9: **Members who believe their congregation or denomination has serious needs give more. Members of congregations in debt or in the midst of capital campaigns give more. Members of congregations with endowments give less.**

Here we have a collection of four distinct hypotheses.

1. Do members who believe their congregation or denomination has serious needs give more? We found that this belief about congregational needs has no consistent effect on giving, but this belief about denominational needs has some effect. Among Catholics, Lutherans, and Presbyterians, members who think the denomination had serious needs clearly tend to give more; among Assemblies of God and Baptists, there was no pattern.

2. Do congregations with debts experience higher levels of giving? Only in some denominations. The answer is yes for Baptists, Lutherans, and Presbyterians but not for the others. The correlations at the congregational level with average self-reported giving were .28 for Baptists, .38 for Lutherans, and .25 for Presbyterians.

3. Do congregations in the midst of capital campaigns receive more contributions? For the Lutherans and some Presbyterians the answer is yes, but elsewhere it is no. Members of Lutheran churches with capital campaigns clearly gave more dollars—an average of $535 last year, compared with an average of $366 in Lutheran churches not holding capital campaigns. The pattern occurred in both small and large churches. Members of large Presbyterian churches, but not small ones, gave more if the church was in a capital campaign. In the large churches, the averages were $678 for those in campaigns, $547 for the others.

4. Do congregations with endowments receive lower contributions? We looked at each denomination separately, and we required that an endowment total $100,000 or more. Although we made multiple tests of the hypothesis, there is no link between endowments and contributions. This surprised us. Having an endowment is not associated with either higher or lower giving.

Hypothesis 10: **Members with stronger and more traditional doctrinal beliefs give more.**

We asked three questions in the lay questionnaire and offered three ratings of the congregation in the Congregation Profile Booklet. We found that traditional beliefs are important determinants of giving. The hypothesis is strongly supported.

Let us look at the lay questionnaire items first. Two of them took the form of statements, with five responses ranging from "Strongly agree" to "Strongly disagree." See Table 3–2 and Table A–15 for a listing of these statements.

Table 3–2 demonstrates that the stronger the orthodox belief and faith, the higher the giving, except among Catholics. Also, the more emphasis there is on helping others to commit their lives to Christ, the higher the giving—except among Catholics. (We return to the Catholics below.)

The associations between these beliefs and giving were also tested by correlations, and the results are shown in Table A–15. These results show again that evangelical beliefs and self-reported importance of religion in one's life are clearly associated with higher levels of giving. The most

TABLE 3–2.
RELATIONSHIP OF CONGREGATIONAL GIVING
TO RELIGIOUS BELIEFS

	Assemblies of God	Baptist	Catholic	Lutheran	Presbyterian
Individual Level: Self-Reported Household Giving to the Congregation					
Only followers of Jesus Christ can be saved.					
Strongly agree	$3,475*	3,015*	934	1,690*	2,158
Moderately agree	2,180	2,085	1,027	1,291	1,985
Neither agree nor disagree	—	2,116	854	1,506	2,015
Moderately disagree	—	—	954	1,174	1,550
Strongly disagree	2,305	2,213	1,214	1,420	2,228
What is the *primary* duty of Christians?					
Helping others commit their lives to Christ.	$3,222	3,095*	1,033*	2,008*	2,420*
Helping change unjust social structures.	—	—	1,023	1,639	1,660
Following Jesus as the basis for spiritual growth.	$3,379	2,442	936	1,411	2,066
Participating in tradition and sacraments.	—	—	1,336	1,157	1,194

*Significant at .05. Groups of fewer than fifty members are not shown.
Based on Lay Questionnaire items 20 and 33.

striking associations occur when the data from all five denominations are pooled. When all five denominations are studied together, the patterns are very strong, telling us that denominations with high giving are also those holding these theological views.

Remember that the denominations vary on these beliefs. The percentages agreeing with the statement "Only followers of Jesus Christ can be saved" were as follows: Assemblies of God, 86 percent; Baptists, 83 percent; Catholics, 35 percent; Lutherans, 52 percent; and Presbyterians, 49 percent. The percentages saying that a Christian's primary duty is helping others to commit their lives to Christ were as follows: Assemblies of God, 60 percent; Baptists, 56 percent; Catholics, 6 percent; Lutherans, 14 percent; and Presbyterians, 16 percent. The denominations are very different, and their levels of giving vary in the same way.

The Catholics are unique. The highest-giving laypersons were those saying that the *primary* duty of Christians is "faithfully participating in the tradition and sacraments of the church" (Lay Questionnaire item 33), as seen in the bottom line of Table 3–2. Since tradition and sacraments are central teachings in the Catholic Church, we can summarize that in *all* denominations, persons committed to central teachings tend to give more. But the distinctiveness of Catholics should not be overstated, since in correlational analysis, pattern was fairly weak. Although the general theory is consistent with our data, the strength of the evidence is too weak to make much of it.

To sum up: The hypothesis about strength of belief and type of theology is strongly supported. It is central to understanding denominational differences in giving. Protestant churches which stress that salvation is only through Jesus Christ and emphasize the goal of helping others to commit their lives to Christ have the highest level of giving. For Catholics, the patterns are different and weaker.

Hypothesis 11: **Members who feel alienated from denominational leadership and teachings give less.**

Many church members today have intense feelings about the moral teachings of their denominations. Both Catholics and Protestants are polarized by debate over such issues as the role of women in the church, the morality of abortion, and the ordination of avowed homosexuals. Do these feelings predict giving? Very little. We included four questions in the Gallup poll that asked about denominational teachings with regard to abortion, birth control, ordination of women, and ordination of self-described homosexuals. (The Gallup poll had only three denominations—

Baptists, Catholic, and Lutherans. See Table A–16.) The correlations were as follows.

For Catholics, only one correlation was strong enough to be noteworthy: Catholics who agree with denominational teachings about abortion tend to give slightly higher percentages of their income to their parish. Catholics' attitudes about birth control, ordination of women, and ordination of homosexuals were unrelated to giving.

For Baptists, espousal of the ordination of women and the ordination of homosexuals was moderately associated with *lower* levels of giving. That is, agreement with present denominational positions predicted higher giving. The issue of ordination of women is a bit complex for Baptists in that the denominational statements favor women's ordination, while in practice it is discouraged, and few women are ordained. So the association with higher giving seems to exist with current *practice*.

For Lutherans, none of the attitudes about denominational moral teachings was associated with level of giving.

Hypothesis 12: **Members who plan their giving by the year or by the month give more than those decide week by week.**

All past research strongly supports this hypothesis, and our data agree. In the lay questionnaire and the Gallup poll, we asked respondents how they made decisions about giving (see Table 3–3).

Clearly, the way lay members plan their giving is associated with the amount given. Persons who say they give 10 percent or more of their income of course give the most. But in addition, those who decide on a percentage of income or a dollar amount to be given in the next year give much more than those who decide on a weekly amount or decide week by week. (For correlations, see Table A–17.) One of these findings has a clear practical implication: Persons who decide to give a certain *percentage* of their income annually give more than those who decide on an annual dollar amount.

We saw in chapter 2 that tithing is done mostly by members of the Assemblies of God and Baptist churches; 73 percent of the Assemblies of God lay respondents and 44 percent of the Baptists said they tithed. For Catholics, the figure was 4 percent; for Lutherans, 7 percent; and for Presbyterians, 9 percent. The Gallup poll asked the same question and had similar results: 45 percent of the Baptists, 4 percent of the Catholics, and 9 percent of the Lutherans said they tithed.

Which characteristics of parishioners influence these decisions about giving? *Who* tithes? *Who* decides on an annual percentage of family

TABLE 3–3.
EFFECTS OF DECISION MAKING ON AMOUNTS GIVEN*

	Assemblies of God	Baptist	Catholic	Lutheran	Presbyterian
Individual Level: Giving to the Church in the Previous Year					
I give 10% or more of my income.	$3,847*	4,042*	1,883*	3,990*	4,471*
I decide on a percentage of my income annually.	3,544	3,120	1,630	2,181	2,508
I decide on an annual dollar amount.	—	2,778	1,373	1,711	2,289
I decide on a weekly dollar amount.	1,671	1,882	1,109	1,320	1,347
I give what I can afford each week.	937	869	621	561	624
Individual Level: Proportion of Family Income Given					
I give 10% or more of my income.	.10*	.10*	.06*	.10*	.09*
I decide on a percentage of my income annually.	—	.06	.04	.05	.04
I decide on an annual dollar amount.	—	.05	.03	.04	.04
I decide on a weekly dollar amount.	.04	.05	.03	.03	.03
I give what I can afford each week.	.03	.03	.03	.02	.02
Gallup Poll: Reported Giving to the Church in the Previous Year					
I give 10% or more of my income.	$3,158*	1,962*	1,820*		
I decide on a percentage of my income annually.	—	—	—		
I decide on an annual dollar amount.	—	1,113	1,910		
I decide on a weekly dollar amount.	1,011	822	893		
I give what I can afford each week.	817	456	517		

*Column is significant at .05.
Based on Lay Questionnaire item 11 and Gallup poll item 10. In individual breakdowns, groups with fewer than fifty cases are not shown, and in the Gallup poll, groups with fewer than ten cases are not shown.

income? In the lay survey responses, we checked the associations with age, family income, education, and frequency of church attendance. Age is definitely a factor in two denominations. Older members of Assemblies of God and Baptist denominations tend more often to tithe, while younger members more often give what they can afford each week.

The pattern with family income is complex. Assemblies of God members who have lower incomes are slightly more inclined to tithe, while higher-income members more commonly decide on an annual or weekly dollar amount. Higher-income Baptists, Lutherans, and Presbyterians do not tithe more than others, but they tend more often to decide on an annual or weekly dollar amount, less often to decide week by week. The relationships between higher education and giving were similar to those between higher income and giving.

The single strongest predictor of tithing and annual planning in all the denominations was church attendance. Regular attenders much more often tithe or plan their giving annually, while those who do not attend church regularly commonly give what they wish each Sunday.

Hypothesis 13: **Younger and more educated members**
  prefer designated giving to specific missions
  over unified giving to denominational missions.
  Persons who prefer designated giving give more.

Support for both parts of this hypothesis varied from denomination to denomination. The lay questionnaire included two questions concerning who should make decisions about allocation of mission funds. One asked who should select the projects: (1) denominational leaders, (2) individual givers, or (3) a combination of both. Another asked if the respondent preferred more local decision making about missions and outreach, more denominational decision making, or no change from the present situation (see Table 3–4).

The five denominations produced different results on the first question. The Baptist and Lutheran members who prefer denominational decision making give more, while the Assemblies of God members and Presbyterians who prefer individual decision making give more. Among Catholics there is no difference.

On the second question, all five denominations are the same: Laity who like the present situation tend to give the most. The Baptists, Catholics, and Presbyterians have an additional pattern in that members who would prefer more local decision making give far more than those who would prefer more denominational decision making. For Assemblies of God and Lutherans, the difference is small.

Are attitudes on these questions affected by background factors? Using the lay questionnaire responses, we looked at the effects of age, family income, education, and frequency of church attendance. The findings were mixed, and they varied from denomination to denomination. Among Assemblies of God members, Catholics, and Lutherans, younger persons preferred more

TABLE 3–4.
ASSOCIATION BETWEEN PREFERRED MISSION FUNDING
AND AMOUNTS GIVEN

	Assemblies of God	Baptist	Catholic	Lutheran	Presbyterian
Self-Reported Giving by Households					
For supporting mission projects of your denomination, either overseas or in this country, which do you prefer?					
I prefer that the denomination select the projects.	$2,861*	3,278*	1,009	1,804*	1,899*
I prefer giving to missionaries and projects that I select.	3,373	2,170	1,080	1,280	2,291
I prefer a combination of both.	3,490	2,804	1,035	1,482	2,062
Would you prefer that congregations make more decisions about funding programs, rather than having denominational leaders decide?					
I would prefer more local decision making.	$2,949*	2,790*	994*	1,411*	2,023*
I like the situation now.	3,683	3,241	1,251	1,846	2,292
I would prefer more denominational decision making.	2,848	2,217	795	1,493	1,843

*Column is significant at .05.
Based on Congregation Life Survey items 16 and 19.

local decision making while older persons tended to like the situation now. For Baptists and Presbyterians, there were no differences by age. Higher-income and higher-educated Baptists, Catholics, and Lutherans would like more local decision making, but among Assemblies members and Presbyterians there were no patterns. Catholics who attend church weekly or more frequently tend *less* than others to recommend more local decision making, possibly because they are more traditional Catholics who prefer the status quo.

On the question of who should select which mission projects are to be supported, older members of all denominations disproportionately preferred that the denomination select the projects. Also, among Baptists and Presbyterians, those who have regular church attendance disproportionately preferred that the denomination select the projects.

In this chapter we have seen that individuals vary in their giving according to family income, age, religious beliefs, level of involvement in the congregation, feelings about the church, and practices regarding planning their giving. In chapter 4 we look at congregational factors that also influence giving.

4

Congregational Factors and Combined Factors Influencing Giving

In chapter 3 we reviewed evidence for or against thirteen hypotheses regarding characteristics of individual church members. In this chapter we do two things. First, we test nine hypotheses about congregational factors that affect giving (numbered from 14 to 22). Next, we look at the importance of the specific factors when all are tested simultaneously.

HYPOTHESES ABOUT CONGREGATIONAL FACTORS

Hypothesis 14: **Smaller congregations have higher per-member giving. Recently founded congregations have higher per-member giving.**

We have heard observers say that the large size of Catholic parishes is a major reason Catholic giving is lower. Is it true? If it is, we might also expect large congregation size to be associated with lower giving in all denominations. To see if this was the case, we drew graphs showing per-member giving for each size of congregation within each denomination.

The findings were weak and mixed. Also, to our dismay, the results drawn from the Congregation Profile Booklet data were somewhat different from those in the self-reported contribution data. The actual graphs (shown in the *Research Report on the American Congregational Giving Study*) contain a few patterns, but they are never clear and consistent. We conclude that the size of congregations, by itself, is not important in trying to understand levels of giving.[1] It is true that per-member giving is a bit lower in the largest Catholic parishes, but the large size of Catholic parishes is not important in explaining the low level of Catholic giving.

Is the number of years since the congregation was founded a factor? Are giving patterns higher in younger congregations? Among Assemblies of God and Catholic churches, we found no association between level of giving and years since founding. But among Baptist, Lutheran, and Presbyterian churches, we found that the newer the church, the higher the per-member giving. This pattern was fairly strong for Baptist churches and less strong for Lutheran and Presbyterian churches. The associations were not explainable by a higher level of family income in newer congregations, because when we controlled for family income, the relationship between newness and higher giving remained.

Hypothesis 15: **Members of congregations with a wide array of programs give more.**

This hypothesis is based on the theory that members will contribute more if they perceive that their congregation is supporting more and better programs.[2] We saw in chapter 3 that members' enthusiasm for the work and programs of their congregations was, to a small degree, associated with higher contributions. Here we look at the number of programs being offered.

The Congregation Profile Booklet asked about thirteen specific programs. We added up the number of programs sponsored by each church and found that the sum was linked to congregation size in every denomination. For example, for Baptists, the average number of programs ranged from 7.7 for congregations with fewer than one hundred members to 11.8 for those with more than six hundred. For Catholics, the average number ranged from 6.5 for parishes with fewer than five hundred members to 10.1 for parishes with more than six thousand.

Does the presence of more programs affect contributions? The answer is yes, except for Catholics. Of the five denominations, Catholic giving is the least affected by the number of church programs. (See Table A–18.) On this topic we need to be cautious, since the statistical analysis is troubled by theoretical circularity: that is, if programs in a church are appreciated by the laity, the laity will agree to contribute more, and if they contribute more, more programs will be put on. Other factors may underlie both phenomena, especially the level of wealth in the community. One way to control that factor is to focus on the *percentage* of income given, not the number of dollars given. When this is done (see Table A–18), the correlations become very weak.

Another way to exclude prior factors is to control for church size (also in Table A–18). When this is done, the correlations do not change. In sum, contributions are higher in churches with more programs, but the percentage of family income contributed is not higher. In further analysis, we looked at correlations with the presence of specific programs (such as adult Sunday school or women's groups), but we found no relationships with giving.

Hypothesis 16: **Congregations that use annual pledge
   drives and pledge cards have a higher level of giving. If the stewardship committee contacts all
   members, the giving is higher.**

Both parts of the hypothesis were supported. For the first part, see
Table 4–1.

Table 4–1 clearly shows that members who make pledges give more
money. Is the higher giving due to pledging or to some other, prior factor?
Perhaps these members are the wealthier persons in the congregations, or
perhaps their congregations are more business-like. One test of prior factors is to examine the percentage of income donated. When this is done
(see Table A–19), more than half of the association between pledging and
amount given is explained away, telling us that level of income is part of
the reason for it. Another test is to control for church size, since larger
churches tend more often to use pledging. But we did this and found that
church size is not an influence.

It is important to ask *which* laypersons make annual pledges. We looked
to see if frequency of church attendance, church size, age of members,
household income, and education predicted whether members pledged or
not. We found two clear patterns: (1) in all denominations, members who
attend church regularly tend more often to pledge; and (2) except for the
Assemblies of God, members of larger churches tend more often to
pledge. (See Table A–20.)

TABLE 4–1.
RELATIONSHIP BETWEEN PLEDGING AND LEVELS OF GIVING

	Assemblies of God	Baptist	Catholic	Lutheran	Presbyterian
		Church Contributions			
In the last year, did you or another adult in your family fill out a pledge card or commitment card?					
Lay Questionnaire Responses					
Yes	$3,656*	3,950*	1,248*	1,836*	2,306*
No	3,001	2,318	792	907	923
Gallup Poll Responses					
Yes		$2,422	891*	1,311	
No		1,804	503	904	

*Column is significant at .05.

Two other background factors were only weakly predictive of who pledged. The first factor was age. Among Presbyterians, older persons tended more often to pledge; the opposite was true for Assemblies of God members, and there was no association in the other three denominations. With the second factor—affluence and education—among Baptists and Lutherans, more affluent and more educated members tended disproportionately to pledge, while in the other denominations there were no relationships.

Do stewardship efforts, such as testimonies during worship services, canvassing, use of commitment cards, and use of numbered envelopes, affect levels of giving? Some of the stewardship efforts we asked the pastors about in the Congregation Profile Booklet seemed to be associated with higher giving levels, especially encouragement of pledging and canvassing the membership. They had measurable effects among Baptists, Lutherans, and Presbyterians. The use of numbered envelopes had little association with level of giving. (See Table A–21.) Three of the specific stewardship efforts that we asked about had no associations with level of giving—sermons on stewardship, distributing promotional materials, and providing postal envelopes to encourage contributions by mail.

This form of analysis is not decisive, since any assessment of the effect of church programs requires that background variables be controlled. We did this in later analysis, as we report below, and found quite weak independent effects of these stewardship efforts.

Hypothesis 17: **Congregations in which the whole membership controls budget setting have a higher level of giving. Congregations that send out monthly or quarterly reports to members on the amount received from them have a higher level of giving.**

This hypothesis has two parts, and both were unsupported. For the first part, about budget setting, we solicited information on who decides the final budget in each congregation. All Baptist and Lutheran churches do this in congregational meetings. Presbyterians make final budget decisions in the lay governing board. Assemblies of God churches vary, but in most of them the final budget is decided by the pastor or by a lay pastoral council. In most Catholic parishes, the pastor sets the final budget.

Are these procedures related to levels of giving? The answer is no. In addition, in the Congregation Profile Booklet we asked who in the congregation was "involved in the preparation of the budget," and we again found no association between the responses and the level of giving.

Does sending out monthly, quarterly, or annual reports to members on the amounts they have given have any effect on giving? We found no association with the level of giving. To reiterate: Both parts of this hypothesis were unsupported.

Hypothesis 18: **Members who prefer that laypersons handle the finances have a higher level of giving than those who prefer that clergy handle the finances.**

True. We asked laity and Gallup poll respondents if they had preferences about whether clergy or lay leaders "handle financial matters" in their congregations. These matters include management and some decision making. In chapter 2 we saw that the majority preferred either that the laity do it or that a combination of clergy and laity do it. Here, we found that the preference for laity handling finances is associated with higher levels of giving (see Table 4–2).

The hypothesis is supported in all tests. Those members who would prefer that laity handle finances tend to give more. We looked to see if a

TABLE 4–2.
PREFERENCE FOR CLERGY OR LAITY
IN HANDLING FINANCIAL MATTERS

	Assemblies of God	Baptist	Catholic	Lutheran	Presbyterian
	Average Contributions				
Do you prefer that clergy (priests or ministers) or lay leaders handle financial matters in your congregation?					
Reported by Individuals:					
I prefer clergy	$—*	—*	714*	—*	—*
I prefer a combination of clergy and lay leaders	$3,146	2,604	1,121	1,449	2,022
I prefer lay leaders	5,396	3,604	1,110	1,758	2,256
No preference	1,784	1,089	497	795	989
Reported in Gallup Poll:					
I prefer clergy		$—*	715	—	
I prefer a combination of clergy and lay leaders		$1,967	739	1,194	
I prefer lay leaders		3,313	1,025	1,293	
No preference		1,185	508	760	

*Figures in the column are significant at .05. Data are not shown for lay questionnaire groups of fewer than fifty or Gallup poll groups of fewer than ten.

preference for laity handling finances was associated with a higher percentage of income given. It was.

There remains the question of *which* laypersons prefer clergy or laity to handle finances. Is some other factor underlying this relationship? We looked to see if age, family income, and frequency of church attendance predicted attitudes on this question. The results were not very informative. There were no effects of age in any denomination. As for family income, Baptists with higher income preferred more often than others that laity handle finances; and Catholics with higher income preferred more often than others that laity or a combination of clergy and laity (as opposed to clergy alone) handle finances.

As for frequency of church attendance, Baptists and Lutherans who attended church regularly disproportionately prefer that laity handle financial matters, and the opposite pattern (although weak) occurred for Catholics.

In summary, the higher level of giving associated with a preference that laity handle finances is not explained by any of these background factors.

Hypothesis 19: **Congregations that use stewardship programs and stress stewardship as an aspect of Christian living have a higher level of giving than do congregations that focus on supporting programs as a reason for fund-raising.**

Our Congregation Profile Booklet asked three questions to test this hypothesis, and our lay questionnaire asked one question. In the questionnaire we asked if the congregation actively promoted a "stewardship approach," which teaches the spiritual meaning of how we use God's gifts, to the giving of time, talent, and money. (The alternative, not stated in the question, is a fund-raising approach, which simply asks for money to support church programs.) The laypersons' responses indicate that a stewardship approach is moderately associated with higher giving. The effect of a stewardship approach was especially strong among Baptists.

In the Congregation Profile Booklet, we asked pastors about stewardship efforts, such as the use of lay testimonials, Bible study classes, and Sunday school classes on stewardship. The results were generally weak, though for Baptists and Lutherans, the use of lay testimonials was associated with higher giving. (See Table A–22.)

This form of data analysis is not conclusive, since background variables were not controlled while assessing the effects of stewardship efforts. As we see below, when we introduced controls, our estimate of the effect of stewardship programs decreased.

Hypothesis 20: **Congregations or denominations that
   stress giving as an obligatory aspect of Christian
   living have a higher level of giving.**

In the Congregation Profile Booklet we asked, "What is your congregation's emphasis with regard to the biblical standard of tithing (i.e., giving at least 10 percent of income)?" As reported in chapter 2, two of the denominations teach the tithe as obligatory: 99 percent of the Assemblies of God churches and 81 percent of the Baptist churches said they did. In the other denominations, this teaching is uncommon.

Does the teaching affect the level of giving? Yes, in some denominations. (See Table A–23.) Teachings about tithing had some effect within two denominations—Catholics and Presbyterians. Baptists and Lutherans seemed unaffected by teachings about tithing, and for Assemblies of God churches no test could be made, because every church stresses tithing. When we pooled the data from all five denominations, the effect on giving was clear and strong, indicating that differences *between* denominations are greater than patterns *within* each denomination.

Hypothesis 21: **Denominations and congregations that
   maintain distinctive lifestyles have a higher level
   of giving.**

This hypothesis comes from the writings of Dean Kelley and Laurence Iannaccone, who argue that churches which have distinctive rules for living that set them apart from other people will experience higher levels of commitment.[3]

An important element in distinctive lifestyles is rules concerning abstinence. Our Congregation Profile Booklet asked, "Does your congregation teach that Christian life should be safeguarded through abstinence from certain kinds of food; alcohol and/or tobacco; gambling; certain kinds of entertainment, such as movies, nightclubs, or dancing; or some other behavior or activity?" We saw in chapter 2 that the vast majority of Assemblies of God and Baptist churches taught abstinence from alcohol, tobacco, gambling, and certain kinds of entertainment. The other denominations stressed abstinence much less.

Are these factors associated with giving? Yes. When all five denominations were pooled together, the associations were strong: churches teaching abstinence from certain behaviors have higher levels of giving. Within each denomination, however, the associations were very weak, largely because churches in each denomination did not vary much in teachings about abstinence. The Congregation Profile Booklet did not ask pastors about other consequences of committed Christian living, such as charity to the poor or social responsibility, as we discussed in chapter 2.

We cannot infer from these findings that the teachings of abstinence *cause* higher giving. Most likely, the teachings are one element among others employed to maintain a high-commitment congregation that is clearly distinct from the surrounding culture.

Hypothesis 22: **Congregations or parishes with five-day-a-week religious schools have a lower level of giving to the congregation or parish.**

This hypothesis is unsupported. It is often voiced in discussions of Protestant–Catholic differences in giving, where it is frequently argued that the presence of Catholic parochial schools depresses giving to the parishes that have them. In chapter 2 we showed that the level of giving per member, as reported in the Congregation Profile Booklet, was little different in Catholic parishes with schools from the level in those without schools.

When we looked at our lay questionnaire data, we found that self-reported giving to parishes with and without schools was the same. For parishes with schools, giving averaged $1,023; for those without schools, it averaged $973. The percentage of family income contributed was 3 percent in parishes with schools, 2.8 percent in parishes without. These figures are not significantly different, besides which they are in a direction opposite to that predicted by the hypothesis; therefore it is false. There is no evidence that the presence of a school lowers giving in a Catholic parish.

ANALYSIS OF
ALL FACTORS COMBINED

To understand the impact of various factors in context, we analyzed the data using multiple regression, which is the most realistic statistical procedure available. It is a bit technical for some readers, so we present the findings here in simple terms.

Up to now, we have looked at factors one at a time. We did not control all other factors when looking at each one. But normally, a researcher wants to assess the independent effect of each factor. When an analyst controls all other factors, the importance of each factor can be expected to diminish, partly because the various factors overlap with one another. This is the usual outcome in multiple regression analysis.[4]

First, we reviewed all the factors available and selected the twenty most important. We did not include level of church attendance as a predictor variable, because it is an alternative measure of church commitment and thus not important for explanatory purposes; to a great extent, whatever explains attendance also explains giving. Nor did we include the question about how individuals decide how much to give, because the response to the question is too closely associated with the amount given to be seen as a predictor of giving.

The top twenty variables were arranged in six sets:

Set 1: Personal Characteristics of Members, Self-Reported
    Average family income
    Percentage with college degrees
    Percentage sixty-five or older
    Percentage under age forty

Set 2: Religious Commitment of Members
    Percentage agreeing that only followers of Christ can be saved
    Percentage saying that the primary duty of Christians is helping others commit their lives to Christ

Set 3: Attitudes toward the Congregation
    Percentage saying they feel high enthusiasm for the congregation
    Percentage saying that opportunities to serve in lay leadership are available to all

Set 4: Characteristics of the Congregation
    Number of members in congregation
    Number of programs and groups sponsored by the congregation
    Congregation has a mortgage debt

Set 5: Theological Emphasis of the Congregation
    Congregation teaches the importance of helping others commit their lives to Christ
    Congregation teaches that it has the only true interpretation of biblical teaching
    Congregation teaches abstinence from certain foods, beverages, and entertainments

Set 6: Congregational Stewardship Program
Percentage of members reporting that they pledge
Percentage saying the church uses a stewardship approach
to the giving of time, talent, and money
Congregation canvasses members in person or by phone
Congregation uses pledge cards
Congregation uses numbered envelopes
Congregation stresses stewardship in lay testimonials and
Bible study

Sets 1 and 2 measure individual members, not congregational leadership or programs. Sets 3 through 6 refer to factors that can be consciously changed, such as congregational programs or teachings, whereas the first two sets are much less changeable. The regression outcome is shown in Table 4–3.

The numbers in the table (betas) are estimates of the importance of each factor. As a rule of thumb, betas of about .15 or more, either plus or minus, are strong enough to have practical importance, and betas of about .30 or more are strong. Betas listed in the table without an asterisk are so weak that they may be unreliable. "Adjusted R^2," at the bottom of the table, is a measure of total explanatory power of the twenty variables.

Table 4–3 provides some answers to our question about the important influential factors. Undoubtedly, characteristics of members, such as income, education, age, and theological commitments, are the most important predictors of what people give.

Among the congregational factors, size of membership is a modest factor in most denominations (the smaller the church, the higher the per-person giving), and for Catholics, the openness of positions of leadership is a factor (that is, if leadership is seen as open to all, giving is higher). In the category of stewardship programs, pledging by church members is clearly important. For Baptists, canvassing members is important.

Since the congregations surveyed vary widely in size, we analyzed large and small congregations separately within each denomination. For Protestants, several factors had greater explanatory power in small churches; the most important was pledging. The percentage of laity who pledged predicted the level of giving in small churches but not in large churches. For Catholics, whether or not parishioners felt that opportunities for leadership were available was important in large parishes but not in small ones; in large parishes, giving was clearly higher when people felt that opportunities for leadership were open to all.

TABLE 4–3.
PREDICTIVE POWER (BETAS)
OF THE TOP TWENTY PREDICTORS

	All	Assemblies of God	Baptist	Catholic	Lutheran	Presbyterian
Set 1: Personal Characteristics of Members						
Average family income	.38*	.70*	.44*	.50*	.50*	.39*
Percent college graduates	.04	.06	.07	−.13	.08	.20
Percent 65 or older	−.02	.08	−.14	.05	.08	.14
Percent under age 40	−.06	−.01	−.17	−.11	−.16	−.12
Set 2: Religious Commitment of Members						
Agree: only followers of Christ are saved	.27*	.07	.08	.12	.18	.32*
Primary duty of Christians: help others commit	.39*	−.02	.23*	.23*	−.05	−.01
Set 3: Attitudes Toward the Congregation						
Enthusiasm for congregational programs	.01	−.10	.02	.01	.02	−.03
Opportunities for leadership open	.07*	.03	.06	.19*	.03	.03
Set 4: Characteristics of the Congregation						
Number of members	−.13*	−.05	−.18	−.26*	−.17*	.17
Number of programs sponsored	.08*	.08	.05	.17	.13	.00
Congregation has mortgage debt	.07*	.08	.06	.09	.08	.05
Set 5: Theological Emphasis of the Congregation						
Importance helping others commit	−.03	−.13	.00	.03	.11	−.04
Church has true interpretation	.04	.04	.24*	−.13	−.02	.00
Church teaches abstinence	.05	.07	−.07	−.05	.05	−.10
Set 6: Congregation Stewardship Program						
Percent who pledged	.20*	.26*	.14	.25*	.42*	.20
Church uses stewardship approach	−.03	.03	.10	.02	−.30*	.04
Church uses canvassing	.00	−.13	.18*	−.13	.11	.09
Church uses pledge cards	−.07	−.05	.02	−.11	−.10	−.16
Church uses numbered envelopes	−.03	.07	.09	.01	.04	−.07
How stewardship is emphasized	.03	.04	.05	−.14	.14	−.03
Adjusted R^2 for All Six Sets	.634	.638	.537	.394	.453	.442

*Beta is significant at .05.

THE FACTORS
THAT MOST AFFECT GIVING

The Big Five Factors

Let us summarize. When we asked, "What are the main factors that influence giving in Christian denominations?" and looked at all our data on five denominations, we found five main factors common to all denominations. In identifying them, we took into account all of our findings. The factors are as follows:

1. High family income (a strong factor)
2. High level of involvement in the church (a strong factor)
3. Conservative theology
4. Planning one's giving by the year—tithing or pledging
5. Small congregation size (a weak factor)

These five factors are foremost when we look at the five denominations together. We might call the factors the "overall big five."

Analysis by Denomination

When we look at specific denominations, however, the summary changes. This is because *within* each denomination the factors are different, and also, within denominations some factors are invariant. For example, evangelical theology is present in *all* Assemblies of God churches; hence it is not a factor predicting variations in giving within that denomination. Analysis within each denomination is useful to persons working within that tradition. The main factors are as follows:

Assemblies of God
1. High family income (a strong factor)
2. High level of involvement in the church (a strong factor)
3. Planning one's giving by the year—tithing or pledging
4. Spouse attends the same church

Baptists
1. High family income (a strong factor)
2. High level of involvement in the church (a strong factor)
3. Evangelical theology
4. Planning one's giving by the year—tithing or pledging

5. Spouse attends the same church
6. Age about forty to sixty-five
7. The congregation uses canvassing (a weak factor)

Catholics

1. High family income (a strong factor)
2. High level of involvement in the parish (a strong factor)
3. Small parish size
4. Planning one's giving by the year—tithing or pledging
5. Conservative theology
6. Opportunities for lay leadership are open

Lutherans

1. High family income (a strong factor)
2. High level of involvement in the church (a strong factor)
3. Planning one's giving by the year—tithing or pledging
4. Small church size
5. Spouse attends the same church
6. Evangelical theology (a weak factor)

Presbyterians

1. High family income (a strong factor)
2. High level of involvement in the church (a strong factor)
3. Evangelical theology
4. Planning one's giving by the year—tithing or pledging
5. Spouse attends the same church (a weak factor)

We repeat again that our analysis here has looked at giving to one's church. We have not looked at any specialized form of religious giving, such as to missions or denominational programs. The factors encouraging such specialized religious giving may be different. They are not studied here.

DIFFERENCES IN GIVING BETWEEN
CATHOLICS AND PROTESTANTS: WHY?

It has been long known that Catholic giving is lower than Protestant giving. Many writers have proposed explanations.[5] We set out to test some of these ideas, and now we can state our conclusions. Here we list the proffered explanations and evaluate their empirical support. Many of them turned out to be no more than myths.

Six Explanations for Lower Catholic Giving

Explanation 1: **Catholic parishes are much larger than Protestant congregations, and this accounts for the lower level of giving.**

It is true that Catholic parishes are much larger; in our data, they averaged more than eight times as large as Protestant congregations. First, we looked at level of giving as it related to congregation size in each denomination, and we found no overall pattern. We did, however, find a small impact of parish size for Catholics when controlling for other factors; the largest parishes had a slightly lower level of giving.

We conclude that the large size of Catholic parishes is at most a secondary factor in the lower level of Catholic giving. Size accounts for only a small portion of the Catholic–Protestant difference. The main explanation must come from factors common to Catholic parishes *of all sizes* versus Protestant churches of all sizes.

Explanation 2: **Catholics give less because they are angry with church leadership, especially over teachings about birth control.**

This assertion has been made in the past by Catholic writers, but we found no evidence for it, even in direct tests. Catholics are no more angry with denominational leaders than members of the other four denominations are angry at their leaders. Also, Catholic attitudes about birth control have no influence on their giving.

Explanation 3: **Catholic giving to the parish is lower because Catholics give much more to other, non-parish Catholic causes, and also because they have children in Catholic schools.**

Both explanations are false. As we saw, Catholic giving to nonparish Catholic causes is no higher than its equivalent in the other four denominations. Also, families with children in Catholic schools do not give a smaller average amount than other families of the same age. One should remember that parents of children in Catholic schools are, on average, among those more active in the parish and more interested in it.

Explanation 4: **Catholics give less because their parishes are less democratic in decision making.**

We often hear people say that if the Catholic Church were more democratic, giving would be higher. We tested this idea and found it was true in only one sense. Democracy in itself is not a predictor of giving in any of our denominations, but dissatisfaction with leadership *is* a predictor. If church members feel no need for democracy, introducing it will have no effect. But if they are dissatisfied with the current local or denominational leadership, a policy change to alleviate the dissatisfaction—whether or not it involves democracy—would have an effect on giving.

Explanation 5: Catholics give less because they are less convinced that their parish or denomination has serious needs.

This has been argued by observers who talk about the wealth of the Vatican and assert that people will not give to a denomination that parades countless gold-plated sacred objects, silk robes, and art treasures. Yet our data show that this explanation for low Catholic giving is false. In our study, Catholic laity are not less convinced than others that their parish or their denomination has serious needs.

Explanation 6: Catholic giving is lower because of less emphasis on stewardship and less effort given to stewardship campaigns.

We tested numerous elements of stewardship education and stewardship campaigns, and we were surprised by the weak and mixed results. The most important stewardship program was the use of pledge cards; in all denominations, laity who fill out pledge cards give more to their churches. Catholic parishes use pledge cards less than Lutherans and Presbyterians. Also, we found some evidence that Catholic parishes emphasize stewardship less than Protestant churches. A substantial percentage of Catholic parishioners do not even know whether or not their parish has such an emphasis. We conclude that the lower emphasis on pledging and stewardship does explain a portion of the difference between Catholic giving and mainline Protestant (Lutheran and Presbyterian) giving.

The Catholic–Protestant differences in giving are quite large, and none of the explanations above can account for more than a portion of them. The main explanation for the differences lies somewhere else. One factor of undoubted effect, yet not clearly visible in our hypothesis testing, is the emphasis on tithing and the theological meaning attached to financial giving in the various denominations. The five denominations studied talk about tithing and giving in quite different ways. We return to this topic later.

Catholic Parish, Protestant Congregation:
What If They Were More Similar?

We had another statistical method for penetrating differences in giving between Catholics and Protestants. We were able to estimate what the Catholic level of giving would have been if Catholic parishes resembled Protestant congregations in specific ways.

It is sometimes asserted that "Catholics would give as much as Protestants *if only* they had smaller, more personal congregations, as Protestants do" or "Catholics would contribute as much *if only* they emphasized stewardship to the same degree." We analyzed these types of "if only" questions by looking at the six sets of predictors outlined above. We calculated what Catholic giving would be if Catholic characteristics were the same as Protestant characteristics on each of the six sets, taken one at a time. As we did this, we divided the Protestant denominations into two groups—high-giving, conservative denominations (Assemblies of God and Baptists) and medium-giving, mainline denominations (Lutherans and Presbyterians)—in order to produce more comparable analyses (see Table 4–4).

In the first line of the table, we see that, under present conditions, Catholic giving is 27 percent as high as Assemblies of God and Baptist giv-

TABLE 4–4. PREDICTED INDIVIDUAL
CATHOLIC GIVING IF CATHOLIC CHARACTERISTICS
RESEMBLED THOSE OF OTHER DENOMINATIONS

	Catholic Giving as a Percent of Assemblies of God and Baptist Giving	Catholic Giving as a Percent of Lutheran and Presbyterian Giving
Under Existing Conditions	27	46
If set 1 (Personal Characteristics of Members) was the same	23	47
If set 2 (Religious Commitment of Members) was the same	78	66
If set 3 (Attitudes toward the Congregation) was the same	29	49
If set 4 (Characteristics of the Congregation) was the same	34	56
If set 5 (Theological Emphasis of the Congregation) was the same	23	56
If set 6 (Congregational Stewardship Programs) was the same	18	37
If sets 1, 2, 3, 4, and 5 were the same	81	88

ing and 46 percent as high as mainline Protestant giving. What if Catholics resembled Protestants in specific ways? If all else were equal but Catholics resembled the other denominations in personal characteristics (family income, education, and age), giving would change little (line 2). If all else were equal but Catholics resembled the others in religious commitment—that is, attitudes about who can be saved and about the primary duty of Christians—giving would rise markedly (line 3).

If Catholics resembled the others in attitudes about their parishes, giving would change little (line 4). If Catholic parishes were the same as the others in size, number of programs offered, and level of debt, giving would rise slightly (line 5). If Catholic teachings regarding the primary duty of Christians, the interpretation of the Bible, and forms of abstinence resembled those of the other denominations, giving would change little (line 6). (Note the distinction here between the personal belief and the congregational emphasis concerning the primary duty of Christians.)

Last, if all else were equal but Catholic parishes had the same stewardship programs as the others, giving would not rise at all (line 7). (This conclusion is misleading in that it mixes the positive effect of pledging with the negative effect of other stewardship efforts. Taken alone, pledging has a positive effect.)

The bottom line in the table adds up the effect of all sets except set 6 (line 7, which had no effect), to see if this exercise identified the sources of Catholic and Protestant difference in giving. The exercise was successful with regard to Catholic versus mainline Protestant differences in that it accounted for 88 percent of the Protestant giving level.

The most important column in Table 4–4 is the right-hand column, since the Catholic Church is much more similar to Lutherans and Presbyterians theologically than to the Assemblies of God and Baptists. From the results, we can conclude that the theological commitment of their members is the most important difference between Catholic and Protestant churches. Second most important are theological teachings by the churches, and third most important are church size and the number of programs offered. With adoption of certain Protestant characteristics, most of the Catholic–Protestant gap might be closed.

To understand differences between Catholics and Protestants more clearly, we need to look closely into the different theologies of community life, leadership, responsibility, and personal justification. This is the main topic of the next two chapters.

5
Tithing, Pledging, and Offering Churches: Case Studies

A research project that looks solely at numbers and statistical tests misses information on matters such as leadership, theological emphasis, and style. These factors are important in understanding patterns of giving and must not be neglected. To gain some understanding of their impact, we carried out a series of case studies of successful churches.

Which churches should we study? We did not want simply to pick the churches in our sample that had the highest levels of per-member giving, since those are greatly affected by the level of wealth in the congregation—a topic that is not our concern here. We decided to speak to judicatory officers in the five denominations and ask them which churches they considered successful in the area of financial leadership and which would be instructive to study. It turned out that the officers generally nominated churches that were much larger than average. This happened for two reasons. First, churches that have been growing steadily year by year are obviously successful in their ministry; if they are growing, they must be doing something right! Second, large churches are more visible. In choosing churches to study, we initially resisted taking large churches; yet in the end, the churches we studied were larger than average.

We explained to the judicatory officers that we wanted to visit the churches over a period of time and interview the pastor and lay leaders. The officers phoned ahead to introduce us. The case studies involved visiting the churches over either a period of weeks (if they were near our places of residence) or a period of intensely filled days (if farther away). We asked to see each church's financial records, and we taped the most important interviews.

We completed twelve case studies. Three were of Assemblies of God churches, two were Baptist, four were Catholic, one was Lutheran, and two were Presbyterian. We gave more attention to the highest- and lowest-giving denominations (Assemblies of God and Catholic) than to those between. The names of all of the churches, individuals, and cities, listed below, have been changed to maintain confidentiality.

Northway Assembly of God—A suburban church in the South; 1,100 members and many frequent attenders.

Springfield Assembly of God—A suburban church in the Southeast; 321 members and many frequent attenders.

Seaside Assembly Fellowship—A suburban Assemblies of God church in the West; 115 members and many frequent attenders.

Medford Baptist—A suburban church in the Southeast; 501 members.

Faith Baptist—A suburban church in the Southeast; 433 members.

St. Benedict Catholic—A suburban parish in the West; 1,660 registered households and an elementary school.

St. Peter's Catholic—A suburban parish in the East; 2,100 registered households and an elementary school.

Mount Calvary Catholic—An urban parish in the East; 3,200 registered households.

St. Ann Catholic—A suburban parish in the East; 1,130 registered households and an elementary school.

Grace Lutheran—A suburban congregation in the East; active membership of about 1,200.

Westminster Presbyterian—An urban church in the West; more than 4,000 members.

Oakland Presbyterian—A suburban church in the East; 1,300 members.

THREE TYPES OF CHURCHES

We found three philosophies of giving in these churches, and we identified the churches according to these three philosophies. We call the first type *tithing churches* and the second type *pledging churches.* The third type we call *offering churches,* although the name and definition are less clear, as we shall see. Offering churches have few or no formal giving programs, such as an annual stewardship drive. The three types fit a spectrum in one important respect: giving is high in tithing churches, medium in pledging churches, and low in offering churches. In reality, not all churches fit into one of the three types. Some fall between the types or contain elements of two different types. We begin by describing the three types and the theological views underpinning each. Please note that these descriptions are purer and clearer than the churches are in reality.

Tithing Churches

The defining characteristic of tithing churches is that they see their financial support as coming mainly from members who tithe. All leadership energy is given to ministering to the people and strengthening their commitment to tithing as a part of a life devoted to God.

A tithing church has no annual stewardship program, no pledging, no annual appeal telling about budget needs, no other mention of money, aside from appeals for specific missions. It maintains an understanding that members who desire to be in good standing with God and the congregation need to tithe. Efforts by clergy to increase church income are limited to preaching that tithing is expected by God and that it wins rewards from God.

Examples of tithing churches in our study are Seaside Assembly Fellowship, Northway Assembly of God, Springfield Assembly of God, and Faith Baptist.

Pledging Churches

Pledging churches favor tithing, but believe it is unrealistic to expect most members to tithe. The crucial characteristic of these churches is that they have annual stewardship programs asking for pledges, normally in the fall of the year. They usually strive to have all members pledge, and they ask members to think in terms of a percentage of household income when considering how much to pledge. Another name for this category might be "stewardship churches," since stewardship teachings and appeals are centrally important.

Examples of pledging churches in this study are Grace Lutheran, Westminster Presbyterian, and Oakland Presbyterian.

Offering Churches

Offering churches believe in tithing and pledging, but they do not stress either. The pastors usually wish that the people would tithe or pledge, but they are not forceful in talking about it, and the congregation has no overall sense that tithing and pledging are needed to be in good standing with God and the congregation. When asked, the clergy of these churches told us they would like their congregants to tithe and pledge more than they do, but the laity resist.

These churches have little teaching about the theology of stewardship and the spiritual meaning of gifts to the church. Efforts to increase giving tend to stress the quality of the program, the costs of maintaining the building and property, the future vision of the parish leadership, and special projects. In effect, the program to encourage giving is not much different from those of secular organizations who stress their valuable work, their service to the community, and their future vision.

All the Catholic parishes we studied fell into this category, and one Baptist church is halfway between an offering church and a pledging church.

In our twelve case studies, the Assemblies of God congregations tended to be tithers, mainline churches tended to be pledgers, and Catholic parishes tended to be offering churches. But note that the identification of denominations with tithing, pledging, or offering types is only a matter of general tendency, with plenty of exceptions on all sides. We have no doubt that a few Catholic parishes can be found that are tithing churches, a few Assemblies of God churches can be found that are offering churches, and so on.

The three types of churches differ in theology. Tithing churches tend to be evangelistic. They preach strong biblical authority for guiding one's life today. They have altar calls in most services. Typically, they do not emphasize social witness or social reform, except on a few issues such as divorce, pornography, abortion, and homosexuality. Most preach abstinence from alcohol, gambling, and extramarital sex.

Pledging churches are not as unitary in these respects. They may or may not be evangelistic. Most mainline Protestant churches are in the pledging or offering category; few are tithing churches.

Offering churches are not very distinctive theologically. They resemble mainline Protestant churches, and of course, if they are Catholic, they give great importance to sacraments, tradition, and liturgy.

Television Preachers

At this point, we need to comment on television evangelists. This topic came up in all of our discussions, and a word about them will help clarify our typology of churches. Pastors of all theological types were unanimous in condemning the methods television preachers used to raise money. Nobody defended Oral Roberts, Jimmy Swaggart, or Pat Robertson. All the pastors made it clear that *they* are not like the TV evangelists, who tell the viewers that God will reward them for any gift they give and that giving a gift to the program is really a sound investment, because God pays the money back in other ways. Everyone condemned the typical appeal of "Give to me and God will repay you more than dollar for dollar." Likewise, everyone opposed "prosperity theology," which says that God wants the believer to be rich and will repay the person for any gifts. This theology interprets gifts to the evangelist as joining a kind of investment club, in hopes of future gain.

We repeatedly heard TV evangelists likened to the medieval peddlers of indulgences. The evangelists claim that a financial gift will elicit God's favor, forgiveness, and blessing. They parade their own fancy cars and houses as if to give proof that "investing with God really works. Look what it has done for me! See, I invested with God, and God gave me all this. It will work for you too!" In addition, TV evangelists' constituencies are always changing, so they can do things that border on manipulation. They are not like a local church, where the people will be there for years to come and the leadership needs to build up trust for the long haul.

For theoretical clarity here, we could have made television evangelists a fourth type of church. They are clearly different in that they teach that God reciprocates in specific ways for specific gifts. We decided against this, however, because TV evangelism is much different from local congregational leadership.

To illustrate the three main types—tithing churches, pledging churches, and offering churches—we describe two of each type in some detail.

TWO TITHING CHURCHES

Springfield Assembly of God and Seaside Assembly Fellowship are clear examples of tithing churches in that they stress the importance of the tithe and have no program of stewardship, pledging, or annual appeal.

Springfield Assembly of God has a favorable location in a growing suburb in the Southeast. It was founded in the 1950s, and its current sanctuary was built in 1978. Five years ago, it added a large educational wing. The church has 321 members, even though average attendance on Sunday is between 900 and 1000. There are five full-time pastors, including the music minister, the director of counseling and recovery programs, and two ministers who are in charge of religious education and youth. Senior Pastor Nichols came in 1988.

The sanctuary seats six hundred and is always packed for the 10:30 A.M. service, with people sitting in aisles and on steps. The 9:00 A.M. service is less popular. The sanctuary is in modern Assembly of God style: an amphitheater form, with three steps across the front leading up to the platform. A large choir section is directly behind the pulpit, and a section to one side is devoted to the band and the electronic synthesizer. During the music worship that begins every service, the words of hymns are projected onto a screen in front.

Springfield downplays speaking in tongues except in times designated for praying aloud. Pastor Nichols believes that speaking in tongues may frighten visitors and play into the stereotype that Pentecostals are "cra-zies." So the gifts of the Spirit are kept subdued and channeled in ways that are uplifting to the congregation.

Services combine Pentecostal and evangelical traditions, emphasizing music, prayer, and preaching. The services are often emotional and touch-ing. They have a constant theme: "Give your life to Jesus Christ, and you will be delivered from your sins and your burdens. Christ accepts you, and this congregation accepts you in Christ's name. Come just as you are and find new life. Decide now." People raise their hands during the hymns, and most services end in a call for people to come forward and kneel if they feel the need for prayer or rededication of their lives to God.

Pastor Nichols stands firmly on literal biblical authority and is opposed to modern reinterpretations of the Bible, evolution, and ecumenism. Nichols does not see denominational identity as really important; being an Assembly of God church is a huge advantage for the church because of the freedom and autonomy it provides, but Nichols gives the impression that he would also be happy in several other denominations.

Springfield Assembly of God has a full range of programs for children, youth, and families. The church has the Assemblies of God version of Boy Scouts and Girl Scouts. It has counseling, support groups, and healing groups. It puts on musical shows at Christmas and Easter. The pastors try hard to serve the people through innovations in programs and ministries. In 1994 they hired a church planning group to do a survey and analysis to guide them in future planning. In addition, they do periodic surveys of members.

Seaside Assembly Fellowship is a storefront church of approximately 115 members, located in the West. Pastor Jim Robinson and Karen, his wife and co-pastor, both in their mid-thirties, have a flourishing ministry, mainly to college-age young people. The congregation is less than ten years old. Seaside's attendance varies between 100 and 130 on any given Sunday, with fewer on Wednesday evenings. As in the Springfield church, every service opens with music. Co-pastor Karen plays the synthesizer, backed by bass and drums. The singing is always enthusiastic and usually lasts a half hour. Pastor Jim tries to keep the gifts of the Spirit subdued in the worship service, so there is little speaking in tongues. The services emphasize giving one's life to Jesus Christ, and they always end in an altar call.

Seaside focuses on evangelizing young people in the community, di-recting the energies of its college-age members through its Master's Com-mission program, which trains young men and women in ministry. Youth ministers reach out to gang members in the community, an involvement that led Pastor Jim to invite city council and school board candidates to visit the congregation one Sunday evening so that each candidate could explain what he or she intended to do for inner-city youth in Seaside. The church members we interviewed all praised the pastor for sponsoring this event, which drew an overflow crowd to the storefront meeting room. They told us, "He cares about what is happening in our community."

Other Seaside ministries include Heart to Heart, which brings women together to share problems and hopes; a church-building mission to Mexico; and Chi Alpha, which helps young adults decide on careers of service as well as address other problems they are facing. Pastor Jim and Karen were repeatedly praised for acting as ministry facilitators rather than directors, yet both "keep an eye on everything that's going on in this church."

Both the Springfield and Seaside churches are basically run by the pastors, and everyone knows it. The members seem to accept this as proper.

The tithing churches are clearly evangelical. The two Assemblies congregations subordinate Pentecostal gift expression to the "basics" of evangelical theology: Accept Jesus Christ into your life, and you will be saved from your sins and burdens. Biblical authority undergirds the seriousness of a tithing commitment, seen as an acknowledgment of the Lord's dominion over members' lives and a gift returned to God in thanksgiving for blessings constantly received. Discipleship is a serious matter and, indeed, costs members in very tangible ways.

Teaching about Tithing
in Assemblies of God Churches

Not all Assemblies members are willing to tithe, nor do all tithing churches rigidly require it. One lay leader in an Assemblies of God church told us that some churches preach that people need to tithe to be saved, but he is opposed to this teaching, and his church does not preach it. Tithing, he believes, is a pledge or an indicator of one's faith, not something that causes or enables salvation.

A psychological benefit of tithing is that it is proof to oneself and other parishioners that the tither is committed to God and in good standing with God. A tithing person is "fully paid up." Even though everyone knows that salvation cannot be bought, payment of a tithe gives the tither a sense of well-being and satisfaction that the person will be saved. Tithing thus has a powerful spiritual benefit, akin to Max Weber's understanding of the early Protestant work ethic.[1] It doesn't produce salvation, but it gives assurance and relief.

Our conversations with Assemblies members about tithing almost in- evitably included clarification about trust in God. To them, tithing carries with it a conviction that once you have incorporated the practice into your life, a reciprocal relationship of trust has been established. God will not let you down; you will be blessed and cared for in ways you do not expect and that transcend rational calculation. Tithing is a sign that "you have your priorities right"— and if you do, you will be taken care of. Pastor Nichols explained:

> We teach tithing. Our giving is theologically based. When we accept Christ, we acknowledge that He becomes the Lord of our life, includ- ing our resources. And the scriptural pattern was to bring what I call in worship "the lordship portion" or "the first fruits." We teach a tithe.

Assemblies of God churches do not push hard for people to become members, but they do have expectations for those who do. One pastor ex- plained:

> Assemblies of God churches have a kind of membership that I would call a "covenant," in which they commit themselves to certain things—doctrinal agreement, agreement to tithe, and so forth. We don't push membership. What we do is to say periodically that if you are interested in knowing about membership, there will be a pastoral class in which we will talk to you about what membership involves. What happens is that some people may not want to commit them- selves to being a tither. Some may say, "I'm not going to lie. I'm not going to say I will tithe and then not tithe." There is that requirement: If a person becomes a member, he pledges to tithe. So it's a matter of conscience. And there may be a doctrinal problem. Because we ask members to agree with the doctrine.

No one is criticized if he or she remains a nonmember for a long time, even for years. That person is still entitled to pastoral care, marrying, burying, and full participation, but not entitled to take any leadership role.

Pastor Nichols elaborated on tithing:

> Now, we don't say that if you don't tithe, you're going to hell. I don't believe that. I don't think the scriptures teach that. But we teach the principle that I believe Jesus taught—of sowing and reaping, of reci- procity, that has to do with faith and with an attitude of heart, that what I have is being entrusted to me, and I am responsible for where it goes. And that's the reason why we also preach against gambling: that we're responsible for what we do, and that we trust God, not the lottery, or whatever, for our life.

Both pastors are typical of other pastors in tithing churches in that they claimed not to know which parishioners tithe. In Pastor Nichols's words,

"I can't tell you what any person in this church gives. I make it a point not to know what anybody gives!" Pastor Jim rarely, if ever, preaches a full sermon on tithing. In one sermon he spoke of "returning to the Lord for all He has given us. I know you'll all do what you can." The sermon continued:

> Some of you have never tithed. The challenge of the Word of God today is "Test me. Prove me. See if I won't bless you in a thousand ways." (Mal. 3:8.) Read Deuteronomy 28 about what God promises to do in your life. Give your life to the Lord and see what God will do! God will bless your business, He will bless your family, He'll bless your plans for the future. He'll rebuke the enemies; He'll rebuke those people who are kvetching about you in the office and the plant, those people who are spreading bad rumors about you as a businessman. God will rebuke them and be on your side and cause you to prosper. God says, "Test me."

No Stewardship Effort

Neither Springfield nor Seaside has an annual stewardship effort or announces an annual budget that must be met. Neither has sermons saying what the church wants to accomplish in the next year if giving is high enough. The only letter that goes out from the Springfield church is an annual thank-you letter for tax purposes. Pastor Nichols explained his philosophy:

> We really are of the principle that "money follows ministry." People vote two ways in a church, with their feet and their pocketbook. So if they're giving and coming, we're scratching where it itches. And if they stop showing up and stop putting money in the plate, then we're failing. So you can come up with all these programs and visit everybody's house with a card and have a stewardship committee and say, "What can we count on you for, Sister Jones, to give in 1994?" and if we're not scratching where Brother and Sister Jones are living, and we're not providing a ministry to their youth and to their children, and if they don't feel fed on Sunday morning and feel that people care about them and feel spiritually empowered, that card is not going to make them give! That's my conviction.
>
> I think that, in our church, we really touch people, so that their faith is central in their life. If you talk to people who come to this church, they're going to talk to you about their walk with the Lord. They're going to talk in very personal, subjective, pietistic terms about a relationship with Jesus. They mean that they're trusting the Lord for their finances, and they believe that what they have God has put in their hands, and they are honoring Him with their tithe.

In Nichols's view, once a person has committed himself or herself to
God and begun tithing, the church should not talk further about money.
Rather, the pastor should convey that the person is now right with God.
In fact, Nichols had preached on stewardship only once in the past two
years. A pastor may, of course, make special appeals for specific projects,
but on a day-to-day basis, a church should teach tithing and not talk about
money needs.

Nichols told about his experiences in Assemblies of God churches:

> In our churches you can count on $800 to $1,200 giving per person at-
> tending per year. I have studied this personally over the years. Count
> the babies and everyone, and depending on the economics of the area
> and the times, you will have $800 to $1,200 per person average atten-
> dance in an Assemblies of God church that tithes. We at Springfield
> are on the high side. We have one thousand folk attending and we had
> $1,200,000 in giving last year.

We asked Nichols if it follows that denominations with a low level of
giving are in that situation because the people are not being ministered to;
this would seem to follow from his theory. He thought a moment and hesitated to respond. Then he cautioned:

> Well, it's not like you can isolate one thing and say, you do this one
> thing, then people will feel ministered to and therefore will be faith-
> ful in giving. It's a whole perception of the dynamic and the life of the
> church, that people feel like something's happening there, they're
> committed to it, so therefore they're committed to supporting it.

Reciprocity with God
and with Church Members

A basic tenet of psychological theories of philanthropy and gift giving
is that many gifts are made in a spirit of reciprocity—belief that a gift will
somehow help the donor in the long run by setting up a relationship of
reciprocity with another person.[2] For the Christian, there is also reciprocity with God.

The tithing churches teach reciprocity with God. This is a sensitive
theological topic at the heart of Christian teaching about money. The issue, put simply, is as follows: Can a gift benefit the donor by establishing
reciprocity with God, so that God will repay the gift later? Does God reward gifts?

Denominations and preachers take varying positions on this question.
The topic is rife with tensions and temptations, and in various meetings
we have seen that it evokes strong emotions among pastors. Church
leaders may be tempted to promise parishioners that God will reward

generous givers, yet when asked directly, they will say there is no direct reciprocity with God.

The topic is even more subtle because of the ways in which God may pay back the giver. Is it by returning the money later, dollar for dollar, in business success or some other income—perhaps twofold, fourfold, or tenfold? Is it through good life experiences, such as health, happiness, and freedom from tragedies? Is it through spiritual blessings, such as inner joy, contentment, and well-being? Is it through eternal salvation? The interpretive issues and opportunities are too numerous to spell out. In the tithing churches, we heard preachers saying that God indeed reciprocates for gifts. A person who tithes may be assured that God will take care of his or her future needs, material and spiritual.

We asked a lay Sunday school teacher in Springfield Assembly of God why the people give so much. He replied that people give a lot because they are receiving a lot:

> People give in thankfulness and also in expectation. They have a sense of reciprocity. My wife and I give because of our faith that God will take care of us. I believe that God knows our needs and will take care of us. And I'll pay God for that, and God will repay me for that.

The attenders at Seaside Assembly Fellowship are sure of at least two things. First, tithing does cost. When we asked one member how he could possibly tithe on a college student's income, he simply told us, "You do without lunch sometimes."

Second, tithing involves a kind of blind trust in God. Specific material rewards are not in question, but being taken care of by the Lord (in some way) definitely is. One Seaside member said, "It never fails. I have heard so many stories of how God blesses me because I tithed." We asked, "So what do you get back?" "I don't really look to get something back, but what I do receive is more than just monetary benefits. It's not a question of, if I give ten you will give me twenty. That is *not* how it works. But I can see it in small ways, like I don't have lunch money, what am I going to do, and someone says, oh, let me take you out to lunch. Just in ways like that, God provides."

We talked with Pastor Nichols about the two kinds of reciprocity. We began our conversation with this comment: "Some fund-raisers assume that people give because of reciprocity and hopes of setting up a relationship. There are two kinds of reciprocity, reciprocity with God and with the social group." He replied:

> Yes. We would like to de-emphasize reciprocity with the social group to the zero level, if possible. That's the reason even I don't know who

gives what. We have some businessmen of substantial means in our church, and I have absolutely no idea if they tithe! I have *no idea*.

We asked again, "So it's your policy to remove reciprocity with other people as a motivation for giving?"

> Yes. I think if we started doing that sort of thing I would get calls and letters from unhappy people. People would say, "Pastor, that's not right!" And it undermines everything else that we're trying to teach people about their Christian life, about God not being a respecter of persons, about our honoring and preferring one another above ourselves, and a lot of Christian virtue that we want to see in the bigger picture of relationships.

One sermon stated Nichols's view clearly: Following God's commandments and giving our lives to God is not something we do just for altruistic purposes; it is something we do *in our own interest*. Any intelligent person, when he or she understands what is at stake, would do it. It is for our own good! It is really the only way to live, since God is in command of the world. Do not forget that. And God will determine how your life goes. You can't afford *not* to give your life totally to God! No intelligent person would ever refuse to do it. God is all powerful and can give blessings overflowing.

A twenty-three-year old at Seaside remarked, "You see how thin Pastor Jim and Karen are? They don't spend a lot of money on eating out or on a lot of stuff. They know that God will take care of them if they have the right priorities."

How to Increase
Giving in All Churches

We asked Nichols what it would take to increase giving in all the Assemblies of God churches, by maybe 5 or 10 percent. He replied:

> Number one, there needs to be a vision and sense of purpose in that church. Let's call it "vision casting." So we know who we are and what we're about. And second is the whole relational issue, so people feel confident in the pastor and his team and the board. A sense of confidence that we have a vision and the pastor and board are leading toward that vision.
>
> And the third thing is consistency. The people need to know where you are going. I had a friend who grew a church up to the attendance range of maybe 2,000 or 2,200. And it was exciting. Full of people, all around! And then, they changed direction in emphasis two or three different times; and that church has basically evaporated—almost disappeared. Because you have to keep people on track. You can't say,

"Our emphasis is family ministry and providing a full ministry to the family," and then the next day say that we're going to be just an evangelistic center, with big rallies. What this pastor wanted to do was not what drew the people there in the first place.

TWO PLEDGING CHURCHES

Our examples of pledging churches are Grace Lutheran and Westminster Presbyterian.

Grace Lutheran is located in an older suburb of an Eastern city. It has 2,000 nominal members, of whom about 1,200 are active. Average Sunday attendance is 650. Grace's building is pleasant and elegant, totally air-conditioned, and fitted with a closed-circuit TV system. Its sanctuary is small, so there are three services on Sunday morning.

Pastor Meyer has served Grace Lutheran for nine years, and now he has two associates and more than a dozen lay staff members. He is a relentless booster of the church's programs, mission efforts, and accomplishments. His preaching is both humorous and earnest. He is unfailingly joyful, affirming, and outgoing.

Grace Lutheran has a very full program. Its music program alone includes two music directors, one full time and one half-time, who lead two adult choirs, several youth choirs, and six children's choirs. The church has three bell-choir ensembles and a string orchestra.

The youth program includes a full range of classes, retreats, and trips. Its flagship is a summer program featuring a high school–age traveling theater group with its own large tent. For one month the troupe goes from town to town in neighboring states, almost like a circus. This program is much cherished by the adult members.

Grace Lutheran owns a retreat center an hour's drive away from the church, which is the site for weekend retreats for families, singles, and youth.

Total pledges at Grace Lutheran in 1994 were $817,000, but total giving was a little less than $1,000,000. Giving per member was about $700. A total of 529 families or individuals made pledges, averaging $1,540 per giving unit. About half of the giving came from 97 pledgers.

Westminster Presbyterian is one of the largest Presbyterian churches in the United States, with over four thousand members. Its annual receipts are close to $4 million. It has a large and lovely sanctuary adjoining an education building that would be the envy of any congregation: five floors of offices; a multipurpose hall and large kitchen; a nursery; thirty-eight

classrooms; recreational areas, including a small indoor gymnasium; re-
hearsal rooms for the music ministry; a graphic arts shop; and a printing
shop. Connecting the education wing with the meeting hall and kitchen
wing is a large foyer reminiscent of a modern hotel, complete with indoor
plants and skylight roof. Across the street is a parking structure. The phys-
ical plant strongly suggests a flagship church.

Senior Minister John Richards has been pastor at Westminster for
twenty-four years. He enjoys a reputation as not only an outstanding
preacher but also an exemplary leader and administrator. His stewardship sermons are models of scripturally based reflection that elicit praise
from congregation members.

Westminster lays claim to one of the largest Sunday school programs
in the nation: more than two thousand attend classes each Sunday before
and after services. Separate programs for elementary, middle school, high
school, and college students, including mission work in both the United
States and Mexico, involve hundreds of young church members.

Westminster's divorce recovery workshops draw hundreds of participants yearly; many in the workshops eventually join the congregation.
The church's music program also is extensive. Aside from performing
each Sunday in the sanctuary, the adult choirs join together several times
yearly to sing with the city's symphony orchestra.

The members of both Grace Lutheran and Westminster Presbyterian include many business and professional persons, for the most part conservative in demeanor and political views.

Teaching about Tithing
in Pledging Churches

We asked Pastor Meyer of Grace Lutheran if he preached about tithing.
He responded:

> I preach more percentage giving than tithing. It's a dash of cold water
> to say to somebody that they must go from a life of self-centered
> spending to a 10 percent tithe. I think it's not realistic, and it's not pas-
> toral. I believe the people have to receive both the law and the joy of
> the gospel. The law may be the tithe, but the joy is reaching a goal that
> one has set for one's spiritual growth. So I preach percentage giving.
> I preach it relentlessly.

Pastor Meyer openly tells everyone that he and his wife tithe:

> Martha and I have long since passed tithing. We're very open about
> that. And we don't give to budgets. Whether the budget is large or
> small doesn't matter. I don't give to budgets. If Grace Church had a

surplus, I would still have to give, since that is who I am. But then I may give more to different causes in the church or in the world. There are so many good places in the world—the hospital we support in Jerusalem, the new churches we are building in Russia.

What if a good church member asked Meyer how much he should give to the church? He answered:

> I'd begin by saying that I can't give you a dollar amount. I would start by talking about a tithe. The Bible has taught 10 percent, which leaves 90 percent for your use. I also understand that you need to start low. I'd ask, "What are you giving now? Why don't you start at 2 or 3 percent, and raise it 1, 2, or 3 percent a year until you get to that level? Two, to 3, to 4, until you get to 10. And then we'll tell you, you will never stop giving."

One longtime member asked Meyer how much the average person in the church gives, so that he could know how much he himself should give. Meyer wrote him a letter that refused to answer the question and explained that it is irrelevant what other people give. Giving is a spiritual matter between the individual and God, not a matter of church needs or matching the average contribution. Meyer told us that at the time he hoped the man would not be offended, and in fact, the man was not.

Pastor Richards at Westminster believes you cannot be biblical about stewardship without bringing in tithing:

> I even believe in storehouse tithing, which is really controversial. The whole tithe should go to the local church or storehouse, which becomes a collection and distribution point. The accountability then resides in the local church. If people give part of their tithe to parachurch organizations, there is no accountability. If we distribute the tithe in an inappropriate way, we can be called to account right away.

Richards preaches tithing but doesn't push it or insist on it. There is no checking up. Richards has no idea how many people tithe. "The secret of this church's financial situation is that we have a large number of people giving, and many give at a high rate, considering their capacity."

Pastor Meyer feels strongly that all clergy must be tithers:

> They have to do it, and they have to lay it on the counter! Be open. Not because it's a prideful thing, but because no mountain was ever taken by any army with the guy carrying the flag being in the rear! You just can't do it that way!
>
> You can't teach what you aren't. The biggest fraud practiced by the clergy today is that they are poor givers. That's only a suspicion; I don't have data on it. But I have seen some reports, and I believe it. I

see seminarians in this parish, and, I suspect, other parishes, who don't give a cent to their home church, even though they're asking the church for scholarship support. There's not a spirit of generosity. I always say, you can't begin preaching stewardship until you're giving yourself. You've got to be a first-person witness to the truth of what you preach.

We asked Meyer why some clergy are afraid to talk about money from the pulpit. He offered this analysis:

Some pastors are scared to death of it! They see it as meeting budgets, and also, they're poor performers in giving themselves. They think, "I can't climb the pulpit steps and ask for a tithe if *I'm* not a tither." And they are right. The people will sense it, even if the financial records are locked up tight. It's a lack of integrity.

In several denominations, ministers are either required or strongly urged to tithe. Assemblies of God pastors are required to send one-tenth of their income to district and national offices. They are urged to tell their congregations openly that they tithe. Baptist leaders told us the same. But we heard repeatedly that Protestant ministers are often conflicted over the topic of giving and how to challenge members to give. One Presbyterian leader said that most pastors are terribly afraid of offending members by asking too forcefully for higher giving; pastors who feel insecure in their positions would like to avoid the whole matter of giving. Another told us that many pastors do not have their personal finances in order; they are financially strapped and see themselves as unable to tithe.

Teaching the Meaning of Stewardship

Pastor Meyer stresses the joy of giving:

I preach stewardship. I talk about it as a response. I often announce the offering on Sunday morning as a kind of response to the Word. The creed and the offering are both part of our responses.

I also believe that giving is *fun*. It makes us feel more important. It's having a reason to be alive that's larger than ourselves and feeling like we make a difference someplace else. It's a great affirmation of our reason to exist. And I think most people feel that way once they have experienced giving.

The gospel is finally a call to *serve;* it is not a call to *receive.* And we begin to live in that gospel when we spend ourselves. The greatest joy of the gospel is when we begin to serve!

Meyer acknowledges that it may pain a person to make a large gift, but he maintains that the joy of making the gift is much greater. Stewardship is essential to the Christian life. It is a part of being a disciple. Meyer continually stresses giving as an *opportunity*, not giving to meet a specific need or to the budget.

Stewardship is much different from secular fund-raising for an organization. Meyer remarked:

> If we get into fund-raising, we're dead. This is a God thing. We can't just talk about raising funds for an institution. The church is not just a social institution. This is what God is all about. This church is owned by the Spirit, and we're doing God's work here.

Annual Stewardship Programs

Westminster Presbyterian has the most carefully orchestrated stewardship program of the churches we visited. Its policy is to concentrate everything on a once-a-year campaign and avoid any other special offerings during the year. Yet one portion of the stewardship effort is ongoing throughout the year—the weekly church newsletter, which is mailed to everyone. It constantly carries stories of Westminster's programs, showing people how their money is being used. A stewardship committee member described it:

> It's done in a way that is highly pictorial or visual, with the minimum amount of words. The idea is that someone could read it from the mailbox to the house, because once it gets to the house, it will get put on the kitchen counter and not get looked at. But in the course of a year, there's a lot of exposure in there to what's going on, going back to the idea that people today give only when they believe something's happening that meets their needs or what they're committed to or interested in. So what we try to do throughout the year is say, "There's a lot happening here," so that when we get to stewardship time in the fall, we don't have to do the impossible and try to tell the whole story in one piece.

The fall campaign begins slowly and climaxes in the last two Sundays in October and the first Sunday in November. The stewardship committee adopts an annual theme that is used in all mailings, materials, and appeals. In October, a pictorial brochure is mailed out that highlights all the ministries. The 1994 brochure stressed the importance of growing from a stance of "getting," which most persons have before they know Christ, to one of "giving," which comes only when people mature in Christ. A massive prayer campaign also begins in October, and the stewardship team instructs all Sunday school teachers to enlist people for the prayer campaign.

Everyone who agrees to join the prayer campaign is given a devotional booklet with daily messages, put out by the church printing shop. An example of the daily devotional message is as follows:

"Then your barns will be filled. . . . " There is nothing wrong with fund-raising, but the primary focus for stewardship campaigns should not stop with raising dollars for a mission. Fund-raising is a financial matter, but stewardship is primarily a spiritual one. Fundraising is concerned with raising money for the budget, while stewardship relates to how we live out our commitment to Jesus Christ. Pray for our children and youth, that giving to the Lord would become a habit early in life and that they would learn the joy of giving.

A second mailing in October discusses the tithe as a basic scriptural idea. Then there are testimonies and skits in worship services on the benefits people have experienced from sacrificial giving or tithing. One well-rehearsed skit included the line "I was a single mother and I didn't think I could possibly tithe."

On Stewardship Sunday in October, the senior pastor holds up a pledge card at the end of his sermon and urges everyone to pray all week to see what the Lord is asking their commitment to be. A week later during the service, the Stewardship Commitment Team comes to the sanctuary with pledge cards. The pastor dedicates them to the Lord, then the committee members hand them out and collect them as the choir sings "When the Saints Come Marching In." On the following Saturday, the Stewardship Commitment Team makes house calls and phone calls to members who did not pledge.

The 1994 campaign emphasized stewardship themes while also promoting the church's many programs. The message was a mixture of spiritual and practical.

Westminster's business manager told us that pledging is basic to the church's financial success. In 1994 almost two-thirds of the church's membership family units agreed to pledge, with the average pledge coming to $1,098. Approximately fifteen families pledged $10,000 or more. Every two months a computerized statement goes out to each pledging unit, indicating what has been given and the balance remaining for the year. Members who maintain their pledge commitment are acknowledged and thanked. Those delinquent are reminded that "we are counting on you to keep your commitment up to date."

At Grace Lutheran, a modest stewardship campaign is carried out each fall, comprised of a letter and set of envelopes sent to every giving unit. The letter asks for a pledge. The content of the letter varies from one category of person to another, depending on the person's past pledging.

Pastor Meyer admitted that this approach is not very effective. Sending letters is next to useless, he told us, since people don't read them. It would be immensely better to ask people to pledge one on one. Stewardship programs ideally, he believes, should be face to face, but this is too difficult; there are too many people to visit, too few laypersons willing to visit them. Meyer explained:

> In a large parish a face-to-face campaign is really difficult, and you have to use other models. My model is acknowledging every pledge—every pledge!—with a personal note. I mention the amount of the pledge. This does two things. It gets out the word in the neighborhood that "the pastor wrote me a note about my pledge. I only pledged five dollars a week, but he wrote me a note!" And what I say in that note is "You've made the first step, bless your soul! The first thing in good stewardship is setting a goal. And when you find the joy in it, you'll want to give and give and give. I'm celebrating that with you. We think that's a great gift. There's room to grow." Nobody's going to be offended by that.

Meyer assured us that one-to-one, frank communication is the way to teach people to give. "If I had time to sit in every home, most of this congregation would be pledging. I have no doubt about that." He is not shy about talking plainly to loyal and regular church members who have poor giving records.

At Grace Lutheran the lay leaders are asked to pledge first, before the start of the annual stewardship drive. The total of the pledges by the staff and church council (but not individual pledges) is then announced at the start of the campaign. In Meyer's words:

> The staff and the council must pledge and announce the total pledge first. They know it. And we publish the increase—1 percent, 2 percent, 10 percent, whatever. And I say to the council, "If you increase the budget by 5 percent, your giving had better show an increase of 5 percent when you announce it to the congregation."

We asked an associate pastor if Lutherans generally like or dislike pledging. He said there is a lot of hostility to pledging in the denomination. It has taken a long time to get Grace Lutheran members to accept annual pledging.

Pastor Richards of Westminster Presbyterian discussed the difficulty of keeping the stewardship ideal distinguished from fund-raising in people's minds. He assured us that stewardship is a tough thing to teach. Repeatedly he stresses "acknowledging the Lordship of Christ" and "expressing our discipleship." At Westminster there is no talk of raising funds to support the budget. No budget is prepared until the results of the stewardship campaign are in. There is no thermometer in the foyer and no victory celebration afterward. The pastor explained:

You never "arrive" under Christian stewardship. It's not fund-raising we're into, it's vision-raising. It's more biblical to talk about steward-ship as it is in scripture than to talk about your church's needs, no mat-ter how big or small you are.

The concept here is that everything belongs to God. Everything you have is a gift to you. And we make that the foundation of our thinking, rather than "How much should I give?" You know, we come naked into the world, so everything we have is a gift. As Christians, we are gifted *and* redeemed. This is anti- what society says, and you have to bang away at it every year, against "What's mine is mine." With the new mind-set, it's a whole different game, a celebration of all you have been given.

The stewardship or pledging churches, in urging their members to give sacrificially, lean heavily on the New Testament themes of awareness of what God through Jesus Christ has done for members individually, for their families, and for the congregation itself. Above all, stewardship is taught as a joyful experience. Growth in stewardship requires time for the believers truly to grasp the implications of stewardship as a total way of life.

Resistance to
Preaching about Tithing

We asked Meyer why so many mainline pastors don't preach tithing. Don't they believe in it? Are they afraid? He replied:

First of all, Protestants have always been uneasy about legalism, and there's a certain legalism and inequity about tithing. Tithing is much more difficult for a family with five children than for a family without children. Therefore, when I am preaching to a family that has five chil-dren that they need to tithe, the same as another family with two pro-fessionals and no children, I'm really preaching what I believe to be an inequity. It's legalism; and because it's legalism, it doesn't address every issue and opportunity with any creativity. Therefore we talk about percentage giving, not tithing. The tithe is the goal. In our new members' classes here, I talk very frankly and openly about tithing. I talk about the need to give, to be invested beyond ourselves.

Meyer believes that giving arises out of community life, and it should be seen as part of community life. Therefore he is opposed to denomina-tional appeals which ask that money be sent directly to national offices. Giving is an act of the community in the context of the community. He told of his anger at a letter, written by a denominational officer, that was ad-dressed to members and asked for special gifts to be sent directly to the national headquarters:

I did not distribute those letters. Stewardship is a celebration of the community that gives! Every gift is a joy to the community. Every gift is a response to the gospel. There is no such thing as mailing away our gifts when we have a congregational life out of which to give, out of which gifts need to arise. You will never support the denomination with mailed-in gifts. It will never happen.

He wrote a letter to the denominational officer, voicing his objections:

Why do we have to mail the gift directly to you? Why isn't it coming down the center aisle every Sunday as our response to preaching the gospel every Sunday? It bypasses worship and response to the gospel. We teach stewardship as a response to the gospel! Givers in the community generate gifts in the community.

Resistance to Pledging

We talked with Pastor Meyer about his experiences with pledging. Since research shows that pledging enhances giving, we suggested that Lutheran churches should perhaps expand pledging. He agreed. But then we asked if there is resistance from lay members to pledging, to which he responded:

Yes, there is. When people look at the amount they give to the church, they are embarrassed. When people are asked, "If the Lord is really the Lord of your life, can somebody tell that by your check stubs?" they're embarrassed. They don't want to face it.

Pledging isn't popular with a portion of the church members; both Meyer and Richards told us this. But making a pledge has a definite spiritual side. When you fill out something and sign on the line, they note, it's a serious matter. Also, churches today need a better idea of what financial resources they can turn to, and pledging accomplishes this.

Pastor Richards said, "I like to know what I can count on. We have lots of businesspeople in our church, and they don't like things vague. I'd have a hard time working with trustees if I didn't run things this way."

Pastor Richards rejects the strategy that starts with a budget and then asks people to pledge the amount indicated. He believes this is the wrong approach. Keep in focus the biblical notion of stewardship, he argues; say to people, "We'll prepare a budget on the basis of what you commit yourselves to give. We're not raising a budget here; we're raising the issue of Christian stewardship." Stewardship is a matter of personal commitment to God. Richards said, "People respond to this. If you make stewardship a bigger thing than money, make it discipleship, a life commitment, not financial, then you give people something big to grab onto."

Reciprocity with God
and with Church Members

We explored with Pastor Meyer what motivations he thinks are important in giving. Does God reward big givers? He replied:

> No. People give out of the joy of the gospel. Well, there is anticipation of the *joy* of giving and of being part of a worthwhile thing. But reward for a specific gift, no. If I want something, I don't think making a gift to God will make it come; I don't think so. The real joy is the giving itself. *That is* its reward.

We mentioned to Meyer that we had visited an evangelical church and heard the minister preach on Malachi 3:8–10, saying that no one should put God to the test by withholding one's tithe. Meyer commented:

> "Yes, I know that passage in Malachi. I would never say that. That's *fear*, not generosity. It's not joy. That's terror! I hope I never get heard saying that.
>
> Lutheran theology has never accepted that there is any reciprocity with God. Lutheran theology says that we are incapable. All humans have sinned and fallen short of the grace of God. There is nothing we can do about it. You can't ever get right with God. Only God's grace can do anything. And we have God's promise of grace.

Meyer was clear that Lutheran theology was different from the theology of many evangelicals:

> I believe the whole Baptist and evangelical approach is fundamentally different from ours. They talk about money very openly, but Lutherans don't talk about it openly, because we are afraid of it. We're afraid of justification by works.
>
> Lutherans are uncomfortable with reciprocity. We are *basically* uncomfortable because it's the wrong reason to give. From our standpoint, you don't give because you want something. You give because it's your nature to give. That's a harder piece to sell. It's not as natural. But Lutherans tend to think that, theologically, intellectually, and biblically, it is more honest.

Westminster's church members, when asked why they give, reflect their pastor's spiritual interpretation of stewardship. According to one member:

> I read recently in a book a friend gave to me that if you give to God, you get ten times over. I knew this was wrong. I give because Jesus Christ is real to me and has called me to a life of stewardship and discipleship. The Lord says that I will take care of you if you trust in me.

And you have to. He does promise to be there and to help us work through any situation.

Another member, a car dealer, put it this way:

> The necessary thing for every Christian is to elevate his or her thinking to a sense of trust and dependency on God, and one way to bring this about is to "disable" the things that inhibit that sense. You come to see stewardship as a way of making daily decisions—like a customer in the dealership showroom: Do we really want to buy this car now? I think it really grows on you. It's not something you get into right away. It's the outcome of faith commitment over time. And no, you don't cut deals with God. Stewardship is a response to what you have already been given. In fact, God may send you a blow and know it will help you grow in faith and understanding. Disasters can be for your spiritual growth. Protection, no.

TWO OFFERING CHURCHES

The offering churches were those without full-blown, formal stewardship or tithing programs. All of the Catholic churches we studied fall into this category. The Catholic churches were much larger in membership than most of the Protestant churches we studied and had much lower levels of giving. We studied Catholic parishes that were relatively high in giving, realizing that this level was high relative to other Catholic parishes but not to all churches.

Our examples are St. Ann and St. Benedict. Both are slightly larger than average for Catholic parishes. They both demonstrate sound fiscal management, multiple ministries, and a sense of ownership by the parishioners.

St. Ann is a parish of 1,130 families, established in 1960 in a new suburb. Its neighborhood is a mixture of white-collar and blue-collar folks. At first the parishioners built a school and had their worship services in the school's auditorium. Then, in the late 1980s, the pastor started a planning process, out of which the decision was made to build a new church. It is now finished. Average worship attendance on a weekend is twelve hundred in five masses.

The current pastor, Father Gregory Wills, has been at St. Ann for fourteen years. He has successfully led St. Ann in a period of growth. He achieved parish consensus about its building program, then presided over two capital campaigns that raised $1.6 million and oversaw the construction of the church building.

Father Wills believes in making full use of volunteers in running the parish. The workers are treated not as volunteers but as people who have taken on a ministry. He described the difference to us:

> A volunteer is someone who gives of their time and needs some kind of recognition. If I know someone is a volunteer, I thank them for what they did. If I know someone has a ministry, I affirm them: "What you are doing is an inspiration to the parish," rather than merely thanking them. I am in no position to thank them for their ministry, because that comes from their baptism.

By encouraging his parishioners to take on a ministry, rather than merely serving as volunteers, Pastor Wills is able to instill in them a heightened sense of ownership and, ultimately, stewardship. One parishioner described Wills:

> He has made us not into just volunteers. What we really are is ministers. We see ourselves as ministers, and we are committed as ministers. This is a high-priority part of our lives. This is not just some hobby or some good thing that we are doing. We are called, and we know it.

Pastor Wills believes in having as much work as possible done by laypeople with a sense of ministry. About three hundred are now active. He thinks other people like seeing the laity in leadership: "That helps people with their giving. They know somebody is putting in those hours and not getting paid." The only paid staff in the parish are the pastor, the youth minister, and two secretaries.

Wills ties lay ministry into stewardship:

> For someone who is in a ministry, their time already belongs to God, so they can't "give it." The same holds true for money. Someone in a real stewardship does not really "give" their money, they are only returning to God what already belongs to God.

St. Benedict is a suburban parish in the West. It was established in the mid-1950s as the city grew rapidly after World War II. The parish is attended by largely middle-class families and retired senior citizens; it has 1,660 families.

Father Don Blackman came to St. Benedict as pastor in 1987. Blackman's background is somewhat atypical in that he studied engineering before becoming a priest, then served as chaplain in the National Guard, where he took management courses and rose to the rank of colonel. He later obtained a doctorate in education. He enjoys a reputation as a very competent administrator and a priest of sound judgment.

When Father Blackman came to St. Benedict, annual giving per family was $93. In seven years he revitalized the parish and increased giving to

$425 per family. Part of this increase was achieved by removing more than one hundred inactive families from the parish registry.

Blackman brought along Jim McGarran from his previous parish. Jim, whose background is that of finance officer for a large retail chain, now serves as business manager for St. Benedict. Though his position is salaried, he returns his entire salary to the parish each year.

*Parochial Schools
in the Two Parishes*

Both parishes have schools. St. Ann's school currently enrolls three hundred students, from kindergarten through grade eight, and it has a long waiting list. It could easily double in size. Of the school's annual budget, 30 percent comes as a subsidy from the parish, an amount that comes to 15 percent of the parish budget.

Some parishioners argue that the school is a drain on parish finances and energy, but these people concede that the school produces commitment to the parish and enhanced activity in the parish by students' parents. Furthermore, they admit, the school provides an opportunity to reach new people. Pastor Wills evaluated the school in terms of how it affects overall parish life:

> It depends on how the school is used. If this school is really used to renew people, to call families to renewal, if the long run goal of the school is evangelization, then it is a tremendous investment. It is a terrific vehicle for getting the message across.
>
> At one point the parish school was run like an academy, and it was a drain, because the parish was not offering it as a vehicle for renewal and evangelization.

Prior to 1987, St. Benedict's parochial school was administered by a lay board, most of whose members had children in the school. When Blackman came, he thought this was a recipe for disaster. Business manager McGarran reflected on the situation:

> The school had an artificially low tuition and consequently high enrollment, since parents found it such a bargain to enroll their kids. The parish was always in need of money. A small group of school board members had charge and were content to see the school strongly subsidized by the parish.

Instituting a "management by objectives" approach to the entire parish, the pastor and business manager first calculated the real cost of the school. Costs such as maintenance, insurance liability for accidents, and heating and cooling had never appeared in the budget. School buildings were rented free of charge to other groups. It was impossible to tell the true cost of education per pupil without knowing first the entire range of costs incurred by the school and its buildings.

Father Blackman and Administrator McGarran, in consultation with a newly established parish finance council (appointed by the pastor), decided that tuition needed to be raised. Over several years, they raised it from $800 per pupil to $2,000. They improved the school and promoted it widely. By 1994, 460 children were enrolled, with 140 on the waiting list. Teachers' salaries were raised substantially. New classrooms were added, providing 250 more places for students. In 1994, school subsidies represented only 9 percent of the total parish budget.

Ministries in the Parishes

In St. Ann parish, about 40 percent of the households are involved in activities in the parish, and about one-third use offering envelopes. But more than half pledged toward one of the two building campaigns to pay for the new church. To secure pledges for the new building, teams of parishioners went out to visit all the families. People were asked to complete a questionnaire about various elements of parish life, and they were presented with a list of specific items, worth specific amounts, that they could contribute; for example a new pew would cost x dollars and a crucifix would cost y dollars. During the capital campaigns for the new building, no decline in offering collections took place.

St. Ann has a clear policy that all funds raised, by whatever program or club in the parish, go into a common pool, to be spent as the parish leadership decides. There are no separate checking accounts for groups within the parish. The purpose is to help unify the parish and encourage a sense of parish ownership. One finance council member explained:

> For example, in dealing with the Parent–School Association, normally you would find an organization that raises money and then spends it on the school. That is accepted nationwide. But that does not happen at St. Ann. We go to the PSA on an annual basis and explain that we are a family and whatever any of us does to raise money goes into the central parish fund. That mentality carries over; you start with the money, but you begin to think like that about everything.

Pastor Wills openly stresses efficiency and accountability in parish management. A council member told us:

> What our parishioners know is that there is very little waste. The money is spent well for things that will be to all of our benefit. The parishioners know that and feel very good about how their money is treated.

At St. Benedict, our interviews with worshipers elicited praise for the many ministries and organizations. "There is something here for everybody." "It's a place that makes you feel welcome." "There's a lot done for kids here." One man claimed that the church had forty-five different groups.

A full-time youth minister helps plan activities, including late Friday and Saturday activities in the parish gym and hall for high school students. Cub Scouts, Boy Scouts, Brownies, and Girl Scouts are active. Father Blackman was commended for opening up the rectory on weekend evenings and making popcorn and serving hot chocolate "to kids who want to come in and just talk with Father."

Stewardship and Pledging

We discussed tithing and stewardship with Pastor Wills of St. Ann. Does he ever preach about tithing? we asked. He told us:

> No. Because I've watched the parishioners move along at a certain pace in giving that is healthy. I suspect tithing is something that shouldn't be preached but should be discussed at our weekend renewals with small groups. It would be more effective if you were communicating it to the people who have a capacity for it. Then, once you had, say, fifty families tithing, it might be good to let that be known—that fifty families are tithing. Then I think other people who are not as plugged in spiritually but maybe could afford to tithe might hop on.

Wills favors pledging for both spiritual and practical reasons, though he is aware of opposition among parish members. Now he is trying to introduce the idea gradually.

For several years, St. Ann had a stewardship committee that accomplished little. But recently the diocese instituted a diocese-wide stewardship program to increase giving. The diocesan leadership encouraged door-to-door canvassing at stewardship time, and St. Ann is considering it. Pastor Wills would like to do canvassing each year, if possible. He would like to talk to all the people personally about their money and their talents.

Now the stewardship committee is trying in other ways to educate the parishioners about the need to give time, talent, and money. As one member put it, "Our stewardship committee is trying to get people to understand the economics of the parish. There are people here who think God just put these buildings here." Another said:

> It is a lot easier to give money than to spend the time and talent. That is one thing we keep stressing. We don't just want people's cash. Just

giving cash does not do anything. It is a lot harder to get people to participate than to get them to contribute cash.

Now the annual stewardship effort at St. Ann includes a letter sent to
every parish household and talks given in masses by members of the stewardship committee. Everyone agrees that stewardship talks given by
laypeople are more effective than talks by priests. The stewardship committee told us:

> It is the people talking to the people [that works]. There could be a
> negative reaction having the pastor talk. Like, okay, he wants more
> money again.

> It comes across really well when the parishioners themselves do the
> solicitation. The priest is not a fund-raiser. He is here for other reasons.

> It is our responsibility, not the priest's, to make sure this parish is fi-
> nancially sound.

Pastor Wills gave his opinion: "People give to people. The issue is, who do
they feel the most connected with, a layperson or the pastor?"

Wills has mixed feelings about fund-raising events and carnivals at
St. Ann:

> Carnivals and gambling cause deterioration because there is a certain
> mind-set that says, "Oh, all we have to do is have a bigger carnival.
> We don't have to bother with stewardship efforts to make sure our
> parish is financially sound."

The approach at St. Benedict is a bit different. There are no Stewardship
Sundays, no requests for pledges, and no mailings. Yet the weekly bulletin
carries ongoing information about parish income and how the money is
spent. Pastor Blackman continually congratulates the people in the bulletin and from the pulpit on their level of giving. He teaches that the minimum giving is $1 a week. Anyone falling below this in envelope giving is
sent a letter each quarter, and if they give nothing at all for a year, they are
sent another letter, then dropped from the parish roll.

The financial accountability introduced by Father Blackman, spelled
out in sermons and the Sunday bulletin through graphs and charts, re-
sulted in the retirement of a $300,000 debt within two years and the com-
pletion of a $1.3 million church. The parish is now debt-free. This fiscal
success is attributed by members partly to Blackman's preaching. "He
really lays it out there," one said. Another added, "We know what's going on because he plays things so straight." McGarran reflected on Blackman's stewardship preaching:

I think it's Father's constant repetition from the pulpit that the Lord will not and cannot be outdone in generosity to us. He refers to sacrificial giving and delivers it with such sincerity that it is overwhelmingly believed: the idea that your need to give is greater than our need to receive. You give time, treasure, and talent—time through volunteering, treasure through your weekly offering, talent that you share in the choir or some other ministry.

Blackman refuses, in his words, "to nickel-and-dime people to death" through cake bakes, rummage sales, and car washes. "None of that stuff is allowed." But he does emphasize the annual archdiocesan appeal. The parish's goal in 1993 was set at $65,000; the parishioners came up with $108,000.

At St. Ann, the parishioners generally oppose making formal pledges. Some people dislike the sense of obligation that it entails, and others feel that giving should be spontaneous. One parishioner said:

I do not think anybody should be forced to give. I have a personal problem with those organizations that force that on you and make you feel that you do not belong or have ownership until you have given. It is not that way here. Here you can have full ownership, full membership, and not give a dime.

In spite of opposition by many members, St. Ann has begun a low-key, informal pledging system. Wills explained:

Every year we send them a card. We tell them, "So that the budget committee will know what they are working with, would you be so good as to write down your expectation for giving for the coming year?" It causes people to stop and think: What am I giving?

A Sense of Ownership

At St. Ann, Pastor Wills has tried hard to create a sense of community. The pastoral council members described what he tried to do and how it has worked:

When he first came here, it was such a turnabout because people were saying, "Father Greg wants *us* to decide this or that!" This was a totally new concept. Instead of something coming down from on high, it was "We may do what we want to do with this parish." It really was very different, and people have adjusted well to it.

Father Wills made the budgeting process very participatory. It comes from the bottom up, with each subcommittee forming its own budget and sending it up. Hearings are held by the parish council, and the whole parish is kept informed. Wills explained:

> Budgeting is not something that happens in a corner with a little group of people. Instead, it is something that happens parishwide. Lots of people have input into the budget because of the organizations that they work on. As people get more conscious of the budget, when you say we are going to plan for next year's budget and ask what they are going to give, that word means something: It has flesh. The fact that people are involved in the spending side makes them more willing to commit themselves to the giving side.

A parishioner agreed:

> One of the biggest things that Father Greg has taught us is to be servants to one another and bring Christ to one another. When you do that, the community and spirit can be felt. When people feel a real part of the community, and when people meet God in a more intense way, then the giving just happens.

Another parishioner said, "I have to go back to our leader, Father Greg, who has brought out the best in us, and shown us how to be closer to God, and by doing that, to be closer to one another."

Pastor Wills wants a strong sense of ownership, but it has to be ownership of the entire parish and not just of one program or one group. He explained:

> There are two kinds of ownership. There's an unhealthy ownership and a healthy ownership. The unhealthy ownership comes from a parish divided into little kingdoms. Then each will work for its own turf, but you won't get one group to work for another group's turf. It is an unhealthy ownership. The healthy ownership is when we feel, "I own the project in the sense that I feel responsible to make the best thing happen to this parish." And that is for the *whole* parish, across the board.

Wills clearly thinks the sense of community is important for giving:

> Knitting our people together is the main thing. People give to people. If you knit people together, they will be giving to each other. Get them to have a sense of community, a sense of communion with each other. That takes time. A pastor has to be in a parish for a certain amount of time before he can effectively call people to stewardship. When we ask people to give, they have to know that they are giving to each other and that they want to give to each other. The giving has to be rooted in people. The ownership needs to be very broad-based. Everyone has to be included in the ownership.

We asked Wills what the main impediment is to increasing giving in the diocese. He responded:

A lack of ownership in the parish; when people have no control over what happens with the money or no good reporting on what happens with the money. You see, people need to be part of the decision making, and it has to be done through consensus and discernment.

SUMMARY

Churches are different. They differ in tradition and theological beliefs. They differ in style and culture. Their parishioners differ in habits and expectations. And levels of giving differ.

We have divided churches into three types, based on their teachings about finances, in hopes of emphasizing the characteristics most important in encouraging or discouraging giving. We tried to portray exemplary churches, carrying out their mission in diverse settings and traditions. Were there similarities? Yes. In all the settings, the successful churches had participatory leadership, a sense of forward movement, a feeling of lay ownership, strong trust in leaders, and a full array of programs.

In chapter 6, we discuss themes that came up repeatedly in the case studies.

6

Motivation and Theology

MOTIVATIONS FOR GIVING

Why give at all? Understanding motivation is central to any analysis of religious giving, yet it is the most difficult topic of all to penetrate. Human motivations are mixed and partly hidden; psychological studies are unanimous on this point. Freudian psychology has shown that motivations are partly unconscious and thus not totally visible to the person, even when the person tries to be "totally honest" with himself or herself. No researcher can come up with a precise inventory of motivations for religious giving. All we can do is make educated guesses from inferential research and observations.

We hold one assumption that needs to be explained clearly. Most religious giving is rational, not irrational, behavior. But there are borderline instances, and some religious giving is impulsive and only partly rational. For example, when a traveling missionary tells a moving story and asks for contributions to his orphanage or clinic, the story will often touch the heart of the hearer and elicit a gift that was not planned. Yet this sort of giving is a small proportion of total religious giving. Most is rational and long considered.

We emphasize this point because it guides theorizing. Religious giving makes entirely good sense to the giver and is felt by the giver to be totally rational. We take it as axiomatic that billions of dollars are given to religious bodies each year for what the givers feel are rational and well-considered motives. An observer who finds religious giving baffling is standing too far outside the theological worldview to comprehend the motivations of the giver.

To understand religious giving, we need to penetrate the specifically religious worlds of the donors. This distinguishes the analysis of religious giving from the analysis of secular fund-raising. The latter assumes a common secular culture, in which most affluent Americans live and move today. But religious people are usually (though not always) different. Religious people may or may not inhabit the broad, mainstream secular worldview of higher education, politics, and business in the nation. Whether they do or not is an empirical question, and both individuals and groups vary in this regard.

Let us look at gift giving in general. If we assume that gift giving is rational behavior, how can we explain it? Put simply, why would anyone give money away? A person who gives money away has less left for his or her own use. How is it different from throwing money into the sea? Why would a rational person do such a thing?

The answer normally given by theorists of economic behavior is that what appears to be, or purports to be, giving money away is actually something else. "Gifts" of money are, to a great extent, made in exchange for something. They are actually transactions, entered into rationally in hopes of an expected return. A gift is usually a "purchase" of something or a "reciprocal exchange" made in the expectation of receiving something back later.[1] For example, a businessman giving a thousand dollars to the city hospital drive and a church member sending a thousand dollars to a missionary are hoping to buy something they want. The task of the theorist is thus to identify conditions under which religious gift giving *is* rational in the actor's eyes, for when properly understood, these conditions will be able to explain actual levels of giving.

The optimal approach here is not one of logical calculation of the game theory type. Rather, to understand religious giving, we need to conceptualize a thoughtful actor who takes a wide set of influences into account, including feelings of family belonging, identity, love, and hope. The religious giver is not oriented to winning a game or making a profit today or this week but usually is thinking long and hard about the future and about what human life really should be. We need to stretch typical rational-actor analysis in the existential direction, including what Max Weber called the "rationality of ultimate ends" and not just instrumental rationality.[2]

Four Kinds of Motivations

We believe there are four basic kinds of motivations for religious giving: (1) reciprocity with God, (2) reciprocity with the religious group, (3) giving to extensions of the self, and (4) altruism and thankfulness. These motivations are phenomena not directly observable and measurable, and furthermore, they are mixtures and alloys of motives, never pure ones.

If, by some means, we were able to score an individual on these four motivations, we would go a long way toward explaining that individual's level of religious giving. The logic is similar to explaining the life expectancy of any American. Everyone has come across scorecards in magazines and newspapers that predict length of life. Typically, these will assign one point (plus or minus), two points, and so forth to the person's present age, habit of smoking or lack thereof, amount of exercise, body weight (too high or too low), and the like, and all the points add up to a prediction of life expectancy. The logic here is the same; we can identify motivations and add them up. It is impossible for anyone to come up with a precise formula predicting the religious giving of any individual, but the general idea guides our discussion here.

We begin with reciprocity. Reciprocity is important because it is a primary motivation for financial gift giving in the United States. Analysts of secular philanthropy and charitable giving see it as the primary motivator of donations. Basically, the donor makes a large gift in anticipation that reciprocity with others will eventually buy something for himself or herself or for some extension of the self. This motivation may be less than noble, but it certainly exists in many places.

There are two important kinds of reciprocity—reciprocity with God and reciprocity with the religious group.

Reciprocity
with God

Reciprocity with God is a simple notion with endless variations. It is rational behavior for a person to give gifts to powerful people—such as kings or lords—in hopes of setting up relations of reciprocity for the future. This practice is plainly visible in America today in the large gifts lavished on politicians. Hundreds of corporations and wealthy individuals bestow "gifts" on U.S. senators in hopes of buying influence later. These gifts (actually payments) are made only when specific conditions are met: if the donor wants something, if the donor believes that giving a gift will help to get what is desired, if the receiver appears willing to enter into reciprocity, and if the receiver clearly knows that the gift was given.

Human nature encourages people to think about God in the same way: God is immensely more powerful than any earthly politician, and God can bestow rewards and blessings of limitless value. The theological question here is whether God enters into reciprocity with individuals and whether God feels an obligation to reciprocate for gifts. A church that believes and teaches this kind of reciprocity with God can expect to elicit higher levels of giving. But is this teaching theologically valid and correct? Is it honest, or is it manipulation?

During our visits, we heard preaching about God's reciprocity in evangelical churches but not in mainline Protestant or Catholic churches. The most frequent scriptural reference in the teachings in the evangelical churches was Malachi 3:8–10:

> Will anyone rob God? Yet you are robbing me! But you say, "How are
> we robbing you?" In your tithes and offerings! . . . Bring the full tithe
> into the storehouse, so that there may be food in my house, and thus put
> me to the test, says the LORD of hosts; see if I will not open the windows
> of heaven for you and pour down for you an overflowing blessing.

This passage specifically mentions tithes and also promises that the Lord
will repay tithers with an overflowing blessing. We could cite many New
Testament passages as well that have this theme. To take just one example, Luke 6:38:

> Give, and it will be given to you. A good measure, pressed down,
> shaken together, running over, will be put into your lap, for the mea-
> sure you give will be the measure you get back.

This is no place for entering into an exegesis of the hundreds of New
Testament references to money and almsgiving.[3] Our point is simply that
because of the variations of emphasis in the biblical passages, we should
expect to hear many versions of teaching about giving in the churches today. In one Assemblies of God sermon, we heard the pastor, quoting
2 Corinthians 9:6, repeat over and over, "As you sow, so shall you reap."
He went on to say that if you sow generously, you will reap generously; but
if you sow selfishly, God will be selfish with you. If you don't give, it will
catch up with you later. If you don't give your first fruits to God, he will
send bad fruits in return, but if you do give, God will send good fruits in
return. That is, not only is giving to God an opportunity for future reward
but failure to give to God is likely to bring something bad. In the pastor's
words, "If you don't give God his due, I can promise you that sooner or
later it will show up in problems in your life. This is one of the spiritual
principles of life."

The sermon continued:

> You cannot be victorious as a Christian, you cannot be overcoming,
> you cannot be the kind of disciple who falls under the lordship of
> Jesus Christ if you are selfish with the funds that God has entrusted to
> you. . . . But if you take from the resources that God has given you, and
> be faithful and obedient to him on a simple level, then you will begin
> to see him at work in your life in many ways that will enrich you, that
> will cause you to mature, to grow; and yes, we as a congregation will
> then be able to do so much more for Christ and his kingdom.

Later in the sermon, the pastor clarified what God will do for the giver:

> Jesus promised us that if we are generous and obedient and following
> through on the things he has given us to do as Christians, then we will
> not be wanting. And there is a great discrepancy between the *needs*

that all of us have, that Christ meets regularly, and the selfish, greedy *wants* that some of us have. We would never give to the kingdom of God hoping that we get back a hundredfold so that we could drive a different kind of car, or have a bigger house, or do this or do that.

An analyst studying sermons like these should not hope to find consistency and clarity. In the sermons we heard, the messages varied. Some sermons took two different sides, in effect saying, "On the one hand . . . but on the other hand . . ." The mix of messages is not accidental. The Bible itself is not consistent on the question of rewards for gifts and therefore opens the door to different interpretations.

Another Assemblies of God pastor pointed out that giving one's time, talent, and treasure to God is not something people do just to be altruistic, it is in the person's own interest. According to this pastor, since God is in command of the world, God will ensure a positive outcome in people's lives when they commit fully to God:

> We Christians can live with confidence that God will take care of us. It is in our interest to love God and keep his commandments; it is in our interest not to love the things of the world, since God is in command. This is not just a fire insurance policy to keep us out of hell. This is a promise to us for eternity. Once we give our lives to God, we can be assured from God's promises that he will guide our lives for eternity.[4]

The pastor then mentioned Malachi 3:10 and commented:

> Will a man ever want to rob God? No, never. Then bring your full tithe here to God. This is what God expects. Who in his right mind would ever dare to test God? God is all powerful! A person who gives his life to God and gives his tithe to God, that person can have total confidence in God's word that you will have "an overflowing blessing." It's right there in the Bible! People who tithe never need to fear about finances.

On this point, a Baptist pastor talked about his own preaching and that of other Baptists: "I used to hear tithing testimonies when I was young, and some people said that when they tithed, they became rich."

"Do any preachers today say that?"

"A lot of people, especially television preachers. Oral Roberts and that type."

"How about Baptist preachers you know?"

"I expect that for a lot of them, if they don't say it, they imply it. I have heard some Baptist preachers say, 'You either give God the tithe, or he's going to take it. You either give it to God to be used in the church, or you're going to spend it on doctors' bills and hospital bills.' No one has said that in *this* church, but I've heard it among Baptists in a lot of places.

"Do you think a Baptist parishioner *should* give with the intention of getting?"

"No. I'm totally against that. Because, one, I don't think God is into the 'I'll scratch your back if you scratch mine' kind of mentality. 'If you do right by me, I'll do right by you.' I don't like the view of God that he's running a kind of barter or trade thing. I don't think God is into cutting deals with people.

"But the Oral Roberts mentality—he says flat out, absolutely, the bigger the check you write, the more the guarantee that you're going to heaven. This gets into salvation by works, not salvation through grace. It's totally wrong! Every time something like that comes into public view, I try to instruct the people otherwise from the pulpit. Remember when Oral Roberts said that if people didn't give, God was going to kill him? On a smaller scale, you have this kind of manipulation of people going on all the time!"

"So you don't leave people the impression that reciprocity with God is possible."

"No." (Laughs.) "You know, as in every church and every pulpit, I may be preaching strongly one theory and one philosophy, but the motivations of the people may be something different."

Later we took part in a discussion in a Sunday school class in the same Baptist church. The teacher put forth a rhetorical question: "What do we get when we give?" One man, who attended the class regularly, said, "We get a check mark." He meant in the Book of Life. "And someday we'll be held accountable for our lives, and we will need as many good marks at that time as we can get." He was not joking. He was totally serious, and the other class members nodded in agreement. This occurred in the same Baptist church where the pastor stressed to us over and over that salvation is by grace and not works. We assume that the pastor, had he been in the class, would have argued against the idea of the check mark. But the class members all agreed. Apparently, the idea of reciprocity with God is deep in these people's minds, in spite of the preaching in their church.

The question of whether we get something back from God when we give is filled with subtleties. What kind of reward? The Oral Roberts theology promises that each dollar given will be returned later, along with many dollars more. Another theme is that if we give, we will be rewarded by spiritual, not monetary, blessings on earth or that we will be rewarded by eternal life. Yet another is that our reward is the joy of giving itself.

As an example of the confused message, John Wesley at times preached that giving money lays up treasures in heaven, even though Methodist theology is very wary about asserting this. In his famous warning about

how the accumulation of riches produces love of the world, he said that
Christians should freely give money to God:

> What way, then, can we take, that our money may not sink us into the
> nethermost hell? . . . If those who gain all they can, save all they can,
> will likewise give all they can, then the more they gain, the more they
> grow in grace, and the more treasure they lay up in heaven.[5]

We asked a Presbyterian pastor if, in his opinion, people tend to give
with hopes of getting something back. He said that he wishes it were not
the case, but he believes it is, especially with young people: "They expect
some kind of return on what they are investing, not necessarily directly to
them personally, but they are expecting that they will see something happening. And if they don't see it, they aren't very motivated."

"But you don't let anything like that come through in your sermons?"

"No. No. That's a very dangerous and misleading thing. We say you
will be blessed, but it won't necessarily show in terms of worldly rewards."

A Catholic pastor discussed with us his attitude about the idea that God
will reward a giver: "God might do that, but that's a small, minute thing.
He doesn't have time to have a book up there, you know, checking each
person. I wouldn't expect God to turn around backward to make up for a
sum of money that I gave him. Giving doesn't require that attitude."

"So you never preach that."

"No. No. When you preach that, then it's too commercial."

A sermon at Medford Baptist Church dealt with reciprocity. It argued
that people should not give money in order to get anything; it's not a give-
and-take deal with God. But God has promised to take care of us. God
knows our needs. When a person gives, he or she receives the grace to see
how the money is being used and what good it does. That is joy in itself.

We discussed the issue later with the pastor.

"So you are saying that we give out of thankfulness."

"Yes."

"Not as a matter of expectation; we shouldn't give in expectation."

"No. And I don't try to play to guilt and I don't try to be manipulative,
or to use gimmicks. I try to present giving as a matter of thankfulness, as
a matter of one's Christian walk and one's commitment to God."

"What do you say about this argument: If you give to God, God will
give back to you later?"

"No. I don't think it's a quid pro quo. I'm not one of those who buys
into the appeal that if you give a dollar to the church, God will return to
you ten dollars."

"But it may be more subtle. If you give to God, God will watch over you *spiritually*—not just give you ten dollars."

"No, I'm not into that. What I do say with integrity is, if you're faithful to God, you will receive a blessing. But the blessing may not be quantifiable. It may not be that if you give one, you get back one, or you get back two. Or if you give, your life is going to become perfect and happy. The blessing comes from the satisfaction of giving, the satisfaction of participating, the satisfaction of helping others."

"Are you alone in this, or is it typical of Southern Baptist pastors?"

"I'm not *alone*, but among Southern Baptists you will find the whole gamut. Some play on guilt. Some use gimmicks."

Later, the same pastor talked about motivations for giving:

> I think some people give because they think there's a formula in God's will. I think some people give because they feel, "I've got more than I really deserve, and I feel uncomfortable with that because, theologically, I really should not have it, and I don't know what to do about that, so to assuage these feelings, I'll give more to the church." And I see people who give because they truly love the Lord and truly believe that God has blessed them in many ways, and this is a positive response. It is a way of saying thank you, of saying it feels good to be a Christian. It feels good to do something that's good and positive.

In chapter 5, we quoted Pastor Meyer of Grace Lutheran Church as saying that God does not reward financial givers. Meyer was totally opposed to preaching that says tithing buys blessings or that not tithing leaves one open to a future famine of blessings. He continued:

> The medieval concept of the storehouse of grace, where saints had surplus grace, was really some of the problem that started the indulgences, irritated Luther, started the Reformation, and split the church. The issue was money—surplus grace and how you buy it. So Lutherans are really uptight on that issue, even 450 years later.

Reciprocity with God is a powerful motivation for some Christian people but not for others. It is powerful only if the person believes that God is open to reciprocal relations and can be trusted to come through later. Some people think of God as too distant or too impersonal to allow the possibility of such a relationship, and other people are uncertain what their beliefs about God are in the first place. The book of Job is the *locus classicus* for the theological issues that arise here. Job's distress came because he believed in reciprocity with God and acted in good faith, but the rewards did not come.

Furthermore, are we sure that God wants financial gifts and not something else, such as personal faith or acts of charity? Maybe gifts of money don't really matter.

In brief, the theological issues here are numerous, and they have a definite impact on people's behavior.

Reciprocity
with the Religious Group

Secular fund-raisers have as a bedrock axiom of their profession the belief that most big donors desire recognition for their gifts. The most precious recognition is from the donor's peers, especially peers who are important (that is, their "reference group"). Anyone raising funds for a worthy cause needs to set up situations that facilitate peer group recognition.[6] For this reason, a financial campaign requires careful planning about asking for gifts.

The all-important concern is *who asks whom* for a gift. The person asking his or her friend for a philanthropic gift is implicitly offering reciprocity with the friend. If the person doing the asking is powerful and influential, the request carries greater weight. Even if an anonymous gift to a hospital, a college, or the YMCA is a result of the asking, at least the person asking for the gift will know about it, and probably his or her associates will too. These people matter. Take an example from the muddier field of politics: If the chairman of the Republican National Committee asks a major corporate lobbyist for a large gift, it is a request that cannot be refused.

Reciprocity with one's religious group occurs in many ways. It is common, for instance, for leaders to develop an informal sense of what a family's "share" should be in supporting the budget. Then each family is faced with a choice of paying the proper amount and receiving social approval or paying much less and risking group opprobrium if the others find out.[7] Reciprocity with the group is also a motive in any pledge campaign, in which everyone knows that the campaign committee (and perhaps others, too) will look at the pledges. The pledger will be mindful of how other congregation members will react to the pledge.

The theological issue is not whether this kind of motivation is present among Christian church members when making gifts. It is present. Rather, the theological issue is whether churches should encourage or discourage it. Is peer recognition for gifts theologically valid? The New Testament has numerous passages on this question, and the main thrust is that peer recognition in giving is not a motivation that is rewarded by God. Rather, God prefers alms given without any eye to social approval. Here are two New Testament passages that illustrate this point:

Whenever you give alms, do not sound a trumpet before you, as the hypocrites do in the synagogues and in the streets, so that they may be praised by others. Truly I tell you, they have received their reward. But when you give alms, do not let your left hand know what your right hand is doing, so that your alms may be done in secret; and your Father who sees in secret will reward you. (Matt. 6:2–4)

When you give a luncheon or a dinner, do not invite your friends or your brothers or your relatives or rich neighbors, in case they may invite you in return, and you would be repaid. But when you give a banquet, invite the poor, the crippled, the lame, and the blind. And you will be blessed, because they cannot repay you, for you will be repaid at the resurrection of the righteous. (Luke 14:12–14)

The topic of recognizing gifts comes up in real life in many ways, and we discussed the issue with clergy. We asked their views: Should large gifts by individuals be made known to the congregation or to the leadership? Should a pastor thank a big donor publicly for the gift? Should a building campaign promise plaques or names on future windows, rooms, or furniture, telling who paid for them? Should a pastor look over the list of pledges to see who are the big givers and who are not? Should lay leaders be given access to the list? Should church leaders make clear who will be looking at the list?

We found diverse viewpoints. On the question of whether or not a pastor should look at the list of pledges, empirical reality seems to be that the majority of pastors do not look at such lists. We did not survey pastors methodically, but this is our impression. Yet we have experienced spirited debates among pastors as to whether or not they should look at the pledges. Important research by John and Sylvia Ronsvalle on this question shows that most laity do not want the pastors to do so.[8]

People with ambivalent feelings about peer reciprocity may make distinctions about when it is or is not defensible. Several denominational leaders with whom we discussed this issue distinguished between a capital campaign for a new church building and annual stewardship appeals. They thought that peer recognition for large gifts for a new church building is theologically legitimate, whereas in annual stewardship campaigns it is not.

We asked an Assemblies of God pastor if he recommended recognizing gifts publicly. He replied:

No. If you go through this building, you won't see any tags or plaques on pews or doors. When you start appealing to that, you're locked into it. And we would say that a certain carnal motivation comes in, where it's not purely spiritual. We want people to feel like they're in a closet;

as Jesus said in the Sermon on the Mount, don't let your left hand
know what your right is doing. We believe that. We teach that.

We asked, "Some churches have occasions when donors who would
like to be known have an opportunity to be recognized: for example, an
auction or an event in which people make pledges for a program. Do you
favor that?"

"Well, we have fund-raisers for youth events, youth workdays, and so
on. But people know that that's not the way the work of the church is done.
It is for specific things."

Another Assemblies of God pastor gave a similar report:

> We have public events, such as an annual auction for world missions,
> and there some people who are really generous and very public. They
> publicly bid up prices. They bid! It is nothing for some of those guys
> to spend six or seven thousand dollars at that auction. Everyone is
> watching! But otherwise, no one knows who is dropping how much
> into the offering plate.

The pastor of Medford Baptist Church told about whether he would
give public recognition to big givers:

> I don't have any strong feelings. I guess what we do is more geared to
> the customs of the community. I guess if somebody proposed it and
> the idea became accepted, I would agree. I don't see that it would vi-
> olate any principle. But I don't think it fits the customs of our com-
> munity. It's just something that is strange and something we have
> never done before, and probably it wouldn't work for us. But it is done
> in some Baptist churches in a more subtle way. I have been in a church
> where everything had a plaque on it.

We asked another Baptist pastor about putting plaques on pews and
windows. He said, "I'm against that. Because I think it allows some well-
to-do people to go on ego trips. It may get the job done, and it may get you
the pews! But in this church we have never saluted anybody for the size
of their gifts."

"So the reason you are against it is that it sets up divisions."

"Yes. I think it divides the fellowship. Again, the gift is to the Lord, the
gift is not to the church. In putting up this building, we told people there
was a need for specific gifts, and some people did that. But we never said
who the donors were. One man gave the grand piano, which cost ten
thousand dollars, but nobody knows who it was. He may have told somebody, but it was not announced."

The Lutheran pastor had a slightly different attitude. We asked him if
he would announce a large gift, for example, if Mrs. Jones gave ten thousand dollars.

"I would first say to Mrs. Jones, 'May I share the good news of this gift?' I would say to her, 'Mrs. Jones, you understand that your generosity primes another person to be generous. Someone else will search their soul. Because if you can do it, someone else will say to themselves that they can too.' "

"One would think that there is some joy in having one's name mentioned in the church."

"There is, and that's fine! And some do it just to get the announcement, and that's not the best motivation. But you start with where the people are. All the motivations may never be clean! But the person has made the gift! That's far ahead of what the other 90 percent are willing to do. So if they want their names read, I'll do it."

"Do you favor putting plaques on the windows and so on, saying who donated them?"

"No. You'll find no plaques here. We *will* do a memorial book, listing the gifts. But to have plaques really does generate the wrong motivations and reward the wrong motivations for stewardship. It does indeed pander to the wrong reason for giving—for recognition, not for generosity. Well, if we have a dedication service, we will say in the program who gave this thing or that thing. But never the amounts."

"So you are not totally against recognition, but you want to keep it subtle, is that it?"

"Exactly. We want to keep it in line. I understand that all giving is done with mixed motivation. But you don't *pander* to the wrong motivation. You pander to the right one."

We asked a Catholic pastor if he would recommend putting plaques on windows or doors in a new building. He said, "I have no objection to that, but at the same time, I would hate to see the place littered up with plaques. In our new education center we have one room named after a parishioner who gave a sizable amount of money. That was the only thing, though."

We probed the issue. "There are some organizations that raise funds by giving recognition to the big givers. Some churches and synagogues do this."

"As a matter of policy, we do not do that. If we had a building program, we might do something like that. Otherwise, no. We don't want to clutter up the building with a lot of plaques. It's an aesthetic issue. I don't have an objection to it otherwise."

"Do you have something like an annual banquet, where you say something like 'We've had a good year, and thanks to Mrs. Jones and Mrs. Smith, who gave us large gifts this year'?"

"No. The names are never given. For a church, there's something unsatisfactory about doing that. A church is different from other organizations."

"Are there any Catholic churches around here who have such a list, with 'Mrs. Jones gave five thousand dollars,' and so on?"

"No, not that I know of. Only in building programs, if there are major gifts. Then people who give a certain amount for the building are recognized."

Giving to
Extensions of the Self

As mentioned earlier, economic theory begins with a basic assumption that the economic actor tries to maximize the rewards gained for himself or herself. In short, most behavior revolves around self-interest. But who is this self? It cannot be merely the individual in isolation. Certainly, the actor thinks about his or her spouse and family members—at least. The needs and desires of these other persons are typically so important that they are felt to be little different from the actor's own needs. And doesn't the same apply to the extended family or ethnic group? How about a long-time circle of friends in the community?

Our point is simply that the self is not clearly bounded. It extends outward and includes other people and even material things. The self has a core and a periphery, with gradually decreasing intensity of feeling at the outer edges. The key to understanding the extent of the self, according to psychologist William James, is whether the actor feels elated or injured when his or her family member or kin or estate is praised or blamed. If so, that person or thing is a part of the self. For example, if one's college alma mater is criticized and the person feels a little pain on hearing it, the college is a part of that person's self.[9]

The family is usually a part of one's self. To illustrate: Suppose I give a thousand dollars to my spouse. Is this a philanthropic gift? It doesn't feel like it. Really it is not a gift at all, since it is to an extension of myself. My spouse is a part of my self, and I do not have the feeling that the money is gone. Suppose I give a thousand dollars to my grown son or daughter. Is this a gift or merely a transfer of funds within the self? It certainly feels different from throwing money into the sea. What if I give a thousand dollars to my nieces or nephews? What if I give a thousand dollars to my college alma mater? What if I give a thousand dollars to my church?

The point here is simple: Gifts to the self—including extensions of the self—are rational acts. To the donor, they are hardly felt as sacrifices at all, because the money is, in effect, paid to oneself. On the contrary, gifts to extensions of the self produce feelings of joy, not pain.

This way of analyzing the self pushes beyond traditional economic thinking. We are talking here about love and devotion. Much gift giving, both religious and secular, is actually giving to the extended self. A gift of a thousand dollars from an alumnus or alumna to the beloved alma mater is a clear example. It is a rational act, and it brings forth positive feelings. Even if there is little expectation of reciprocity, there is joy in an act that benefits a part of the self. People who love their church will feel joy when they give to it.

Altruism
and Thankfulness

The discussion about extensions of the self helps us disentangle the debate today over altruism. Some theorists deny that altruism in human behavior exists at all. The debate over altruism arises because economic models normally have a narrow definition of the self and do not believe in the existence of pure altruism (except in the actions of a few saints, who are too unusual to bother economic theorists).

Some theologians distinguish economic and spiritual models of human behavior. We have heard the argument made that economic analysis should not be applied to church giving, because church giving is done for more altruistic and spiritual reasons than other gift giving. One pastor told us that human life has a spiritual economy in addition to a financial economy, and church giving needs to be analyzed in spiritual terms, not economic terms. In our opinion, there are spiritual factors in all human life, and clearly so in the lives of church members; but that does not mean we need to posit separate spiritual and financial economies. It is more fruitful to expand the economic model to allow spiritual factors.

Researchers who test human behavior in search of instances of altruism always find it. The debate over altruism should not be over whether or not it exists—it does exist. The issue is how, where, when, and under what circumstances altruism exists.

Researchers who study altruism usually insist on distinguishing types. For example, ecological theorist Garrett Hardin distinguishes five types of altruism—familialism, cronyism, tribalism, patriotism, and universalism.[10] All are forms of transcendence of the individual, but they differ greatly. Most altruistic acts involve family and cronies in one way or other. Seldom do they involve broader, undefined domains of humanity. Numerous psychological studies confirm that behavior involving relatives, ethnic group members, or people perceived as similar to the subject is more often altruistic than behavior toward other people.[11] The majority of such behavior occurs within the extensions of the self, in James's sense.

Some analysts of religious giving assert that a sense of thankfulness is sometimes a motive. They argue that some religious people (possibly not a majority) develop a sense of gratitude for the many gifts God has given them, and they make gifts to churches and missions as a response. We would expect this motive to occur mostly when an earnest Christian believer experiences a special blessing. People might feel the need to make gifts to God after recovery from a disease, at completion of a successful journey, or at the baptism of grandchild. At these times, a natural human response would be to feel thankful and to make a gift to God in return. Pastors with whom we talked said that some of their parishioners give out of gratitude, and it is part of a person's spiritual development to learn to recognize the many blessings one has from God and to feel thankful.

How about the rest of everyday life, not just occasions of good fortune? Are humans not receiving gifts continually from God? Stewardship theology commonly stresses that we are, and it encourages giving gifts in thankfulness for God's ordinary gifts. This motive might be observed, for instance, in an appeal for gifts to poor Christians in third-world nations or for hapless victims of an earthquake or typhoon. A motive for responding to such an appeal might be thankfulness that we are not in such dire straits, as well as a tinge of guilt that we have good fortune in life through no merit of our own. In principle, gifts given in thankfulness would not be motivated by reciprocity, because they are not given with the belief that the individual should give gifts back to God to ensure that God's blessings continue to come. Yet human motives, as we said, are not unalloyed.

The motive of giving out of gratitude no doubt exists, but we are uncertain if it is a major motive in giving, operating over long periods of time. Proponents of a stewardship approach told us that this motive can *become* salient in church members' lives. The pastors we listened to in mainline churches often preached about giving due to gratitude. Indeed, the pastors whose theology was imbued with a stewardship ideal strove to sharpen people's vision of the gifts God has given them, because this vision is important in spiritual growth and strengthens a person's desire to return time, talent, and treasure in gratitude.

It is difficult to know how strong a motive thankfulness is. No doubt, some giving is done without the self-interest of reciprocity foremost in the giver's mind. The strength of the thankfulness motive is partly dependent on a theological vision of the gifts one is receiving from God, so we would expect it to be more prominent among theologically committed people than among the secularized or the weak in faith.[12] For our purposes here, we include it in the broad category of altruism and generosity.

To summarize: We believe that these four motivations explain most congregational giving. We are sure, at the very least, that a person who experiences all four motivations will give more than someone who experiences none of them.

Appeals to Four Motivations

To exemplify the four motivations, we can give examples of appeals based on each. An appeal for giving based on reciprocity with God could be "Give your tithe to God, and God will take care of your needs now and in eternity" or "Give to God, and God will repay you."

Public appeals based on reciprocity with the religious group might say, "Make a gift, and we will put your name in the list of donors for the project"; "Everyone has to do his or her part to keep our church going"; "Contribute to the church so that you can feel you are doing your part."

A personal appeal to a donor often implies an offer of personal reciprocity by the asker: for example, "Could you make a pledge toward our campaign? The committee and I would appreciate your help on this one."

Appeals based on giving to extensions of the self might say, "Give so that this church can continue to serve your family and your community"; "Remember what this church has meant to you and what it will mean for your loved ones"; "Help us make this church something your family will be proud of."

Examples of appeals based on altruism and thankfulness are "God has blessed you, and you can thank him by helping some of God's less fortunate children"; "Do something good with your money. You can't take it with you"; "You have been fortunate in life, and you can return a portion to God in thanks."

STEWARDSHIP
VERSUS FUND-RAISING

We need to be clear about two technical terms we introduced earlier. *Fund-raising* refers to a process of asking donors for contributions to an organization. It also refers to a profession in American life, often called "development," that elicits gifts for large organizations, such as colleges, hospitals, and art museums. Fund-raising professionals typically manage programs in which potential donors are asked for gifts—if possible in person, at the least by phone or letter. The person asking for the gift communicates the good deeds and effectiveness of the organization, its budget and sources of income, and its future plans. He or she also communicates a personal commitment to the project and asks the prospect for a gift.

Whereas *fund-raising* is a secular term, *stewardship* is biblical. It is most clearly depicted in the parables of Jesus, when he talked about a king or a wealthy landlord who went on trips and left his realm in the hands of a manager, or "steward." The steward was responsible for everything until the king returned and asked for an accounting. Jesus told many parables about unjust and just stewards, about stewards investing their masters' money, and so on. The message is always that God owns the earth and all its riches but leaves it in our hands temporarily.[13] Some stewardship sermons put most stress on the point that God, not we as individuals, owns the earth, and we are only temporary users of God's treasures. Others stress the future return of the Owner, when God will ask each of us for an accounting of our stewardship.

The term *stewardship* today is often used loosely to mean nothing more than "giving" or "teaching about giving." But it always carries a spiritual or theological meaning that distinguishes it from institutional fund-raising. Stewardship involves more than money and more than expecting to be blessed in return. It includes use of time, talent, and treasure, and it includes management of not only personal wealth and church wealth but also the entire human family and the environment. We are asked by Christ to oversee all of humanity and all of planet earth until he returns. Remember, we brought nothing into the world and will take nothing out except our souls.

Giving out of stewardship motivation is different from giving out of self-interest based on reciprocity with God. It is not as intuitive or as persuasive. As Pastor Meyer told us, Lutherans are taught that believers give not for what they receive but because it's their nature to give, and he added, "That's a harder piece to sell. Not as natural." Stewardship motivation requires education year-round, not just during a pledge campaign. The theological topics need to be broached and examined in a situation that is not tied to financial requests, and they need to be taught by the pastor and by Sunday school teachers, not just by a stewardship committee.

Stewardship is different from fund-raising. It puts its focus on the individual's need to give, not on the church's need to receive. It stresses giving as an aspect of spiritual life and of people's relationship to God, not as merely a matter of meeting an institutional budget. In its purest form, stewardship teaching says nothing about institutional needs and about how the money will be spent; these are side issues, to be handled by trusted leaders. Yet a problem arises at this point, since many donors will want to know more specific information about the church—what its needs are, what the budget is for the next year, what its budget trends are, who will decide how to spend the money, and even "what is my fair share" in supporting the church. Any church that declines to answer these questions runs a risk of evoking cynicism or distrust among the laity. The laity feel they have a right to know and may ask, "What do they have to hide?" or "What is this *really* all about?"

The stewardship motive for giving depends on strong faith, and in most churches laity will be found who do not feel motivated by a sense of their role as stewards, except in very general terms of human responsibility to take care of this planet during their lifetimes. A stronger appreciation of stewardship depends on seeing it in terms of one's relationship with God and on feeling gratitude for one's blessings. Some practical, hard-nosed types in any church will see stewardship theology as only high-sounding pious phrases and a distraction from "good, straight talk" about the church's budget and plans. They will say, in effect, "Cut the blah-blah about stewardship and just tell me about next year's budget and my fair share." So in most churches, some members respond to stewardship teachings and others do not. Church leadership must work with laity of both kinds, and individual churches may need to employ a mix of approaches, depending on the religious commitments of the members.

A discussion of stewardship versus fund-raising must distinguish between annual efforts to get pledges and appeals for capital campaigns. Capital campaigns are common in all denominations, and as we saw in chapter 2, over one-fourth of all churches are involved in them at any one time. We found repeatedly that opinions about stewardship vary depending on whether one is making an appeal for the ongoing program or an appeal for a capital campaign. Typically, capital campaigns are run more on a fund-raising model than on a stewardship model. It is likely that strong-faith church members respond better to stewardship appeals for the church program, while others of weaker faith respond better to group-reciprocity appeals often used in capital campaigns. We believe this is the case.

We found that church leaders may abandon stewardship theology in a time of perceived crisis. We encountered both congregations and denominations in which the leaders became nervous about short-term financial declines and turned to fund-raising appeals as an emergency answer. This flies in the face of stewardship training, which, by nature, is long-range and constant, and which never focuses on institutional needs. In reality, many local churches use both approaches, as do many denominations. Some denominations end up with separate departments, using different appeals for specific things.

Teaching Stewardship

Many pastors told us stewardship is a year-after-year educational effort that should not be expected to have short-term effects. No stewardship program should be expected to show results in one year. Stewardship education needs to help people grow in the faith and in recognition of God's gifts; it is not just a means to get money out of their pockets. No pastor, they told us, should see stewardship education as only a way to raise money. Its purpose is also to help Christians grow in faith and spiritual maturity. Giving is part of the mature Christian life.

The pastor of Medford Baptist talked about stewardship sermons:

> I preach stewardship sermons four or six times a year. I try not to preach, "We're out of money. Give more." I try to be much more intentional and very biblical. I try to use humor in the sermons to disarm people—since stewardship is an area in which people can get really mousy. But I find that with the right kind of humor, it works. I deal with it biblically, and I am not judgmental. I am positive, encouraging, and motivational, but I make a strong rationale that this is a *positive expression* to God that we are thankful.

We asked, "Some pastors stress selling the program or the church and the budget, and others say no, you should stress stewardship as one portion of Christian spiritual life. What do you do?" He answered:

> It's the second. That's the way I have done it, presenting stewardship as a part of our Christian life, part of our response to God's grace. God's grace affects us in a lot of ways, but one way is that we try to reflect back through our life and our priorities and show appreciation for what God has done.

This pastor actually mixes several approaches. We asked him what he would say if a parishioner asked him how much he or she should give. He replied:

> Well, I think we could provide several things. We can say, if we have *x* average attendance, and if you divide that into the budget and if everybody gave the same, it would be *x* dollars per attender. We have figured that out, and it is about thirty dollars per Sunday per attender. With that we could operate this church at the present level.
>
> There are actually two levels in thinking about stewardship. On one there is a sense that when a person gives oneself in commitment to the Lord, you are giving your total self, and it involves your material self as well as your thinking and feeling self. And second, there is a level in which we need to do stewardship because there are real-world costs involved in providing a building, having a full-time minister available, and so on.

We asked, "Why is there so much talk of grace in relation to stewardship?"

"Remember: Why do we give—to maintain the organization, or do we give out of a deeper or higher sense? We give out of a sense of *gratitude* that we are children of God and we are redeemed, not through anything we have done to deserve it or earn it but simply out of God's love. How do you respond to love? You respond to love in generous ways."

"Okay. I believe a saint would say that, but an average parishioner might say, 'I certainly appreciate God's grace, but does it have to cost me two thousand dollars?'"

"Well, some people will. There are some people who see everything in terms of dollars and cents and costs and benefits. But others are just naturally generous, and if they're grateful for something, they will express that gratitude in some visible, tangible, material ways. If they feel blessed they have a desire to share that blessing, to plow it back in."

We asked if stewardship education should be expected to have a short-run or a long-run effect.

"I think there are some temporary gains that come through a fund-raising program. But that kind of approach burns itself out very soon. What you need to have is a program that is more educational, in which what you are trying to do is to change their values and their perceptions about money and the church and spiritual things. And that's always a much longer-term process."

"It sounds as if you distinguish fund-raising, which is a one-shot affair, from stewardship education, which is long-range."

"Yes. You can't do fund-raising all the time. It's okay if you are putting up a new building. . . . And also, you can't raise money by always saying that the church is in some kind of crisis, like we are going broke. That burns itself out. But to *really* build a solid financial base in a church, you've got to educate people about the relationship between their money and their faith, and that's a long-term thing. You could use a fund-raising approach to extract money from their pockets, but you are not helping them grow in the faith."

In chapter 5, we examined the views of Pastor Richards of Westminster Presbyterian as he discussed the difficulty in keeping the stewardship ideal distinguished from fund-raising in people's minds. The distinction is a tough thing to teach. Richards repeatedly stresses "acknowledging the Lordship of Christ" and "expressing our discipleship" and avoids talk of raising funds to support the budget. At Westminster, no budget is prepared until the results of the stewardship campaign are in.

The stewardship churches, in urging their members to give sacrificially, lean heavily on the New Testament themes of awareness of what God through Jesus Christ has done for them, as members and as a church. These churches teach stewardship as a spiritual ideal in looking at all of life, and it requires time for the believers to achieve this mind-set. A Baptist pastor told us:

> Our people think about giving alongside every other spiritual act, trying to be as responsible as they can. We constantly make it a spiritual

discipline. The people have to grapple with it, wrestle with it, every time they give. "Can I give more? Is there something more I could do to help? What is God telling me?"

The ministries carried out by each church are also important in stewardship education. The churches teaching stewardship often had strong programs of ministering to others, and the pastors could point to these ministries as concrete indicators of "what God is doing among us," justifying a call for the congregation to respond out of gratitude for these visible gifts.

What virtually every pastor told us is that both tithing and stewardship commitment are built up slowly; they are not instantly born out of dynamic preaching or impressive ministries. Stewardship emphases can be effectively taught in all churches—evangelical, mainline Protestant, and Catholic.

TITHING AND PLEDGING:
FOR AND AGAINST

Because all research shows that tithing churches have higher giving, it would seem advantageous for all churches to become tithing churches. Why don't they? Is there a theological reason or a cultural reason? Maybe tithing depends on strong faith, and some churches are filled with people whose faith is too weak. Maybe the laypeople who don't tithe would not do it even if the pastor preached it, so if the pastor asked for a tithe, he or she would only create alienation and division. Maybe the pastor himself or herself is conflicted about tithing.

The same questions arose concerning pledging. Because pledging helps the level of giving, why don't all nontithing churches move to annual pledging? In our interviews we never heard a theological argument against pledging, but we heard from laypeople about how they dislike it. The opposition to pledging, as far as we can discern, is not a matter of principle but a matter of convenience and freedom (and, for some, it is a matter of avoiding detection). Hearing these comments caused us to reflect on underlying factors that affect giving. We need to entertain the theoretical possibility that one's level of giving depends on the depth of one's faith more than anything else, and that tithing and pledging are no more than logistical matters.

Tithing

We discussed the pros and cons of tithing with many pastors. An Assemblies of God pastor discussed what he would tell a good Christian person about financial obligation. He reminded us that tithing is commanded in the Old Testament but not the New Testament:

> Well, the principle of the New Testament is *generosity*. The Old Testament gives us the tithe. But in Matthew 23:23, Jesus said that you ought to do these heavier matters of the law but not neglect tithing. So we say to people, use tithing as a benchmark for your giving. Then you know that you're doing what was required under the law. If you want to do more, it is up to you. The tithe is what the early Christians had to give, and you ought at least to be doing that to be a generous person.

A lay leader in an Assemblies of God church said that whereas some churches preach that you need to tithe to be saved, he is opposed to such a teaching, and his church does not say it. For him, tithing is a pledge or an indicator of one's faith, not something that causes or enables salvation. Tithing has a psychological element in that it is proof to oneself and to others that the tither is committed to God. It doesn't produce salvation, but it gives assurance and relief.

Our conversations about tithing in Assemblies of God churches concluded with the point that a tither trusts God. In their view, the tither can be sure that God will bless and care for him or her in ways beyond human comprehension. Tithing is a sign that the person's priorities are straight, and therefore the tither will be taken care of.

By contrast, mainline Protestant pastors tended to be equivocal about tithing. Lutheran pastor Meyer said:

> We ask for a tithe, but we say to people that "we know some of you are in tough circumstances and cannot do it." You [the researcher] have visited and know our style here. We are confrontational in terms of the Word of God. We tell people what we feel the Word of God says, and it's up to them to apply that. And we have people who want to hear that; it's not a style that they're just tolerating. It's what they want.

We asked a Baptist leader if pastors should recommend tithing to their people. He responded:

> Not tithing. I recommend a *proportionate giving* of money, because there are some people who financially cannot tithe, and it may turn them off completely if you stress ten percent as the minimum. Four percent may be a good minimum for someone really in difficulty. Therefore you should teach money management, in order to move that four percenter up to a four and a half percenter.

In chapter 5 we saw that one reason the pastor of Grace Lutheran does not preach tithing is that he believes it is not realistic and not pastoral. The demand of tithing is too extreme for most church members. We put a question to him: "The way this discussion is going, if you say to a person, 'Is the Lord really the Lord of life?' when you talk about that person's low giving, it suggests that maybe it *isn't* true that the Lord is really Lord for that person."

"I think that's true. How many women today considering an abortion have a biblical discussion about it? Not many. They will think about lots of other issues, but not biblical. They won't ask, 'What does God really want in this situation?' The people in the more conservative churches— the higher givers—tend to do that. But not many mainline Protestants."

We asked, "Maybe mainline Protestants are more hesitant about their faith commitment. Do you think so?"

"Yes. And they're also less biblically informed. The fact of the matter is, even mainliners want to say that the Bible is the Word of God. But they don't know what's behind the covers, and therefore they walk relatively free of it. Now, when you get into the more conservative groups, they're reading the Bible chapter and verse."

We asked the pastor of Medford Baptist if he talked about tithing. He answered, "I do not put a strong emphasis on it. What I have tried to focus on is helping people start where they are and grow. I guess I am theologically not inclined. I guess I see the Christian faith as a growing relationship, and so I don't preach a legalistic kind of dogma. I try to help people grow in their faith and in their relationship with God. So what I try to do is preach that people should start somewhere and then grow."

"Do you ever say, 'God expects a tithe'?"

"I don't think I have ever preached that. I think I have preached that tithing is a *benchmark*. But I have also preached that for some people, less than 10 percent would be a tithe in their situation. Some people have little to live on. And for other people, 10 percent would not *approach* a tithe, since they have far more income than they have need."

"So it sounds as if you define a tithe by the amount of discretionary income the person has."

"Well, I think a tithe is defined more by the level of sacrifice that it reflects than by adherence to a fixed formula."

The mainline pastors seem to be influenced by the giving traditions in their denominations and their perceptions of how a call for tithing would be received. For some laity it seems too much to ask, and it might elicit bad feelings. And anyway, nowhere does the gospel say that a tithe is necessary for a Christian. Tithing is a costly practice, one that people never enter into quickly or lightly.

It seems that for many evangelicals and Pentecostals, tithing is not too much to ask, whereas for most mainliners, it is too much to ask directly, and the pastors adjust. The depth and type of faith seem to vary between evangelicals and mainliners. We have evidence of this in our five-denominational survey, as well as in measures of church attendance, of emphasis on evangelism, and of chuch members' faith that only followers of Jesus Christ can be saved. To a great extent, the issue of tithing is a matter of strength and type of personal faith.

Pledging

In chapter 4 we showed that church members who pledge give more to their churches than members who don't pledge. The act of pledging seems to encourage reflection about church giving, with the result that church members who make pledges tend to give more. If the number of persons who pledge were increased, more financial resources would be available to the churches. All of the pastors in nontithing churches favored pledging. Yet the practice is controversial, and some churches do not use pledging at all. Why not?

Remember that in the churches that strongly preach tithing, pledging is seen as not needed; the committed church members will tithe without any reminding and without any pledges. But let us look at the nontithing churches. Why isn't pledging more widespread?

One Baptist pastor discussed the opposition to pledging:

> People are hesitant to sign up. Somehow or other it's ok when buying a house or buying a car, but to put your name down in black and white for God, people hesitate. As if God takes it more seriously when you sign than if you merely raise your hand. . . . I think some of the opposition is from people who had bad experiences in some other churches, where there was a constant hammering away from the pulpit about people not giving enough or not meeting the budget. People also don't like the feeling that if they get a statement from the church saying they have pledged a thousand dollars but have given only $250, this is a dun or a demand. It's almost like a bill.

Another Baptist pastor spoke of his experiences:

> We have not done pledging, but this year we are moving toward it. I have always been a proponent of pledging, but there was always resistance. I did not push it. I waited four or five years, until we completed this successful pledge campaign for the new building program. I saw that experience as a launchpad for pledging. That campaign was so successful that it dispelled some of the fears and myths and broke the ice as far as annual pledging. People here often see pledging as manipulative. And sometimes it *is* used in that way.

We asked him why there has been opposition to pledging.

> The arguments I have encountered against it are, first, you should not ask people to make a promise; it is between the person and the Lord, and if you make a promise, somehow that invalidates it. I guess then you are giving more for legalistic reasons than for internally motivated reasons. I suppose it makes it more of a transaction and maybe less spontaneous.
>
> And the second argument is that some people feel like they don't want to make a promise because they don't know what their income will be. We then point out that people make a promise when they sign a mortgage or when they buy a car with monthly payments or use a credit card!

We asked, "How about other Baptist pastors? Are there any against pledging?"

"I've never encountered any."

"Why are they in favor?"

"I think the reason is that it creates a sense of commitment. It basically structures the sense of commitment that you are asking the people to make. And on the practical level, it gives you a better handle on what you can expect for the coming year. Today you need to have some basic idea of what you can plan for, since the planning cycles are a little longer."

Next, we asked a Baptist judicatory leader why some Baptists are against pledging. He responded:

> Many of our lay leadership like the idea of anonymity. They do not like the idea that people can know what they give. It is a tendency to go back to years ago, when it was only my business what I gave to my church and my Lord. Signing cards is giving up a little bit of freedom, so that other people may know what I am doing.
>
> Maybe it's because some people don't give very much and are ashamed of how little it is. Maybe people are not giving as much as their neighbors, and they would be embarrassed. Maybe they feel that somebody will tell the community what they are doing. In small rural churches, it is a difficult thing to get commitment cards signed. But we keep saying that the greater the commitment people make, such as with cards, the more the church will grow in total receipts.

In our discussion with a Lutheran pastor, we asked why there isn't more universal pledging in Lutheran churches. The pastor answered:

> For many people, church giving is discretionary giving and people don't want to be bound by it. It's a big decision to pledge, especially if the church asks for a big gift. People don't disagree with pledging as a matter of principle. If people were against pledging, Detroit would never sell cars by monthly payments. People are willing to

pledge when it comes time to buy a car. They just never thought of the church as a place to do pledging.

The Catholic pastors were very hesitant about pledging because of resistance from laity. The pastor of St. Benedict does not ask for pledges at all. At Mount Calvary, the experience with pledging has been discouraging. The parish has done well in getting pledges for building campaigns and for the annual diocesan appeal, but laity are very reluctant to pledge to support annual parish expenses. The pastor speculated as to why:

> What I ascribe this to is that people did not like to put something in writing, or perhaps when people make a pledge, they really feel committed to it. Maybe some people felt that the economy might be a little iffy; if things continued, fine, they would be able to do this. But if they didn't, they wouldn't feel obligated to carry this out.

We asked him if the parish could eventually take on the mainline Protestant model of getting pledges for operating expenses. He hesitated, then said, "I don't know how well that would work. I'd be scared to death to try it. Catholics have this tradition of Sunday offertory giving."

Catholic parish staff members were also skeptical about pledging for annual expenses, for a variety of reasons:

> "It's fear of the unknown."

> "Until we get in danger with our offertory contributions, we're happy to accept these results and keep going, rather than get into something that's new, frightening, and might upset some people."

> "If pledging had come in at the very beginning, when the parish was established, it might have caught on, but after the fact it's too late."

> "We're very happy with the results we get."

> "People would be taken aback if asked to pledge for support of the general budget, because it is a very 'non-Catholic' way of approaching it. No doubt about it."

The following reactions about pledging are from Catholic laity:

> "We have not found it necessary."

> "We do not need to get involved in pledging. Our offertory has increased without pledging."

"To me, it's a negative step."

"I am not sure it would work or not in this parish, but it is not something I would want to do."

"I don't think a pledge would bring any more money in. I would not pledge the amount of money that I give because after I pledge it, I would be giving it because I pledged it, not because I wanted to give."

One Catholic pastor likes the idea of pledging, but he does not push it, due to parish opposition. Each year the parish sends out pledge cards, without any hard sell. Last year it sent out 1,100 and got 250 signed cards back. The pastor added that many people also don't like to use envelopes:

The vast majority of those who don't use envelopes don't want to because somewhere in the past they've had a bad incident with a parish priest over their collection, over being hounded for money, being constantly bombarded with demands for money, because their name was on the envelope list. They are usually older people.

Why are so many people against pledging? The pastor said, "I don't know. I think they want to be free. They don't want that obligation."

We asked the pastor, "What do you think about pledging?" He replied:

Personally, I would like to have pledges. The assurance of getting that financial stability would be a big relief—to know that a thousand people have pledged so-and-so much and that I could count on that for the year. For planning purposes, it would be a wonderful thing. On the other hand, people don't want to do it—and they *are* still contributing to the parish. I don't really want to upset a thing that's working. Even though it's not my ideal, it's working!

You know, we don't have to do it [pledging]. And I don't push it because I don't *have* to push it. Plenty of money comes in voluntarily. I don't like to push pledging, and so I don't do it. Everything is coming along fine here now!

Pledging is not nearly as costly as tithing. It is a relatively small step to take, and yet the members of many mainline Protestant churches and many Catholic parishes are opposed to it. Apparently, many people prefer anonymity in giving.

It is worth mentioning here that unlike tithing, pledging has no biblical reference and little theological content; this may account for some of the lay resistance to it.

We had many discussions with laypersons about whether they felt they were giving to God or to the church. Were they thinking of God or of the church when deciding on their level of giving? These discussions were often indecisive, because people either did not make a distinction or linked the two closely. But one interesting point emerged. Insofar as people think of God rather than the church when making their gifts, the size of the gift is not subject to short-range variation that depends on how much the donor likes the pastor and the church's present policies. Donors who think mainly of God will give constantly whether or not they like the pastor or what the church is doing.

It is possible that constancy of giving varies in identifiable ways. One Lutheran denominational leader told us that, in his experience, Missouri Synod Lutherans, who are more conservative theologically, are more constant givers than the more moderate ELCA Lutherans. A Baptist pastor told us that the most substantial givers in the churches he has served gave constantly, regardless of the pastor or the current state of disarray in the church.

Another clue about whether a donor thinks of God or the church is whether the donor's level of giving changes after he or she moves from one town to another and joins a new church. If the donor feels he or she is giving primarily to the church, the level of giving will depend on the love for the church; when the donor moves to a different town, the level of giving in the new church, like the donor's love for it, will begin low and then rise only gradually.

A Catholic director of religious education had a theory that there are different levels of givers. We state it here without knowing how true it is.

> The top level, the ownership group, contribute no matter what. They don't need to know where the money is going. Part of their spirituality is that it doesn't matter where the money is going. They would contribute anyway, because they feel it's part of their stewardship and being part of the parish. But the next level needs concrete results in order to dig a little further down.

USE OF
STEWARDSHIP PROGRAMS

Our research was not designed to assess the effectiveness or appropriateness of stewardship programs, yet this topic came up again and again. Many parishes have tried specific stewardship programs, either those designed by denominational offices or those offered by outside consultants. The programs typically incorporate a series of letters to church members, talks in church services, special sermons for several weeks, and then, in some cases, a massive effort to visit or phone all the members to ask for pledges.

These programs are in tension with the widely held view that stewardship education must be done constantly, not just once a year. Also they border on using pressure salesmanship, which may irritate church members. Yet all evaluation studies known to us have found increases in pledges after such a stewardship program. They seem to have an effect, especially in the first year.[14] The programs typically increase giving by 5 to 20 percent over one or two years. A recent telephone survey of Catholic diocesan staff concluded that about 50 percent of parishes are using some sort of stewardship program. These parishes usually experience an increase in giving for about two years, then a leveling off. If the program is discontinued, giving often subsides.[15]

Denominational officers promote stewardship efforts of various kinds. But not all pastors like these efforts. A Baptist state officer told us of resistance to stewardship programs by some pastors: "They don't see the need of it. They would rather just stand up and say, 'Here's the budget, let's go from here.' They just ask the people to give."

"Is there some resistance to a stewardship program?"

"Yes. I don't know what the problem is. Some pastors have been relying on the old people, and the old people have gotten to be really old and on fixed income, so they don't give as they used to."

"Does it matter if the minister or a lay leader is up front when it comes to stewardship?"

"I think a layperson has a lot to offer. If a layman says, 'I have grown a lot in my understanding of stewardship,' it has an effect. If a pastor says that, a lot of parishioners will say to themselves, 'He is getting paid for that,' and will turn him off."

"Would you say a layperson is more valuable?"

"Yes, if he talks about himself, his family, his growth, and his commitments. But not everyone agrees with me."

"What do people who disagree with you say?"

"Well, some think that the preacher is the power figure and has to do all the work and all the stewardship, the person around whom everyone else gathers. But I think the laypeople should take the churches back. Pastors sometimes get too much authority."

The pastor of Oakland Presbyterian agreed on the importance of having a lay leader up front:

> I think that when you have a parishioner give a kind of personal testimony as to why the church has been important in their lives, it is much more effective than for the minister to get up there and convince people that they should be giving money.

A Baptist state leader criticized once-a-year stewardship efforts:

With them you raise money but don't raise people. I don't think you are teaching people anything but only getting money from them. It may work. But the church has to be different. That doesn't mean I can't *use* it, but theologically, it is not the best way to get money from people over a long period of time.

The highest goal I have as an educator of churches is to help people grow so they are giving not to things but because of the grace of God in their lives. The reality, however, is that the greatest percentage of people give for three reasons. First, because they are afraid. Second, because they are part of a fellowship and want to stay part of that, like a country club, where they have bought into the process of the church and thus have to continue to be a part of it. And third, they give to things that excite them and interest them. My task, I think, is to help people grow toward the more ideal.

We asked, "You said they have fear. Fear of God or of other people?"

"Fear of having God take it away from them. Many see God as a big guy who gets back at people who aren't good."

Many Catholic churches have tried stewardship programs. St. Peter's Catholic Church used Father Joseph Champlin's Sacrificial Giving program for a time three years ago but does not use it now. The Sacrificial Giving program includes having outsiders come to the parish to talk about how giving has changed their lives. It stresses giving as part of spiritual life, rather than giving as a way of supporting the parish.

Some members of the parish council objected to having laypersons from outside the parish come to talk about stewardship. One critic said that Sacrificial Giving did not emphasize financial accountability enough and that the laypeople wanted more facts about use of the funds. Another told us that Sacrificial Giving came too close to saying that God will reward a gift; he said that this "evangelical pitch" was not well received by the educated and reflective type of person in that parish. After a while, the parish stopped using outside speakers and modified the program to make it more palatable.

In spite of the objections to the Sacrificial Giving program, Sunday giving at St. Peter's increased by 10 percent in the first year it was used, and the pastor thinks the program was a major reason. In subsequent years there was no similar increase. We asked the pastor how he would evaluate the program, and he told us, "It was successful in bringing the collection up in the first year, but it hasn't gone up any more in three years. It stayed at that level."

"Have you continued the program since then?"

"Well, some parts of it. We had the three-year renewal this past fall. The people responded less this time."

"Is that in the nature of the program or an accidental thing?"

"I don't know. First of all, when we first did it, no one had made a push for money for a long, long time. So there was a little slack there, and people said, 'Yes, it's time.' And then everybody noticed that we got an awful lot of things done at the church. We painted the interior of the church, put in new carpeting a year ago, added new restrooms—we spent several hundred thousand dollars on repairs."

"Was that part of the appeal for money?"

"No, but everybody knew that those things had to be done."

"I thought the Sacrificial Giving program does not include appeals for that type of thing."

"No, it does not. But . . . everybody knew the problems were there. We made the effort to get over the whole idea of sacrifice, but it just got mixed up in people's minds. And as we reported the things we did with the money, the idea came out that it's for these specific projects. And I don't know how to get past that. I think we're all mixed up in it ourselves, because the finance committee and I kind of respond to specific needs. And just now we have to get the parking lot paved. That's on our minds, how to raise the hundred thousand dollars to do that."

Not all Catholic parishes are like St. Peter's. Some parishes have strong stewardship emphases. The National Catholic Stewardship Council identifies such churches and encourages the spread of stewardship ideals, particularly at its annual meetings. One Catholic parish nationally known for its stewardship program is St. Francis of Assisi in Wichita, Kansas. One of the authors visited it.

The parishioners of St. Francis give at an impressive level. Sixty-four percent of St. Francis's two thousand households give between 8 and 10 percent of their gross income, yielding a total parish income from regular offerings of over $3.2 million annually. This parish is vivid proof that there is nothing intrinsic to a Catholic parish that inhibits it from adopting a successful stewardship program that will enable it to raise giving at least to the level of mainline Protestant denominations. Indeed, giving at St. Francis is much higher than in most mainline Protestant churches.

St. Francis's pastor, who was installed in 1967, admits that it takes a long time to develop the trust essential to get families to contribute at this high level. The top priority of the pastor is to involve parishioners of all ages in one or more ministries, through their giving of time and talent. Families choosing to give at least 8 percent are assured of tuition-free Catholic schooling for their children from kindergarten through high school. Parishioners are kept well informed of the parish's outreach ministries, which include a free medical clinic for persons without health insurance, through the monthly parish newsletter. A visitor to this church cannot help but sense the vitality and enthusiasm of its membership and staff. With the help of this parish and its pastor, the entire Wichita diocese is implementing a stewardship plan.

THE UNIQUENESS
OF CATHOLIC PARISHES

As previously noted, Catholic parishes are, on the average, eight times as large as Protestant churches; they therefore have a different culture. Over one-third have parish schools. They have a different tradition of clerical control than Protestant churches do. It would seem reasonable to assume that the tasks of leadership are different for Catholic than for Protestants pastors and that attempts to increase giving would require different strategies. Our experience tells us this is so.

One Catholic pastor talked to us about his efforts to give the congregation a sense of ownership of the parish. For example, he made surveys of church members to learn their priorities and discern their interests. "People want to be co-journeyers with you in meeting their own needs. They don't want you to act like the old patron who spoon-feeds them. They want a sense of ownership."

Another pastor told of his philosophy of leadership:

> I wanted the *people* to operate the parish. I felt that the parish belongs to the people and that a pastor is simply a person who tries to oversee the thinking and working of the people. I tried to turn as many things over to the people as possible, and I wanted the people to feel that the church belongs to them; to feel that the people *are* the church.

We asked him what impedes Catholic giving.

> I think among Catholics you're going to have difficulty increasing the giving if you convey the thought that the church belongs to the priest. The moment you say that the church belongs to the people, they will listen to you.

The pastor of Mount Calvary told us that the members felt as if they owned the parish from the day of its founding: "They came here wanting to build something, wanting to put something together, and they have felt tremendously committed to that ever since." In this parish, the priests have tried hard to call forth the gifts of the laity in parish life. The pastor explained:

> Parishes where people do feel ownership are much more vital, more alive parishes. There are all kinds of involvement here. My task is simply to sustain that. You sustain that by allowing people to have voice

in what is important to them and inviting their input, their skills, and their talents.

Financial Reporting

The importance of financial reporting and accountability came up repeatedly in our discussions with Catholics. It was unanimous among clergy and laity we interviewed (as it was in the mainline Protestant denominations) that parish finances need to be carefully audited and open to all. The secrecy of yesteryear cannot continue.

Several Catholic pastors told of new actions they had taken. For example, the pastor of St. Benedict made a rule that employees of the parish should never count the collection. Instead, a randomly chosen group of parishioners were given the task. And he circulated different people through the finance committee and the counters committee, so that more people would know about the parish finances and what's going on. He talked to the people frequently about the financial situation of the parish and the diocese. At St. Peter's, the finance committee took new steps to clarify the distinction between giving to the parish and paying school tuition. The pastor of St. Ann parish introduced bottom-up budget discussions each year, beginning with the needs and plans of specific committees and making final decisions in the finance committee. All of these policies were introduced to increase feelings of ownership and accountability.

Well-managed Catholic parishes seem to be characterized by financial openness, participation in a liturgy that is vital and engaging, sermons that portray a clear stewardship ideal, accessibility of both pastor and staff, and vibrant ministries that parishioners are encouraged to participate in. From our case study experience, we conclude that the combination of pastorly activism, fiscal responsibility, and appealing ministries will go a long way toward ensuring generous financial support.

7

Conclusions

We began this project hoping to understand the differences in levels of giving among five denominations and among congregations within each. The questions we asked have long been debated: Why is Catholic giving lower? Why is evangelical giving higher? Does pledging matter? Do stewardship programs help? What should congregations do to encourage higher giving?

WHAT WE FOUND: A SUMMARY

It was important that our research be cross-denominational, to help each denomination see itself in a wider context. After the data were in, we made several presentations to church leaders in which the usefulness of the cross-denominational approach was confirmed. But this approach also introduced some misreadings and some bafflement. Some of our audiences confused intradenominational and interdenominational differences.

Denominations differ because their theological worldviews differ. Our experiences have taught us that the members of different denominations actually live in different worlds and are shaped by distinct assumptions and distinct experiences. This is shown by the different ways denominational members talk about their own faith and church life, and it is shown by the ignorance they have about other denominations. A researcher in such a situation needs to pass back and forth from one theological world to another, trying to understand the worldviews of devoted members in each while also trying to maintain some objectivity in the hope of being able to comprehend all. We have been impressed repeatedly by how encapsulated church members are in their own religious worlds. For people in every denomination, their own congregation and, especially, their friends in the congregation fashion their understanding of religious reality. Anyone disbelieving this statement can put it to a test: Ask people in any denomination about the theology and practices of other denominations. You will see how little they know.

In general, the evangelicals live more encapsulated lives than the mainliners and Catholics do. Our experience is that evangelicals, more often than others, emphasize that they are different from run-of-the-mill Americans. Their preachers are more likely to say something like this: "We are different from the rest of Americans. We have something that they don't have, and we should be thankful."

Comparing dissimilar denominations—for instance, Assemblies of God and Catholics—is akin to comparing Japanese and American companies. Management writers have produced shelves of books on this topic, and they all say that Japanese and American business leaders live in substantially different cultural worlds. Business leaders of one world who wish to learn from the other find that only a few elements are exportable.

In contrast, the differences among churches within any one denomination are more like differences between Chrysler and General Motors. Both companies exist in the same culture, and only the organizations differ. Elements of each firm are readily exportable to the other.

Hypotheses about congregations within a single denomination must be distinguished from hypotheses that focus on different denominations. In this study we have found important factors that go far toward explaining different levels of giving among denominations, but many of those factors are unimportant within each denomination. For example, a foremost factor in giving is evangelical or conservative theology; it is decisive in predicting levels of giving from one denomination to another, but it is much less important in comparing congregations within a particular denomination. This is because congregations in a denomination differ so little from one another.

In our opinion, the findings in this study of greatest practical usefulness are those that pertain *within* denominations, since church leaders in each denomination operate within a given theological context. Our findings comparing different denominations are less useful at the practical level, since they are less exportable from one denomination to another. Pastors will say, "But we're not Pentecostals. We're not Mormons. We're *who we are*, and we have come to this point after years of prayer and experience." They are right.

Theories That Turned Out to Be Unimportant

During three years of research, our findings and experiences forced us to shift our views about the main factors that influence church giving. Some of our ideas proved to be unimportant. Four hypotheses we began with were not supported in either the congregation survey or the case studies, so they should be abandoned.

The first false hypothesis is that congregation size is crucial in its effect on levels of giving. We initially thought that because Catholic parishes are much larger than Protestant congregations and also have a lower level of giving, parish size was possibly an important factor in giving. This view was supported by observations which contended that large congregations could not achieve the same feelings of ownership and community as small congregations.

The obvious test of the importance of parish size is to look at its importance within each denomination. If the theory is true in general, it should be true within each denomination. As we reported in chapter 4, however, we could not find any general patterns in the data. When we controlled other variables, we did find a modest association among Catholics: Smaller parishes have slightly higher per-member giving. We found slight associations in the same direction for Baptists and Lutherans, but a slight association in the opposite direction for Presbyterians (see Table 4–3). All of the findings were weak and disparate. Differences between Protestant and Catholic giving are, for the most part, not traceable to the larger sizes of Catholic parishes.

Given the influence of feelings of community and ownership in fostering contributions, could these feelings be nourished in large congregations as well as small? We think so. We have seen cases of large churches in which this was done. People who stress the importance of community and ownership are right, but these qualities are not necessarily limited to smaller churches.

The second false hypothesis has to do with democratic procedures. At the outset, we believed that democratic procedures encouraged giving, reasoning this from the fact that Catholic parishes both are less democratic and have a lower level of giving. Some Catholic writers have argued that adopting more democratic processes in parish governance will encourage higher giving. But our study found this to be, at most, a secondary factor.

What *is* crucial is trust in leadership—in whoever actually has the power in the congregation, whether clergy or lay leaders. If that trust is missing, giving will be low. In clergy-led congregations, this means trust in the clergy; in democratic congregations, it means trust in the leadership group and in the decision-making process.

Recall that Assemblies of God congregations are not very democratic. Even though some have pro forma elections of lay officers, the clergy greatly influence the selection of candidates for office. The ministers run the churches, and everyone accepts the situation as proper. Yet in the Assemblies of God churches, the level of giving is high.

We asked people about this again and again, and they were unanimous: The specific constitution of the church and the specific process of budgeting do not matter. What matters is trust in leadership. For example, we asked an Assemblies of God pastor: "Some people say that the more democracy there is, the higher the giving. But apparently you don't say that."

"No, I don't say that. But I think *trust* matters. The more trust, the better."

"And how do you keep trust?"

"Transparency and honesty. And people know that."

"How about constitutional provisions?"

"I'll tell you, I once worked in a mammoth church in Chicago. I was an associate there. It was a wealthy church, with megamillionaires. The pastor was a very strong leader. You might even have people out there who really disagreed with him! There wasn't much democracy. But they sensed something that's there in that church that they were getting. That was crucial. Absolutely."

"So that transcends the issue of democracy."

"Yes, it really does!"

A Baptist pastor discussed how trust relates to stewardship programs. He said that pastors must carefully avoid gimmicks, anything that has only one-time efficacy, and anything that smacks of dishonesty or manipulation. Because a pastor has to face members year in and year out, the pastor needs to build the total confidence of the members. In this pastor's opinion, it takes about three years to build up the kind of trust needed to really lead the people in a congregation. He added:

> Some people demand democracy more than others. There is an interesting phenomenon in the South: often the First Baptist Church is full of white-collar people, and it is totally democratic. The other Baptist church in town—if it is also Southern Baptist—is more blue-collar and is much less democratic because the pastor is autocratic. But the blue-collar people are used to taking orders and are quite compliant, and they don't mind this at all. Even if the people are first-generation managerial, they still have the older mind-set of being passive and having an authoritarian pastor. But the First Church will tend to call a pastor who shares responsibility and is more collegial.
>
> Also, in the whole Southern Baptist Convention, the more fundamentalistic churches are less concerned about democracy than the others. They tend to have strong pastors.

The implication of these responses is that if the people are content and if they trust their leaders, the actual amount of democracy does not matter.

The third false hypothesis is that Catholic giving is lower than Protestant giving because Catholics are angry. This has been asserted by

Catholic sociologist Andrew Greeley, who wrote about Catholic anger over birth control, and newspapers today are full of accounts of Catholics in various places who are angry with the Vatican. Initially, we thought that the theory might be true, but now we conclude that it is largely false.

In our survey, Catholics are no angrier in general than the members of the other denominations. It is true that, as we saw in chapter 2, Catholics, more than others, feel that laypeople have inadequate voice in decisions about parish money, and it is true that Catholics report less often than others that important decisions in their parish are made with open discussion by church leaders and members. On these topics, Catholics are angrier than members of the other denominations. But on other measures Catholics are not unique. Some Catholics are angry about church teachings on birth control and women's ordination, but these attitudes are not associated with level of giving.

We therefore conclude that the alleged Catholic anger is, at best, a secondary factor in explaining the low level of Catholic giving.[1] Also, we conclude that anger about local matters, wherever it exists, has a greater effect than anger about national or international Catholic matters.

The fourth false hypothesis, held by many Protestant denominational leaders, is that the level of giving in a denomination is dependent on policies and actions by the denomination. Church officials tend to think, for example, that Presbyterian unhappiness over the 1993 Re-Imagining Conference (criticized as radical and heretical by many in the church) has taken a toll in Presbyterian giving, or that Baptist unhappiness with the power struggles at the national level has taken a toll in Baptist giving. But we could find no evidence that attitudes about denominational leadership affect giving to the local church. All our findings indicate that giving is felt to be a matter between the church member and God or between the member and his or her congregation. The national denomination is unimportant.

Our study is not the first major stewardship research project to test the importance of denominational policies on local church giving. An important survey of fifteen Protestant denominations was done in 1971 by a team headed by researcher Douglas Johnson.[2] It tested the hypothesis that the extensive social action of denominations at the end of the 1960s was causing Protestant church members to cut down on their contributions. The study found no evidence for the hypothesis. The 1971 study also found, in agreement with ours, that laypersons wanted more say in how church funds are spent.

We need to remind the reader that our study did not include any investigation of congregational decisions about where to *spend* money,

especially about which mission and outreach projects to support. Allocation decisions by church boards are not at all the same as decisions by individual members about how much to pledge or to give. No doubt, happiness or unhappiness with denominational leadership affects allocation
decisions in many churches. But these feelings have no noticeable effect
on the amount given by individuals.

We collected a few more hypotheses during our case studies, and one
merits mention here. It was stated by an Assemblies of God minister,
quoted in chapter 5: "Money follows ministry." We heard it numerous
times. A variant form states that "people vote with their feet and their
pocketbooks." We heard this most often from evangelical and Pentecostal
pastors, who went on to say that people will give only when they and their
families are being well served, when their hearts have been touched, and
when they devote their lives to Christ. If a church experiences a downturn
in attendance or giving, this is a symptom that the ministry somehow does
not speak to the people. Two corollaries of this theory are that the quality
of ministry is the main determinant of financial giving and that stewardship programs are useless. This theory is subtly appealing for high-giving
churches, since it attributes growth to quality of leadership.

We believe the theory is true only *within* denominations. It is not cred-
ible that denominational differences in giving between, for example, Assemblies of God and Lutherans are explained by quality of ministry. To
believe this, we would be required to posit that the Lutheran and Catholic
clergy are of lower quality than Assemblies of God ministers. But this is
not the case. Rather, church members live in their own theological and institutional worlds. Within each denomination, the expectations of leadership and ministry are different.

In our surveys, members of different denominations rated the quality
of their leadership about the same. Catholics and Lutherans were as satis-
fied with their ministers as the Assemblies of God members and Baptists
were with theirs.

Within denominations, however, the theory is much more convincing.
In our case studies, we encountered churches in which members had un-
varnished enthusiasm for the programs and ministries, and we have no
doubt that those members gave more.

Denominations Are Different:
Must We Stop There?

We began this chapter by emphasizing how different the denominations are from one another. Having laid out these differences, must
we conclude that there is little else to say? Have the five denominations

settled into certain giving levels that reflect their respective theologies and traditions and that are therefore fairly permanent?

Not at all. First, we found much variation *within* denominations in leadership, style, and emphasis. Second, there are a few lessons from the research that apply to everybody.

We can demonstrate this by returning to the "overall big five" factors named toward the end of chapter 4:

> High family income
> High level of involvement in the church
> Evangelical theology
> Planning one's giving by the year
> Small congregation size

The first two factors, high family income and high involvement in the church, have similar and obvious impact in all denominations. The third is different; basic theological orientation is a stable bedrock foundation to any denomination's life and not open to change. The fourth factor, habits of planning one's giving, clearly applies to all denominations and deserves attention by all. The fifth factor, small congregation size (the least important of the five), is not easily influenced.

Much needs to be done to enhance giving today. Our case studies tell us that education and stewardship programs can be helpful in all denominations. And there are other practical lessons for everyone. A Lutheran pastor put the task in these terms:

> There are a number of factors in giving. I think people of any church can be taught the joy of giving. And I believe that that in itself is not impossible to do, regardless of denomination. I think that denominations tend to stumble into the postures they find themselves in and can just as easily walk out of them. They can convince people that there is a *reason* to give, that it is substantially important to them to be able to give. I think people need to give. It becomes a part of good mental health to give something of themselves so that their life is invested more broadly than just in themselves. It is substantially a matter of good health, emotional and spiritual.

THE GOAL
AND THE TASK AHEAD

What is to be done? Throughout the study we have assumed that church giving is a good thing and should be increased. Church giving must not be thought of in isolation but as one component of the total

Christian life. It must be seen in proper relationship to the basics of godly living—as Micah put it, "to do justice, and to love kindness, and to walk humbly with your God" (6:8). Financial giving needs to reinforce the total growth of the individual and community and not detract from it. There can be no working at cross-purposes, no hidden agendas, no manipulation, no dishonesty. The task of stewardship is not merely to transfer money from people's pockets into the church treasury but to build up the whole church community.

Stewardship must be done with full participation of leaders and members, with openness and accountability, and with total responsibility. There is no room for mishandling of funds, secret accounts, or hidden reappropriation of money from one place to another. As we have said repeatedly, church members need to be able to trust the leadership totally. The day for clandestine skimming of funds by clergy or for secrecy in financial matters is over. If we had our preference, we would declare the day of secrecy about clerical salaries and staff salaries to be over; doing so would bolster trust everywhere.

Stewardship must take the long view. Stewardship of time, talent, and money is a lifelong matter, to be cultivated in Christian education and prayerfully considered year by year. There is no room for one-shot stewardship efforts that harp on crises, either real or fabricated, or that make statements that cannot be supported over the long haul. For this reason, we do not favor stewardship programs that have only an immediate focus, and we distrust appeals by TV preachers who, unlike a local pastor, do not need to maintain the trust of their flocks year after year.

Stewardship teaching and stewardship programs everywhere need to be administered with the skill, enthusiasm, and sustained effort we have observed in our case studies. Individual stewardship efforts taken alone, such as canvassing every member by phone, using pledge cards, and using numbered envelopes, are less decisive. Successful stewardship programs involve an entire theology and vision of personal and collective responsibility that goes far beyond particular strategies.

Theology is more important than institutional policies in affecting church giving; this we stated in chapter 4, and we believe it is correct. We came to know many church members who are obviously firm believers in the Bible and who desire to commit their whole lives to Christ. In the five denominations we studied, we found that such people tend to have literal interpretations of scripture and a consciousness that their Christian way of life sets them apart from the mainstream culture. For the most part, these people are evangelicals. But more generally, churches with a clear identity about their teachings and about where they stand relative to the common way of life in their communities tend to generate higher levels of giving.

We have emphasized the theological issue of reciprocity with God, since it is both crucial and sensitive. Pastors and theologians of all types have strong feelings about it. From our research we conclude that church people who believe that God will reciprocate for monetary gifts tend to give more to their churches. Hence it is a keen temptation for church leaders in need of financial support to preach about how God rewards givers, even though it flies in the face of long-held theological prohibitions in many denominations. We researchers have little to contribute to this theological debate, except to remind readers of how consequential belief in reciprocity is financially.

Limiting Alternative Activities

New questions now arise: If evangelical Christians are the high givers within most of the denominations, how can their numbers be increased? Or how might the kind of commitment they possess be extended more widely throughout churches?

One useful lesson on this topic has come from sociological theorists using "rational choice theory." This theory, most often invoked in discussions of church growth and decline, suggests that high-growth churches increase members' commitment and participation by forbidding or criticizing alternative activities that might compete with that commitment. Then "potential members are forced to choose whether to participate fully or not at all."[3] In these churches, the members are told what is required of them to be in good standing.

Applied to church giving, the theory points out that members in some churches are pressured to tithe or to pledge generously, particularly in the presence of fellow parishioners whose commitment is openly expressed, as happens in Assemblies of God churches. "Free riders" and others inclined to only lukewarm participation and giving are screened out. This mechanism occurs in some evangelical churches and partly accounts for the high giving.

The mainline churches, by contrast, tend to demand relatively little of their members, so the costs of belonging are less than in the stricter churches. Far fewer mainliners than evangelicals describe themselves to researchers as "strong" members of their churches. Members of mainline churches are also likely to have more ties and group memberships outside their churches and to feel more competing loyalties. Some of the people we met in Presbyterian, Lutheran, and Catholic churches were tolerant, culturally sensitive persons with experiences in more than one cultural group or nation. Their faith is sometimes tentative and tolerant, because they appreciate other religions besides their own. We met some members who seem to have no faith at all. They are secular people who participate in churches for the benefits to them and their families, and they happily contribute to churches to support the good things churches do. They think of the church as one more good institution in town that deserves everyone's support, like the Boy Scouts, Red Cross, and Goodwill Industries.

Let us be clear that the "faith" we are talking about here is the faith empirically held by the church member, not the theology articulated by the minister or priest. Normally, one should expect a gap between the two. Pastors are generally well aware of this situation and frame their teachings about church giving accordingly. For people of faith, the pastors emphasize stewardship and tithing, and for people of little faith, they engage in secular fund-raising.

Rational choice theorists emphasize that mainline Protestant and Catholic pastors are much less likely than evangelically oriented pastors to make demands that pressure members to make serious either–or choices about their resources and lifestyles. The message of mainline pastors seems to be "This is strictly the choice of you and your family." The result typically is a lower level of church giving. For people in this mindset, the church needs to sponsor and promote outreach programs of compelling humanitarian value.

Communicating a Stewardship Vision

Stewardship needs to be emphasized in all churches. The findings from our surveys and case studies show that high levels of giving *can* be developed when pastors possess a stewardship vision (a vision that will vary in formulation) and successfully communicate it to the staff and parishioners.

In a stewardship vision three of the overall big five factors in giving play a fundamental role:

1. *High levels of involvement* are offered in meaningful ministries and urged in pulpit and newsletter. Involvement in some ministry is an expectation communicated to new members.
2. *Evangelical theology* helps generate motivation to support outreach ministries that aid the needy and support people seeking a more meaningful life "in Jesus Christ." These ministries will "bring them in" to church life. An example is the divorce recovery workshops at Westminster Presbyterian.

3. *Planning one's giving by the year* is communicated to parishioners as an element of high involvement and as a sign of ordering one's long-term priorities to support the congregation's work.

There is nothing in such a stewardship vision, theological or otherwise, that restricts it to evangelically oriented denominations. This is vividly demonstrated by our case study congregations, for example, Westminster Presbyterian and St. Francis of Assisi Catholic. Presbyterian, Catholic, and other mainline churches have enhanced donations by emphasizing "stricter" elements of theology and practice already present in their traditions and by weaving them together into a program that makes demands on church members. Our case studies prove that congregation members can rise to such demands regardless of denomination. It takes time and concentration. The pastors we talked to said that raising such a vision is a challenging task, requiring years to see full fruition.

Catholic parishes differ from Protestant churches in their large size and their heritage of clerical leadership. American Catholics are heirs to a tradition that has had strong clerical ownership of the church, coupled with a tacit message that the laity are not really responsible for the church's finances. The church was defined as someone else's thing, and many parishioners assumed that both the church's leadership and its financial burdens were turned over to the clergy. This was accepted as proper. But in the 1970s, 1980s, and 1990s, the mentality of American Catholics gradually changed toward wanting more lay participation in church life. For Catholics, like other Americans, this feels natural. In this new situation, it should be understood that responsibility for financial support will also shift more and more directly to the laity.[4] If the Catholic parish is the people of God guided by the laity, the laity need to accept greater responsibility for financial support.

Specific Lessons

Our findings lead to several conclusions for all churches that are worth repeating:

1. Having lay leaders manage the finances and lead the stewardship programs will help reduce any suspicions that the clergy are promoting giving solely out of self-interest.
2. Having broad lay participation in the congregation's

budgeting and priority setting will contribute to the sense of ownership.

3. Locally developed mission projects, more than denominational or national mission projects, will tend to excite interest and financial support.

4. Congregations must avoid any perception that small cliques of laity run the place and exclude others from having any part in leadership.

5. Full financial accountability and reporting will allay suspicions that the clergy or a few lay leaders are doing anything in secret.

6. Stewardship teaching about the joy of giving should be coupled with concrete mission efforts by each congregation that add to the laity's sense of ownership and bring about joy in doing them.

Comparisons with Church Consultant Lyle Schaller

Our conclusions agree with the views of Lyle Schaller, the most respected Protestant church consultant today. Schaller has published more than two dozen books on church leadership, including at least two on stewardship.[5] He makes several points that should be mentioned here.

Schaller makes a basic distinction between two types of Protestant churches, "high-expectation churches" and "voluntary associations." They are polar types at two ends of a spectrum, with variations between, and the spectrum describes Protestantism today. High-expectation churches, located at one end, require strict adherence to certain doctrinal statements, agreement on criteria to be used in interpreting the Holy Scriptures, regular attendance at corporate worship, a commitment to tithing, and an additional commitment that the whole tithe will come to the specific congregation. Voluntary association churches, at the other end, have members who retain great autonomy in belief, participation, the right to withdrawal, and financial support. The members resist demands for adherence to rules. Schaller's distinction is similar to ours in chapter 5 between tithing churches and others.

The closer a church is to a voluntary association, the greater the percentage of the members' giving that will go to causes other than to the church itself. Also, the higher the income of a family in a voluntary association church, the greater the percentage of the family's income that will go to causes outside the church.[6]

The voluntary association type of church has the most difficulty raising contributions. The most common problems are inadequate communication of the financial needs of the congregation to the members and a low level of trust by many members in the policy-making processes of the congregation. Often, portions of the membership of these churches feel they are not being heard.[7]

Schaller says again and again that opportunities for giving need to be numerous and diverse. The era of the unified budget of a church (that is, with only one fund and only one treasury) is over. Church members are diverse and are motivated to give to different funds—to the building maintenance fund, to the fund for a new organ, to the fund for building a new church in Brazil, to the earthquake relief fund, and so on. Churches should not fear that numerous special appeals throughout the year will limit the amount of money members will give to the operating budget; special appeals seldom have this effect. Schaller says: Give the members numerous options and let them choose! Giving is not a fixed-sum structure, so that if a large amount of money goes to one cause, less will be available for another. Every church should have special offerings up to six times a year. Special appeals need to be for specific things that are visual, attractive, and comprehensible. If a mission study group comes home from an exciting trip to some third-world nation, a special offering for their favorite project should be taken at once.

Schaller agrees with us that stewardship training needs to be done constantly through the year and should be kept positive, expansive, and concrete. Stewardship has no place for guilt, chiding, or negativism. The best stewardship program involves home visitation, if possible. When establishing such a program, the leadership should build on the church's natural groupings, such as Sunday school classes and congregational organizations. Sunday school classes and organizations should have their own giving programs and their own treasuries. Loyalty to such groups is precious and should never be seen as competing with loyalty to the congregation as a whole.

Schaller makes several recommendations about handling endowments. Above all, keep endowments separate from the annual operating budget and keep management of endowments separate from the finance committee. Endowments should be for special projects and causes, not for supporting the annual budget. A good idea is to form a separate foundation in a church for managing an endowment.

Not all consultants agree on these topics, and this is no place to attempt a comprehensive review. In our experience with different consultants, probably their greatest disagreement is on the value of one-year stewardship programs versus multiyear efforts. We have listened to many sales pitches for one-year stewardship programs, while hearing the advice from others that churches must take the long view and abandon any one-year stewardship programs geared toward quick results.[8] For our part, we are wary of the one-year programs.

Another area of disagreement among consultants is on the importance of the stewardship effort as such, as opposed to the importance of the total faith and community life of the congregation. Some writers put more emphasis on theology than Schaller does, and indeed, our research supports that emphasis.

Church consultants give greatest emphasis to concrete things that leadership can affect. This is useful. Consultants pay attention to church programs and creating bonds between people. That is, people give to people and groups they love, and this giving is joyful. Anything to increase the love for a congregation, a group in the congregation, or a project of the congregation will call forth gifts to it.

PROSPECTS FOR THE FUTURE

In every case study church, we talked with pastors and parishioners about the future: How will the churches survive and carry out their mission in years ahead? Can the old practices continue? Are young people different from their elders? Our interviewees were unanimous that things are changing. Most often our discussions turned to baby boomers (those between the ages of about thirty-five and fifty), and we found widespread agreement on several points.

Baby boomers have less denominational identity and loyalty than their elders. For most baby boomers, it does not matter which denomination, if any, a church is. Boomers will switch denominations without hesitation—and increasingly, they will even cross the Protestant–Catholic boundary.

Baby boomers respond to high-quality programs. They tend to gravitate toward churches with good Sunday schools, good youth programs, good family programs, the best sharing groups, and the like. They want worship and music that touches the soul. Sometimes baby boomers are described as "consumer-oriented" rather than "loyalty-oriented," meaning that they approach churches almost as they approach retail stores—seeking to buy something without expecting to get involved otherwise.

Several pastors told us that, in the future, large churches will have an advantage, since large churches are more able to put on high-quality programs and sponsor spiritually enriching worship. One large-church pastor said:

> All of the statistics show that the large churches are growing and the small churches are dying; because it's a consumer society today. If you come to our church, I can give you a choir for your little kids before

they start school—and stand them up five or six times a year in church to sing. I can give you teenage choirs, a seventeen choir, I can give you a college choir. If you are an adult, you have a choice of two choirs, plus an oratorio choir—just to mention music alone. I can give you a youth ministry program that's staffed with a pastor and an additional layperson. What do you want? We've got it. And if we haven't got it, we can hire people. And when you come here, you expect a certain level of excellence. Things that would be quite permissible in a church of a hundred just wouldn't be tolerable here, in quality.

Baby boomers are more inclined to give to particular projects than older people. They give more readily to specific, appealing, tangible projects, and they are slow to give to large, bureaucratic institutions. One denominational leader told us, "They are wedded to *causes,* and if you have a good cause in a local church, they will respond. But it may be something else next week!"

Baby boomers share in the nationwide tendency toward distrust of large, national bureaucracies. They are more local in loyalties than their elders were. Sociological studies have documented a downward slide in Americans' trust in many large institutions.[9] People who distrust the large institutions will prefer to send money to specific projects and to people whom they know personally. The pastor of Westminster Presbyterian put it this way:

> People will give only to that which they see is doing something, whether directly meeting their needs or something they are interested in. Fewer people today give because it's the right thing to do. They don't just give without asking questions or without seeing results.

A Baptist judicatory officer told us:

> Young people prefer hot items that touch the heartstrings, like an earthquake, floods, families that are poor, or the homeless. Very few of those things are primary ingredients of local church budgets. A lot of money is going out of the local church to these outside causes.
>
> An example is what I heard of two weeks ago. A young man, about thirty-five, gave $26,000 to his church for the employment of a youth director for a church that never had one. This is *his* perceived need, since he has two teenage daughters. So he gave the gift to make sure that what he wants happens. Now *that's* designated giving!

One Baptist pastor described the fundamentalist takeover of the Southern Baptist Convention. Though he himself was not in the fundamentalist faction, he was not alarmed:

> My view is that the fundamentalists took over a dinosaur! I think they have taken over a Convention that was operating in a highly centralized way. It has a highly centralized fund-raising process that, given

the changing trends of society, is in trouble. Centralized processes are going out the window. The fundamentalists are creating *more* centralization when all the other trends in society are moving the other way. They have taken over a dinosaur that was going to fall apart anyway, and they hastened the process.

UNFINISHED RESEARCH TASKS

Research studies such as ours provide new data and new insights, but they do not solve many of the practical questions besetting pastors and congregational leaders. In speaking about our study, we uncovered plenty of questions that went beyond the research. Here are four of them.

First, should pastors look at the pledge cards as they come in? Viewpoints and rationales on this question vary, and feelings can run high. We have heard it argued that pastors should *not* know the size of pledges, since it is too tempting for pastors to treat the big givers with special deference. The New Testament says that God is no respecter of persons, and the church should not be either. In contrast, we heard arguments that clergy, in order to do their pastoral work effectively, need to know the truth about their flock. One pastor contended that when he visits a patient in the hospital, he needs to know the truth from the doctors as to whether or not the person is dying; he needs to know this to carry out his pastoral task. Similarly, he argued, he needs to know the pledges of the members if he is to be an effective spiritual leader for them.

Our tendency on this issue is to prefer that local churches set the guidelines but also to lean toward minimizing any distinction between clergy and lay leaders. Perhaps it is best if the clergy have the same access to the pledge information as the lay financial leadership has. Probably most important, the congregation as a body should agree on the rules about who has access to the pledge cards, and everyone should follow those rules. (We mention again the research by John and Sylvia Ronsvalle, noted earlier, indicating that most church members do *not* want pastors to look at the pledges.)

The second question is about church endowments. Should congregations actively seek to build up endowments for themselves? We have heard arguments on both sides. One common argument in opposition to endowments is that they inhibit annual giving by members. Yet in our study we had a chance to test this hypothesis, and we found no support for it. In most churches and in most circumstances, having an endowment does not diminish a church's level of giving.

Our guess is that whether or not an endowment inhibits giving depends on the extent to which the church's annual income comes from the endowment rather than from pledges. Also, it seems to depend on whether the church's endowment is earmarked for special uses or used to bolster the annual operating budget.

While lecturing, we discovered that many pastors did not believe our finding that annual giving is unaffected by a church endowment. They recounted story after story of churches in which this was not the case. We could only reply that in our sample, after controlling other variables, we could find no negative effect of endowments on annual stewardship.

Another problem is that disparities in wealth from one church to another can be exacerbated by the presence of endowments. We have heard animosity toward endowed churches voiced by pastors of neighboring nonendowed churches, which shows us that the issue of endowments has wider consequences than merely in the endowed church itself. The debate over endowments goes beyond our present research, but it warrants mentioning here because endowments are growing on all sides, and the future will see more of them than the past did.

The third question is how to keep negativity and scolding out of stewardship teaching. Lyle Schaller advises everyone to keep guilt out of all stewardship sermons and appeals. How can this be accomplished?

We found near-universal agreement among Protestants that stewardship sermons are uncomfortable for preachers to preach and for laity to hear. Everyone would love to avoid them, if possible. Church magazines often have cartoons portraying, for instance, parishioners running for the doors when a preacher announces that the sermon is on stewardship. What are the reasons for this distress? They seem to have to do with conflicting feelings, fear of embarrassment, fear of giving offense, and avoidance of being scolded. Pastors need help at this point.

Many pastors also need help understanding the aversion they themselves feel to stewardship programs. Some told us they hate to ask for money. For them it is the most dreaded part of their work. Why? What can be done to ease this aversion? These are questions that need to be addressed.

A fourth question that needs research concerns the shifting attitudes of local church boards. In most mainline denominations, such as the Lutherans and the Presbyterians, there is a decided trend for local lay boards to spend a higher percentage of church income on local church programs today than was the case a decade or two ago. In some denominations there is a second trend toward sending mission money to diverse programs and projects, rather than funneling it all through the denomination. The local boards want to choose mission projects themselves. Why is this occurring?

This is sometimes called the "allocation issue": How and why do local church boards allocate funds the way they do? The present study did not try to research these allocation decisions, but future studies should do so. This topic is complicated by important denominational differences in allocation systems. For example, a typical Catholic parish makes very few decisions about allocating mission money, unlike a typical mainline Protestant congregation. The Catholic parish normally pays a required assessment to the diocesan office, spends small amounts on local mission projects, and uses the rest of the funds for parish needs. Individual Catholics who favor one or another mission project must direct their money by giving to special offerings or giving directly through the mail to the preferred project. A Protestant congregation is different in that a larger portion of the annual contributions (on average, over 10 percent) is allocated by the lay ruling board.

In short, there is work enough for all. Pastors must do their part, denominational leaders must do their part, and researchers must do their part. The team of researchers who wrote these chapters is mindful of what we can offer and what we cannot. We hope the work we have done contributes to a greater future for the church and its mission.

Appendix A.
Details of Sampling and Data Analysis

PRETESTS

During the spring and summer of 1992, we pretested the congregational data collection in eighteen churches, most of them in the Washington, D.C., area. We tested phone interviews and mail questionnaires for gathering data from laity and decided on the latter. By autumn, we felt confident that the methods would work.

SAMPLES OF CHURCHES

We decided on 125 congregations in each of the five denominations, located in sampling clusters in each of the nine U.S. census regions. Since the participating denominations are not evenly spread across the nation, we calculated how many congregations in each denomination we had to sample in each region.

We randomly selected sampling areas in each region, using Catholic dioceses as sampling clusters. They were as follows: Norwich, Connecticut (New England); Pittsburgh, Pennsylvania (Mid-Atlantic); Kalamazoo, Michigan (East North Central); Winona, Minnesota (West North Central); Richmond, Virginia (South Atlantic); Jackson, Mississippi (East South Central); Oklahoma City, Oklahoma (West South Central); Colorado Springs, Colorado (Rocky Mountain); and San Diego, California (Pacific). We maintained confidentiality of all names of congregations, towns, and individuals.

In some regions our sample called for studying only one or two congregations in any denomination. To reduce expenses, we decided on a minimum of four congregations per denomination in any region. Samples smaller than four were assigned to neighboring regions. The resulting sample is shown in Table A–1.

SAMPLING CONGREGATIONS

Between January and July 1993, we visited the judicatory officers in the nine sampling areas. Charles Zech was in charge of Norwich and

TABLE A–1.
SAMPLES OF 125 CONGREGATIONS PER DENOMINATION

	Assemblies of God	Southern Baptist	Catholic	Lutheran	Presbyterian	Total
Norwich	0	0	11	0	0	11
Pittsburgh	14	0	25	25	25	89
Kalamazoo	14	8	25	29	20	96
Winona	13	7	18	34	15	87
Richmond	17	40	10	13	29	109
Jackson	10	33	5	0	9	57
Oklahoma	27	28	12	8	11	86
Colorado Springs	9	4	8	5	5	31
San Diego	21	5	11	11	11	59

Pittsburgh, Michael Donahue of Kalamazoo and Winona, Dean Hoge of Richmond and Jackson, and Patrick McNamara of Colorado Springs and San Diego. Patrick and Dean shared Oklahoma City.

To select the congregations, we gathered information on congregation sizes in each of the five denominations, then decided to oversample large congregations and undersample small ones. The oversampling was done because the distribution of congregation size in all the Protestant denominations is greatly skewed, with a few large ones and many small ones. We took one-half of the sample congregations randomly from the top one-third of the distribution. The other half was taken randomly from the lower two-thirds. Before data analysis, we removed the bias by weighting the data.

It was important that *we* draw the samples and not leave the job to denominational staff. Our criteria for selecting congregations were as follows: (1) all congregations had to be at least five years old; (2) all congregations needed to be typical and not specialized; for example, none should be a campus church or a retirement home church; (3) all congregations had to have at least fifty resident members (for Assemblies of God congregations, a total of fifty members and frequent attenders); (4) congregations needed to represent cities, suburbs, and small towns in correct proportions to represent the region; (5) congregations temporarily without pastors during the year under study should not be included, if possible. We drew random samples of congregations within fifty or seventy-five miles of the judicatory headquarters, with the correct distribution of sizes. In the actual circumstances we made a few errors, due to misinformation: we got nine congregations less than five years old and eight smaller than fifty members. We left them in the data set.

The minimum size requirement was awkward for the Assemblies of God, since the lists of churches from the national denominational office included many smaller than fifty (total of members and frequent attenders). At least one-fourth of the Assemblies of God churches had to be eliminated because they were too small.

We selected and trained field workers with the help of local denominational staff. They visited the congregations and sent in reports. All mailing was done directly from our four research offices. Data collection took place mostly between March and October 1993.

The percentage of congregations we were able to include is shown in Table A–2; overall, it was 84.8 percent. Let us clarify that the first column in the table represents the percentage of the target group we were able to include but not the overall rate of agreement. If a congregation refused, we replaced it with a maximally similar church, but the replacement congregations in turn refused at a disproportionately high rate. This was chiefly a problem among small churches.

During the data collection process, we learned why the level of participation was not higher. The topic of our study was a factor. Some pastors were alarmed by a study of church finances, and others resisted the idea of having us survey a random sample of members. Refusals were most common among small congregations. Some were suspicious of us, partly because they did not trust their denominational leaders.

SAMPLING LAY MEMBERS

The field workers visited all of the churches. Together with the pastor or another staff member, they filled out the nine-page Congregation Pro-

TABLE A–2.
PARTICIPATION RATES BY DENOMINATION AND REGION

	Percent of Target Churches Included	Percent of Lay Questionnaires Returned
Denomination		
Assemblies of God	75.2	55.2
Southern Baptists	78.4	53.9
Catholics	88.0	60.5
Lutherans	93.6	70.1
Presbyterians	88.8	66.7
Region		
Northeast	88.0	59.1
Midwest	88.5	68.9
South	82.1	57.3
West	81.1	59.5
Total	84.8	61.2

file Booklet and gathered names and addresses for the lay questionnaires. (A copy of the booklet is in Appendix B, and a copy of the lay questionnaire is in Appendix C.) In each church we sent thirty questionnaires to a random sample of lay members. We sent a questionnaire to only one person in any family, and if the church had fewer than thirty families, we sent out fewer than thirty questionnaires. In Assemblies of God congregations, we sent one-half to two-thirds of the questionnaires to members and the others to frequent attenders, depending on the local situation. The questionnaires were in two languages, English and Spanish. We asked the pastor of each church to give us a brief letter of endorsement to be photocopied so that we could include copies with the lay questionnaires.

It was important that *we*, not the pastor, select the thirty persons to be sampled. We insisted on this in every case, but we could not totally prevent tampering with the sample. In a few churches the pastors insisted on helping with the sampling and were thereby able to influence the process.

As Table A–2 shows, the overall response rate for the lay questionnaires was 61.2 percent. During the data collection process, we became aware of the biases in the lay questionnaire response. In general, the more educated and more urban congregations had the highest responses rates. Also, the response rate was much lower in Spanish-speaking than in English-speaking congregations. Within congregations, the more committed and more educated members tended more often to return the questionnaires.

WEIGHTING THE DATA

For all analyses using the congregation as the unit of analysis, we weighted the congregational profiles so as to reinstate the proper size distribution. Large congregations were downweighted and small ones upweighted.

For analyses in which the individual member was the unit of analysis, we weighted the cases according to the size of the member's congregation. Members of small congregations were downweighted and members of large ones upweighted so that they represented *all* members of the denomination. The weights are shown in the *Research Report* (discussed below).

NATIONWIDE TELEPHONE SURVEY

As a check on our parish-based sampling, we commissioned a nationwide telephone survey of church members. We selected the Gallup Organization and bought a random survey of one thousand persons, age eighteen or older, contacted through random telephone dialing. The survey included only persons who said they were Catholic, Baptist, or Lutheran and who also said they belonged to a church or parish near where they live. We specified that the final sample would need at least 175 Baptist, 175 Catholic, and 175 Lutheran church members. The data were gathered during September and October 1993. The Gallup technical staff estimated the completion rate at 62.8 percent; that is, of every 100 eligible persons they reached, 62.8 completed the interview.

RESEARCH REPORT AND DATA

Detailed information on research methods and experiences is found in the *Research Report on the American Congregational Giving Study*, available by writing to Dr. Dean Hoge, Life Cycle Institute, The Catholic University of America, Washington, D.C. 20064. It is about 343 pages long and costs $50. Copies have been deposited in the libraries of the Catholic University of America, Villanova University, and the University of New Mexico.

Three sets of data are available to interested researchers. First are data from the 625 Congregation Profile Booklets. Second are data from the 10,902 mail questionnaires. Third are the data from the 1993 Gallup poll of three denominations. The actual questions and codebooks are found in the *Research Report*. The data are available on diskette by writing to Dr. Charles Zech, Department of Economics, Villanova University, Villanova, PA 19085.

TABLES WITH DETAILED FINDINGS

TABLE A–3.
CHARACTERISTICS OF MEMBERS AS ESTIMATED BY PASTORS*

	Assemblies of God	Baptist	Catholic	Lutheran	Presbyterian
Percent Female	60	59	56	57	59
Age					
39 years old or less	48	38	36	35	35
40 to 59 years old	30	30	32	27	25
60 to 75 years old	16	23	22	24	25
Over 75 years old	4	9	9	12	15
Race					
African American	4	4	2	1	5
Asian American	1	1	2	0	0
Hispanic	10	1	7	0	0

(table continues)

Table A–3 *(continued).*

	Assemblies of God	Baptist	Catholic	Lutheran	Presbyterian
Native American Indian	1	3	0	1	0
White	83	90	87	97	94
Other	1	0	1	0	0
Education					
Less than a high school diploma	14	15	12	12	6
High school diploma	67	60	57	60	49
College degree	19	26	29	28	45
Annual Household Income					
Under $20,000	33	28	25	27	23
$20,000–$49,000	57	56	55	53	52
$50,000 or more	10	15	18	20	25

*In percentages.

TABLE A–4.
AVERAGE CONGREGATIONAL RECEIPTS IN MOST RECENT YEAR

	Assemblies of God	Baptist	Catholic	Lutheran	Presbyterian
Averages of All Cases					
Total Receipts	$165,788	181,547	374,833	143,752	230,543
Receipts from regular offerings or pledges	141,506	142,634	268,387	106,946	159,171
Special offerings and appeals	13,715	32,284	52,355	18,582	32,303
Special fund-raisers	2,089	653	16,565	1,252	1,568
Wills, bequests	710	2,267	11,838	7,143	12,369
Investments	705	2,137	12,515	4,218	11,145
Rents and fees	2,205	950	3,730	3,127	4,493
Judicatory subsidies	178	289	1,423	610	874
Other*	4,817	336	8,594	1,876	8,622
Percent of Cases with an Entry in Each Category					
Receipts from regular offerings or pledges	100	100	100	100	100
Special offerings and appeals	65	97	95	88	96
Special fund-raisers	39	20	66	45	39
Wills, bequests	21	23	63	56	47
Investments	18	27	65	62	76
Rents and fees	22	16	54	55	55
Judicatory subsidies	3	2	15	9	12
Other*	14	6	40	23	25

(table continues)

Table A–4 *(continued).*

	Assemblies of God	Baptist	Catholic	Lutheran	Presbyterian
	Averages for Cases with an Entry in Each Category				
Receipts from regular offerings or pledges	$141,506	142,634	268,387	106,946	159,171
Special offerings and appeals	21,174	33,399	55,177	21,110	33,727
Special fund-raisers	5,299	3,274	25,037	2,809	4,015
Wills, bequests	3,399	9,717	18,708	12,839	26,348
Investments	3,850	7,877	19,347	6,871	14,604
Rents and fees	10,263	5,830	6,903	5,651	8,121
Judicatory subsidies	6,068	11,221	9,577	7,180	7,245
Other*	36,217	5,619	21,307	8,145	35,184

Other is composed mostly of money received from parochial schools, day-care centers, other programs, or separate organizations within the congregation. Dollar amounts listed do not add up exactly to total denominational receipts because of insufficient data.

TABLE A–5.
AVERAGE CONGREGATIONAL EXPENDITURES IN PREVIOUS YEAR*

	Assemblies of God	Baptist	Catholic	Lutheran	Presbyterian
	Averages of All Cases				
Total Expenditures	$164,660	179,894	388,486	148,607	229,659
1. Congregational programs and operations	144,075	149,394	266,510	128,609	195,846
2. Subsidies to schools and programs	1,297	110	80,314	1,146	660
3. Denominational missions	16,260	25,840	34,512	15,221	19,267
4. Other missions	2,429	2,401	7,129	3,330	13,885
Parts 3 + 4 as percentage of total expenditures	11.4	15.7	10.7	12.5	14.4
	Percent of Cases with an Entry				
Subsidies to schools and programs	10	1	70	6	10
Denominational missions	97	100	99	98	99
Other missions	46	52	36	79	86
	Mean Amounts for Those with an Entry				
Subsidies to schools and programs	$12,079	10,103	115,985	19,496	6,268

(table continues)

Table A–5 *(continued)*.

	Assemblies of God	Baptist	Catholic	Lutheran	Presbyterian
Denominational missions	16,777	25,840	34,793	15,547	19,433
Other missions	5,280	4,606	19,614	4,210	16,004

*Dollar amounts listed do not add up exactly to total denominational expenditures because of insufficient data.

TABLE A–6.
SELF-REPORTED CHARACTERISTICS OF LAY MEMBERS*

	Assemblies of God	Baptist	Catholic	Lutheran	Presbyterian
Percent Female	56	59	62	63	62
Age					
30 years or younger	10	6	5	5	5
31 to 40 years old	26	19	21	20	16
41 to 60 years old	42	37	36	38	37
Over 60 years old	22	37	38	37	43
Race					
Asian or Pacific Islander	1	0	5	0	0
Black or African American	2	1	1	0	2
Hispanic	5	1	5	0	0
White	91	96	88	99	97
American Indian	1	1	0	0	0
Biracial or bicultural	1	1	1	0	0
Education					
High school graduate or less	34	29	28	28	16
Some college or technical training	41	39	32	35	31
College graduate	17	20	20	22	30
Graduate or professional degree	8	12	20	15	23
Mean Family Income	$39,210	42,686	45,481	44,034	54,237
Do you have any dependent children under 18 years of age in your household who attend religiously affiliated grammar school or high school five days a week?					
Yes	11	4	13	3	3

(table continues)

Table A–6 *(continued)*.

	Assemblies of God	Baptist	Catholic	Lutheran	Presbyterian
How often do you attend worship services at your church?					
More than once a week	66	51	20	4	7
About once a week	27	36	59	51	53
Two or three times a month or less	7	13	22	45	40

*In percentages.

TABLE A–7.
LEVELS OF GIVING AND ATTITUDES TOWARD GIVING*

	Assemblies of God	Baptist	Catholic	Lutheran	Presbyterian
Household Contribution Last Year					
To your church (not including school tuition or contributions to a capital campaign)*					
Under $100	5	6	11	11	8
$101 to $500	12	13	37	28	25
$501 to $1,000	12	14	32	22	22
$1,001 to $2,500	30	31	15	28	29
$2,501 or more	42	36	4	11	17
Average Household Contributions Last Year					
To your church (not including school tuition or contribution to a capital campaign)	$2,985	2,479	819	1,196	1,635
To your church for a special capital campaign	308	371	239	310	452
To groups or causes in your denomination other than the local congregation	270	201	203	127	156
To all religious groups or causes outside your denomination	305	194	129	138	259
To nonreligious charities, community organizations, or social causes	141	220	244	261	401
Total contributions to the congregation	$3,254	2,810	1,032	1,471	2,036
Total contributions to the congregation and denominational causes	$3,514	3,006	1,225	1,591	2,186

(table continues)

Table A–7 (continued).

	Assemblies of God	Baptist	Catholic	Lutheran	Presbyterian
Total religious giving	$3,820	3,194	1,346	1,727	2,443
Total religious and nonreligious giving	$3,994	3,415	1,599	2,000	2,860
Contributions to the congregation as a percent of household income	8.3	6.9	2.9	3.7	3.9
Total religious giving as a percent of household income	9.9	7.8	3.7	4.4	4.8

*Broken down by percentages.
Based on Lay Questionnaire items 11, 10, 37, 38, 39, 40, and 41.

TABLE A–8.
INDIVIDUAL LEVELS OF SELF-REPORTED GIVING BY MARITAL STATUS*

	Assemblies of God	Baptist	Catholic	Lutheran	Presbyterian
Marital Status					
Single	$1,584	2,004	1,068	1,350	1,378
Married	3,667	3,111	1,126	1,565	2,281
Divorced	1,632	1,510	773	769	1,047
Widowed	1,529	1,700	636	1,301	1,410
If married or living in a committed relationship, does your partner attend the same congregation you do?					
Yes	$3,836	3,289	1,087	1,627	2,395
No	1,907	1,087	1,251	829	1,392

*All columns are significant at .05.
Based on Lay Questionnaire items 51 and 52.

TABLE A–9.
LEVELS OF CATHOLIC GIVING IN DIFFERENT TYPES OF PARISHES

	With Parish School	Cosponsoring a School	No School
	Contributions Reported by the Parish		
Per Member	$154	157	186
Per Household	364	400	401

(table continues)

Table A–9 *(continued).*

	With Parish School	Cosponsoring a School	No School
Self-Reported Contributions per Household			
Households Age 50 or Younger with Children in the School	$1,666	—*	—
All Others Age 50 or Younger	895	792	648
All Households without Children in the School	902	901	1,079

*Less than fifty cases. In the top half of the table, no differences are significant at .05.

TABLE A–10.
SELF-REPORTED GIVING BY ATTITUDES ABOUT DEMOCRATIC DECISION MAKING

	Assemblies of God	Baptist	Catholic	Lutheran	Presbyterian
Do typical members of your congregation have enough influence in decisions about the use of church money?					
Yes	$3,524*	3,005*	1,136	1,568*	2,165*
No	3,052	2,385	1,009	1,459	2,034
Opportunities to serve in lay leadership in my congregation are available, if one is willing to make the commitment.					
Strongly agree	$3,501*	3,013*	1,145*	1,631*	2,273*
Moderately agree	2,767	2,004	1,001	1,279	1,430
Neither agree nor disagree	2,124	1,862	569	528	1,888
Moderately disagree	2,355	—	—	—	—
Strongly disagree	—	—	—	—	—
Important decisions in my congregation are made with open discussion by church leaders and members.					
Strongly agree	$3,294*	3,085*	1,363*	1,558*	2,014*
Moderately agree	3,634	2,591	1,036	1,603	2,243
Neither agree nor disagree	2,476	1,540	866	922	1,329
Moderately disagree	3,236	2,137	1,049	1,304	2,046
Strongly disagree	3,030	—	896	1,476	2,400

(table continues)

Table A–10 *(continued)*.

	Assemblies of God	Baptist	Catholic	Lutheran	Presbyterian
Overall, I approve of the decision-making processes in my *congregation*.					
Strongly agree	$3,294	3,075*	1,220	1,587*	2,152
Moderately agree	3,535	2,482	1,008	1,512	1,974
Neither agree nor disagree	2,526	1,885	844	876	1,559
Moderately disagree	2,662	2,617	952	1,508	1,881
Strongly disagree	—	—	742	—	—
Overall, I approve of the decision-making processes in my *denomination*.					
Strongly agree	$3,143	2,886*	1,373*	1,496	1,589*
Moderately agree	3,671	2,818	920	1,519	2,093
Neither agree nor disagree	3,024	2,219	926	1,358	1,733
Moderately disagree	3,369	3,396	894	1,931	2,666
Strongly disagree	—	3,325	1,264	1,366	3,319

*Column is significant at .05. Groups of less than 50 cases are not shown.
Based on Lay Questionnaire 4, 22, 23, 31, and 32.

TABLE A–11.
CORRELATION OF GIVING WITH AVERAGE ATTITUDES ON DEMOCRATIC DECISION MAKING*

	All	Assemblies of God	Baptist	Catholic	Lutheran	Presbyterian
	Congregational Level: Correlations with Self-Reported Giving to the Congregation					
Do typical members of your congregation have enough influence in decisions about the use of church money? Yes.	—	—	—	—	—	−.20
Do lay members have sufficient influence on the decision making in your denomination? Yes.	—	−.25	−.23	—	—	—
Opportunities to serve in lay leadership in my congregation are						

(table continues)

Table A-11 *(continued)*.

	All	Assemblies of God	Baptist	Catholic	Lutheran	Presbyterian
available, if one is willing to make the commitment.	.31	—	.35	.29	.32	.29
Important decisions in my congregation are made with open discussion by church leaders and members.	.26	—	.19	—	—	—
Overall, I approve of the decision-making processes in my *congregation*.	.26	—	.18	—	—	—
Congregational Level: Correlations with Self-Reported Percent of Family Income Given						
Do typical members of your congregation have enough influence in decisions about the use of church money? Yes.	.18	—	—	—	—	−.25
Do lay members have sufficient influence on the decision making in your denomination? Yes.	—	−.22	—	—	—	−.25
Opportunities to serve in lay leadership in my congregation are available, if one is willing to make the commitment.	—	—	.21	—	—	—
Important decisions in my congregation are made with open discussion by church leaders and members.	.30	—	.19	—	—	—
Overall, I approve of the decision-making processes in my *congregation*.	.26	−.19	—	—	—	—

(table continues)

Table A-11 *(continued).*

	All	Assemblies of God	Baptist	Catholic	Lutheran	Presbyterian
Overall, I approve of the decision-making processes in my *denomination.*	.34	—	.19	.27	—	—

*Correlations weaker than .18 are not shown in this and later tables. All correlations shown are significant at .05.
Based on Lay Questionnaire items 4, 12, 22, 23, 31, and 32.

TABLE A–12.
AVERAGE GIVING TO THE CONGREGATION BY LEVEL OF INVOLVEMENT

	All	Assemblies of God	Baptist	Catholic	Lutheran	Presbyterian
Individual Level: Average Self-Reported Giving to the Church						
Attendance more than once a week		$3,510	3,416	1,267	2,840	3,226
About once a week		2,775	2,469	1,166	1,777	2,406
Two or three times a month		3,304	1,692	543	1,256	1,632
About once a month		—*	—	405	670	1,126
A few times a year		—	—	243	421	710
Never		—	—	—	—	—
Individual Level: Correlations with Giving to the Church						
Frequency of church attendance	.38	.23	.36	.34	.37	.30
Volunteer hours attending programs or events at your church, including Sunday school	.28	—	.21	.18	.26	—
Volunteer hours given at the church to teach, lead, serve on a committee, or help with some task	.27	—	.26	.21	.27	.20

(table continues)

Table A-12 *(continued).*

	All	Assemblies of God	Baptist	Catholic	Lutheran	Presbyterian
Congregational Level: Correlations with Average Self-Reported Giving to the Church						
Average frequency of church attendance	.52	.24	.32	.22	.32	.31
Average volunteer hours attending programs or events at the church, including Sunday school	.60	.20	.38	.29	.26	—
Average volunteer hours given at the church to teach, lead, serve on a committee, or help with some task	.52	—	.39	.30	.25	.25
Congregational Level: Correlations with Self-Reported Percent of Household Income Given						
Average frequency of church attendance	.65	.36	.32	.33	.38	.45
Average volunteer hours attending programs or events at the church, including Sunday school	.70	.41	.38	.20	.27	.27
Average volunteer hours given at the church to teach, lead, serve on a committee, or help with some task	.56	.28	.28	—	.23	.22

*Groups with less than fifty persons are not shown. The breakdown at the top of the table is significant at .05 in all denominations.
Based on Lay Questionnaire items 34, 35, and 36. The Gallup poll had relationships between giving and involvement similar to those shown here.

TABLE A–13.
CORRELATION OF GIVING WITH THREE MEASURES OF CONGREGATIONAL ENTHUSIASM*

	All	Assemblies of God	Baptist	Catholic	Lutheran	Presbyterian
Congregational Level: Correlations of Average Attitudes With Average Self-Reported Giving to the Church						
How much enthusiasm do you feel about the work and programs of your congregation?	.30	—	.31	—	.23	—
If I had to change the congregation I attend, I would feel a great sense of loss.	.26	—	—	—	—	—
The budget priorities of my congregation are appropriate.	.28	—	—	—	—	—
Congregational Level: Correlations of Average Attitudes with Self-Reported Percent of Family Income Contributed						
How much enthusiasm do you feel about the work and programs of your congregation?	.22	—	.28	—	—	—
If I had to change the congregation I attend, I would feel a great sense of loss.	.36	—	.22	.18	.24	.19
The budget priorities of my congregation are appropriate.	.30	−.18	—	—	—	—

*All correlations shown are significant at .05.
Based on Lay Questionnaire items 6, 21, and 24.

TABLE A–14.
CORRELATION OF CONGREGATIONAL GIVING
WITH ITEMS ON THE DENOMINATION*

	All	Assemblies of God	Baptist	Catholic	Lutheran	Presbyterian
Congregational Level: Correlations of Average Attitudes with Self-Reported Giving to the Church						
How much enthusiasm do you feel about the work and program of your denomination?	.33	—	—	—	—	—
Do you read any magazines, news- papers, or newsletters published by your denomination?	—	−.23	—	.41	—	—
Overall, the leadership of my *denomination* is doing a good job.	—	—	—	—	—	−.24
Congregational Level: Correlations of Average Attitudes with Self-Reported Percent of Income Contributed						
How much enthusiasm do you feel about the work and programs of your denomi- nation?	.46	—	.37	—	—	—
Do you read any magazines, news- papers, or newsletters published by your denomination?	.29	—	—	.31	.30	.27
Overall, the leadership of my *denomination* is doing a good job.	.27	—	.19	.20	—	—

*All correlations shown are significant at .05.
Based on Lay Questionnaire items 18, 17, and 30.

TABLE A–15.
CORRELATION OF CONGREGATIONAL GIVING
WITH RELIGIOUS BELIEFS*

	All	Assemblies of God	Baptist	Catholic	Lutheran	Presbyterian
Individual Level: Correlation of Attitudes by Self-Reported Percent of Income Contributed						
Only followers of Jesus Christ can be saved.	.27	—	—	—	—	—
My whole approach to life is based on my religion.	.29	—	.19	.23	.26	.23
Congregational Level: Correlation of Average Attitudes by Self-Reported Giving to the Church						
Only followers of Jesus Christ can be saved.	.53	—	.26	—	—	—
My whole approach to life is based on my religion.	.42	—	.25	—	—	.24
What do you believe the *primary* duty of Christians is? (Percent saying, "Helping others to commit their lives to Christ.")	.60	—	.34	.29	—	—
Congregational Level: Correlation of Average Attitudes by Self-Reported Percent of Family Income Contributed						
Only followers of Jesus Christ can be saved.	.66	—	—	.26	.28	.28
My whole approach to life is based on my religion.	.59	—	.30	.23	.29	.39
What do you believe the *primary* duty of Christians is? (Percent saying, "Helping others to commit their lives to Christ.")	.74	—	.39	.23	—	.27

*All correlations shown are significant at .05.
Based on Lay Questionnaire items 20, 25, and 33.

TABLE A–16.
CORRELATIONS OF INDIVIDUALS' AGREEMENT WITH
DENOMINATIONAL TEACHINGS AND GIVING (GALLUP POLL DATA)*

	Baptists		Catholics	
	Amount	Percent of Income	Amount	Percent of Income
Questions				
(five responses; agreement = 5, disagreement = 1)				
Do you agree or disagree with your denomination's teachings regarding abortion?	—	.22	—	.21
Do you agree or disagree with your denomination's teachings regarding birth control?	—	—	—	—
Do you agree or disagree that women should be eligible for ordination to the ministry or priesthood in your denomination?	−.23	−.28	—	—
Do you agree or disagree that self-described homosexuals should be eligible for ordination to the ministry or priesthood in your denomination?	−.25	−.28	—	—

*All correlations shown are significant at .05. The Gallup poll included only Baptists, Catholics, and Lutherans. Lutherans were removed from this table because their attitudes on these questions had no associations with giving.

TABLE A–17.
CORRELATIONS OF DECISION MAKING WITH AMOUNTS GIVEN*

	All	Assemblies of God	Baptist	Catholic	Lutheran	Presbyterian
Congregational Level: Correlations with Average Self-Reported Giving to the Church						
Percent giving response 1 vs. others ("I give 10 percent or more of my income")	.66	.32	.51	.34	.36	.32
Percent giving responses 1, 2, or 3 vs. others ("I give						

(table continues)

Table A-17 *(continued).*

	All	Assemblies of God	Baptist	Catholic	Lutheran	Presbyterian
10 percent or more of my income," "I decide on a percent annually," or "I decide on an amount annually")	.69	.35	.60	.39	.29	.61
Percent giving response 5 vs. others ("I give what I can afford each week")	−.50	−.31	−.49	−.34	−.48	−.40
Congregational Level: Correlations with Average Self-Reported Percentage of Family Income Given						
Percent giving response 1	.81	.50	.63	.39	.32	.50
Percent giving responses 1, 2, or 3	.67	.48	.60	.29	.20	.26
Percent giving response 5	−.37	−.36	−.42	—	—	—

*Correlations weaker than .18 are not shown.
Responses are to item 11 in Lay Questionnaire.

TABLE A–18.
RELATIONSHIP BETWEEN GIVING AND NUMBER OF PROGRAMS SPONSORED*

	All	Assemblies of God	Baptist	Catholic	Lutheran	Presbyterian
Correlations at Congregational Level						
Number of Programs Offered, by Average Self-Reported Giving to the Church	.45	.35	.36	—	.39	.44
Number of Programs Offered, by Average Self-Reported Percentage of Income Given	.28	—	.25	—	—	—

(table continues)

Table A-18 *(continued).*

	All	Assemblies of God	Baptist	Catholic	Lutheran	Presbyterian
Partial Correlations, Controlling for Church Size						
Number of Programs Offered, by Average Self-Reported Giving to the Church	.52	.36	.22	.21	.36	.30
Number of Programs Offered, by Average Self-Reported Percentage of Income Given	.37	.20	.24	—	—	—

*Correlations weaker than .18 are not shown. All correlations shown are significant at .05.
Based on Congregation Profile Booklet item 14.

TABLE A–19.
CORRELATIONS BETWEEN PLEDGING AND LEVELS OF GIVING*

	All	Assemblies of God	Baptist	Catholic	Lutheran	Presbyterian
Correlations for Individuals						
Lay Questionnaire Responses						
Pledging by Contributions	—	—	.27	.20	.29	.27
Pledging by Percentage of Income Given	—	—	—	—	.18	.26
Gallup Poll Responses						
Pledging by Contributions			—	.27	.22	
Pledging by Percentage of Income Given			—	.16	—	
Correlations for Congregations						
Lay Questionnaire Data						
Percent Pledging by Self-Reported Contributions	—	.36	.51	.31	.53	.40

(table continues)

Table A-19 *(continued)*.

	All	Assemblies of God	Baptist	Catholic	Lutheran	Presbyterian
Percent Pledging by Self-Reported Percentage of Income Given	−.19	.28	.21	—	—	—

*All correlations shown are significant at .05.
Based on Lay Questionnaire item 7 and Gallup poll item 7.

TABLE A–20.
PERCENT OF HOUSEHOLDS MAKING AN ANNUAL PLEDGE*

	Attendance at Worship			
	Monthly or less	2–3 times/ month	Weekly	More than weekly
Assemblies of God	7	25	30	43
Baptist	10	15	28	37
Catholic	29	49	58	57
Lutheran	42	59	68	73
Presbyterian	61	76	87	91

	Church Size			
	200 or fewer	201–400	401–800	801 or more
Assemblies of God	22	31	50	32
Baptist	10	21	38	47
Catholic†	36	51	50	58
Lutheran	32	54	72	88
Presbyterian	65	80	86	90

*All relationships shown are significant at .05.
†For Catholic parishes, the sizes are 1,000 or fewer; 1,001–2,000; 2,001–4,000; and 4,001 or more.

TABLE A–21.
CONGREGATIONAL STEWARDSHIP EFFORTS AND LEVELS OF GIVING*

	All	Assemblies of God	Baptist	Catholic	Lutheran	Presbyterian
Correlations for Congregations: Average Self-Reported Giving to the Church						
Stewardship Strategies in the Last Year						
Used appeals or testimonies during worship services	—	—	.21	—	.24	—
Canvassed every member by phone	—	—	.40	—	—	—
Canvassed every member in person	—	—	.21	—	.25	.26
Used pledge cards or commitment cards	—	—	.32	—	.42	.18
Used numbered envelopes	−.29	.22	.22	—	—	—

*All correlations shown are significant at .05.
Based on Lay Questionnaire item 28.

TABLE A–22.
LEVELS OF GIVING RELATED TO STEWARDSHIP EMPHASIS

	All	Assemblies of God	Baptist	Catholic	Lutheran	Presbyterian
Individual Level: Self-Reported Giving						
Has your congregation actively promoted a "stewardship approach," which teaches the spiritual meaning of how we use God's gifts, to the giving of time, talent, and money?						
Yes, and therefore I am likely to give more.	$3,252*	3,322*	1,456*	1,982*		2,341*

(table continues)

Table A-22 (continued).

	All	Assemblies of God	Baptist	Catholic	Lutheran	Presbyterian
Yes, but it has no effect on my giving.		3,181	2,753	981	1,269	1,944
Yes, and therefore I am likely to give less.		—	—	—	—	—
No, my congregation has not.		4,023	2,819	1,132	2,023	2,099
I don't know.		2,485	1,253	1,444	519	1,101

Congregational Level:
Correlations with Average Self-Reported Giving

	All	Assemblies of God	Baptist	Catholic	Lutheran	Presbyterian
Lay questionnaire: Average saying the congregation uses a stewardship approach to the giving of time, talent, and money	.25	—	.46	.22	.38	.30
Church stewardship efforts reported in the Congregation Profile Booklet						
Program to encourage giving stressed giving a certain percentage of income rather than giving to church programs	.23	—	—	—	—	—
Biblical concept of stewardship stressed year-round	.24	—	—	—	—	—
Used lay testimonials	.29	—	.34	—	.36	—
Used Bible study or Sunday school classes	.26	—	—	—	—	—
Used articles in the church newsletter	—	—	.34	—	—	—

*Column is significant at .05. Data from groups of fewer than ten churches are not shown.
Based on Lay Questionnaire item 10 and Congregation Profile Booklet items 29 and 38.

TABLE A–23.
LEVELS OF GIVING RELATED TO TEACHINGS ABOUT TITHING

	Assemblies of God	Baptist	Catholic	Lutheran	Presbyterian
Giving per Member Reported in the Congregation Profile Booklet					
The church's teaching about tithing:					
The tithe belongs to God and is due God. In addition, Christians should give offerings as they are able.	$631	556	—*	—	719*
The tithe is an ideal to be striven for, but it is not obligatory.	—	572	231	432	538
Giving a proportion of one's income, not tithing, is emphasized.	—	—	146	411	682
Proportionate giving is not emphasized.	—	—	148	—	443
Congregation Level: Average Self-Reported Giving in the Lay Questionnaire					
The church's teaching about tithing:					
The tithe belongs to God and is due God. In addition, Christians should give offerings as they are able.	$2,786	2,437	—*	—	2205*
The tithe is an ideal to be striven for, but it is not obligatory.	—	2,407	1,042	1,242	1,451
Giving a proportion of one's income, not tithing, is emphasized.	—	—	1,127	1,379	1,785
Proportionate giving is not emphasized.	—	—	649	—	1,126

*Figures in the column are significant at .05. Data for groups of fewer than ten congregations are not shown.
Based on Congregation Profile Booklet item 32.

Appendix B.
Congregation Profile Booklet

CONGREGATION PROFILE BOOKLET

To be completed by the pastor or financial officer of the congregation and the research staff person.

CONGREGATION NAME _____

CONGREGATION NO. _____

Life Cycle Institute
A Center for Studies in Religion and Culture
Cardinal Station
Washington, DC 20064
1993

DEFINITION OF TERMS

The word *congregation* includes parishes.

Tithe and *tithing* refer to giving 10 percent of one's income in a strict sense. They do not include proportionate giving or planned giving more generally.

Stewardship refers to teachings or programs emphasizing the biblical concept of stewardship of God's gifts, especially of time, talent, and treasure. It does not mean "raising money" or "appealing for funds" generally.

CLARIFICATIONS ON QUESTIONS

Questions 4 and 5: Presbyterian and Baptist congregations should count all persons on the list of current resident members. Lutherans should use "confirmed communing" members. Persons living out of the area should not be included, nor should persons on a separate "inactive" or "affiliates" list. Catholic parishes should use the number on the parish registry, not an estimate of the total number of Catholics living within the parish boundaries. Assemblies of God congregations should enter the number of members in question 4 and the number of non-member affiliates who attend frequently in question 5.

Question 6: Count the number of households using the same method as in question 4 on counting members. Catholic parishes should use the number of households on the registry list.

Question 21 on Receipts:

> *Line b* includes all special offerings, diocesan and national offerings, capital campaign contributions, special mission collections, and other special projects. Collections designed for a particular purpose beyond the operating budget should be included (e.g., CROP walk or special collection for earthquake victims).

> *Line d* includes one-time gifts or bequests.

> *Line e* includes money earned on investments and annual interest on bank accounts.

Question 24 on Expenditures: It has four lines.

> *Line a* includes all salaries, benefits, maintenance, program supplies, utilities, and other expenses to support the program. Money going into reserves or spent on building projects is included.

> *Line c* includes all denomination-sponsored missions and programs, whether evangelistic, educational, or charitable. Support for denominational colleges and seminaries is included.

> *Line d* includes all other mission, outreach, and charitable projects not sponsored by the denomination. For example, gifts to local homeless projects or charitable efforts sponsored by civic groups are included.

> The total of lines *a, b, c,* and *d* should represent total congregational expenditures for the last budget year.

AMERICAN CONGREGATIONAL STUDY OF RELIGIOUS GIVING
CONGREGATION PROFILE
1993

Name of Congregation _____

Address _____

Zip _____

Phone _____

Name of person giving information _____

Name of field worker _____

Denomination
_____ 1. Assemblies of God   _____ 4. Lutheran
_____ 2. Baptist   _____ 5. Presbyterian
_____ 3. Catholic

I. BACKGROUND

1. When did your last complete fiscal (budget) year end?
    _____ , 199_____

2. When was the congregation founded?
    Year _____

3. Which of the following describes the pastoral staff situation of your
    congregation during the last complete fiscal year?
    _____ a. At least 1 full-time pastor.
    _____ b. Part-time pastor.
    _____ c. Position was temporarily vacant.

4. How many members (youth or older) did the congregation have at
    the end of last year? Do not include non-resident members.

    _____

5. For Assemblies of God only: How many frequent attenders are on the
    mailing list?

    _____

6. How many households were registered or represented in your congregation?

   _____

7. What was the average worship attendance on a typical weekend? Give total for all worship services. Persons attending more than once should be counted only once.

   _____

8. Where is your congregation located?
   a. _____ Large city (over 250,000)
   b. _____ Suburb or large city
   c. _____ Medium city (50,000 to 249,000)
   d. _____ Suburb or medium city
   e. _____ Small city (10,000 to 49,000)
   f. _____ Town or village of 2,500 or more
   g. _____ Town or village under 2,500
   h. _____ Rural

II. MEMBERSHIP COMPOSITION

9. What percent of your members are
   a. Male   _____ %
   b. Female   _____ %

10. What percent of your members are
    a. 18–24 years old   _____ %
    b. 25–39 years old   _____ %
    c. 40–59 years old   _____ %
    d. 60–75 years old   _____ %
    e. Over 75 years old   _____ %

11. What percent of your members are
    a. African-American   _____ %
    b. Asian-American   _____ %
    c. Hispanic   _____ %
    d. Native American Indian _____ %
    e. White   _____ %
    f. Other   _____ %

12. What percent of your members have
    a. A college degree   _____ %
    b. A high school diploma   _____ %
    c. Less than a high school diploma _____ %

13. What percent of your members would you estimate have *household* incomes of
   a. Under $20,000   _____ %
   b. $20,000–$49,999   _____ %
   c. $50,000–$99,999   _____ %
   d. $100,000 or more   _____ %

III. CHURCH PROGRAMS

14. What organized groups did your congregation sponsor last year?

	Regular	Infrequent	Did not Sponsor
a. Children Sunday school or religious education	1	2	3
b. Youth Sunday school or religious education	1	2	3
c. Adult Sunday school or religious education	1	2	3
d. Prayer or study groups at church	1	2	3
e. Prayer or study groups in homes	1	2	3
f. Singles' group	1	2	3
g. Men's group	1	2	3
h. Women's group	1	2	3
i. Senior adults' group	1	2	3
j. Youth group	1	2	3
k. Children's groups	1	2	3
l. Music program other than chancel (normal) choir	1	2	3
m. Other _____	1	2	

15. Did your congregation operate a parochial (five-day-a-week) school last year? (Do not include day care center, preschool or before- or after-school "latchkey" programs.)

   _____ Yes   _____ No

If **YES**: Indicate how much money for the school came from each of the following:

a. Tuition $_____
b. Direct congregation subsidy $_____
c. Indirect congregation subsidy $_____
   (e.g., janitor, utilities)
d. Fund raising $_____
e. Other _____ $_____

16. Did your congregation cosponsor, with other congregations, a parochial school?

_____ Yes   _____ No

If **YES**: How much did your congregation contribute?

a. Direct congregation subsidy $_____
b. Indirect congregation subsidy $_____
c. Tuition scholarship $_____
d. Other _____ $_____

17. Did your congregation sponsor a day care center or preschool?

_____ Yes   _____ No

If **YES**: Was the day care center self-supporting, or did it require a subsidy? (Check only one.)

a. _____ It was self-supporting.
b. _____ It provided a surplus to the congregation.
                                    Amount: $_____
c. _____ It required a subsidy.   Amount: $_____

18. Did your congregation sponsor a before- or after-school "latchkey" program?

_____ Yes   _____ No

If **YES**: Was the latchkey program self-supporting, or did it require a subsidy? (Check only one.)

a. _____ It was self-supporting.
b. _____ It provided a surplus to the congregation.
                                    Amount: $_____
c. _____ It required a subsidy.   Amount: $_____

19. Is space in your facility used, rent free, for any community social programs?

_____ Yes   _____ No

20. Did your congregation sponsor or support at least one missionary last year?

_____ Yes _____ No

IV. RECEIPTS

21. For the last complete fiscal year, how much money came from the following? (Include *all* contributions raised by the congregation.)
    a. Regular offerings or pledges $_____
    b. Special offerings, denominational or diocesan appeals, or other special appeals (Include capital campaign and all appeals made in church, even if money was not recorded in budget.) $_____
    c. Special fundraisers (fairs, bingo, bake sales, etc.) $_____
    d. Wills, bequests, and special gifts $_____
    e. Investments $_____
    f. Rents and fees $_____
    g. Judicatory subsidies (Synod, Diocese, Conference, Presbytery) $_____
    h. Other _____ $_____
                    TOTAL RECEIPTS $_____

22. Was your congregation involved in a capital campaign last year for enlarged facilities, new equipment, other capital improvements, or debt relief?

_____ Yes _____ No

    If **YES**:
    a. What is the total goal? $_____
    b. When did the campaign begin?
            Month _____ , 19_____
    c. What is the target date for receiving all payments?
            Month _____ , 19_____
    d. How much was raised last year? $_____

23. Does your congregation have an endowment?
    _____ No _____ Yes; how much? $_____

    If **YES**, how is the income to be spent? (Check all that apply.)
    a._____ General operating budget
    b._____ Capital improvements
    c._____ Special mission or program
    d._____ Other _____

V. EXPENDITURES

24. How much of the income, from #21, was spent on the following?
    a. Congregation operations, programs, and
       ministry. (Include all staff salaries and benefits.
       Also include money put into reserve.)　　　　　$_____
    b. Subsidies to school, day care, or latchkey
       programs.　　　　　$_____
    c. Denominational mission work and programs.　　$_____
    d. Other mission work and programs.　　　　　$_____
    　　　　　　　　　　TOTAL EXPENDITURES　　$_____

25. Last year, did your congregation have a mortgage debt?
    _____ No　　　　　_____ Yes; annual payment　$_____

VI. BUDGET

26. Who was involved in the preparation of the budget?
    (Check all that apply.)
    a._____　Pastor(s)
    b._____　Paid staff
    c._____　Church governing board or pastoral council
    　　　　　(including committees of the board or council)
    d._____　Finance committee
    e._____　Congregation members via channels other than
    　　　　　as indicated above

27. Who had the *final* say in approving the budget? (Check only one.)
    a._____　Pastor(s)
    b._____　Church governing board or pastoral council
    c._____　Finance committee
    d._____　Congregation members
    e._____　Other _____

28. What strategies were used to encourage lay giving to support the con-
    gregation's operation budget last year? For each of the following (a–g)
    check only one answer.

    a. Sermons on stewardship
       _____ Pastor alone　　　　　_____ Pastor and laypersons
       _____ Laypersons alone　　　_____ Did not have sermons

    b. Appeals or testimonies during worship services
       _____ Pastor alone　　　　　_____ Pastor and laypersons
       _____ Laypersons alone　　　_____ Did not have appeals

c. Distribution of promotional material
_____ At church only   _____ At church and mailed
_____ Mailed to members only _____ Did not distribute
                                          materials

d. Canvassed every member by phone
_____ Pastor alone   _____ Pastor and laypersons
_____ Laypersons alone   _____ Did not canvass every
                                          member by phone

e. Canvassed every member in person
_____ Pastor alone   _____ Pastor and laypersons
_____ Laypersons alone   _____ Did not canvass every
                                          member in person

f. Canvassed some members by phone
_____ Pastor alone   _____ Pastor and laypersons
_____ Laypersons alone   _____ Did not do a partial
                                          canvass by phone

g. Canvassed some members in person
_____ Pastor alone   _____ Pastor and laypersons
_____ Laypersons alone   _____ Did not do a partial
                                          canvass in person

29. In your program to encourage giving, which had the greater emphasis? (Check only one.)
    a._____ Giving a certain percentage of income
    b._____ Supporting the programs of the church
    c._____ Half and half
    d._____ No such program

30. Did your congregation use any of the following? (Check all that apply.)
    a._____ Pledge cards or commitment cards
    b._____ Numbered envelopes
    c._____ Monthly or quarterly receipts
    d._____ Annual receipts
    e._____ Other _____

31. What procedures were used concerning mailing in contributions? (Check one.)
    a._____ Postal envelopes were provided to encourage contributions by mail.
    b._____ Contributions by mail were accepted, but postal envelopes were not provided.
    c._____ Mailing in contributions was discouraged.

VII. TEACHINGS

32. What is your congregation's emphasis with regard to the biblical standard of tithing (i.e., giving at least 10% of income)? (Check one.)
    a._____   The tithe belongs to God and is due God. In addition, Christians should give offerings as they are able.
    b._____   The tithe is an ideal to be striven for by all Christians, but it is not obligatory.
    c._____   Giving a *proportion* of one's income, not tithing, is emphasized.
    d._____   Proportionate giving is not emphasized.

33. Which of the following is emphasized most strongly in your congregation? (Check one.)
    a._____   Helping others to commit their lives to Christ. Personal morality and social actions are secondary to this.
    b._____   Helping to change unjust and oppressive social structures or to alleviate human misery. Whether or not this helps people accept Jesus as Savior is not the primary concern.
    c._____   Following the life and teachings of Jesus as the basis for spiritual growth and personal fulfillment.
    d._____   Faithfully participating in the tradition and sacraments of the Church. Other concerns are secondary to maintaining the historical integrity and continuity of the faith.

34. What is your congregation's approach to interpreting and teaching the biblical meaning of Christian faith and the Church? (Check one.)
    a._____   This is one best or true interpretation, and our congregation or denomination comes *closest* to teaching it.
    b._____   There is one best or true interpretation, but no church can legitimately claim to be closer to it than another.
    c._____   There are probably many interpretations which are equally valid, so many churches may be correctly teaching Christian faith.

35. Does your congregation teach that Christian life should be safeguarded through abstinence from: (Check all that apply.)
    a._____   Certain kinds of food
    b._____   Alcohol and/or tobacco
    c._____   Gambling

    d._____ Certain kinds of entertainment such as movies, night clubs, or dancing

    e._____ Other _____

    f._____ No form of abstinence is stressed

36. In general, how would you describe your congregation's teachings in relation to "typical" churches in your denomination? (Check one.)

    a._____ We allow for more differences of opinion in interpreting Christian teachings than do most churches in our denomination.

    b._____ We are similar to "typical" churches in our denomination.

    c._____ We tend to be stricter in interpreting Christian teachings than are most churches in our denomination.

37. Last year, what emphasis did you give to the biblical concept of stewardship of God's gifts? (Check one.)

    a._____ It received year-round emphasis

    b._____ It received occasional emphasis

    c._____ It was emphasized once

    d._____ No emphasis

38. How was stewardship emphasized? (Check as many as apply.)

    a._____ Sermons

    b._____ Lay testimonials

    c._____ Biblical study or Sunday school classes

    d._____ Articles in the church newsletter

    e._____ Other _____

Appendix C.
Lay Questionnaire

GENERAL INSTRUCTIONS:

Choose only one answer for each item. Fill in the circle next to the response that is most correct for you.

I. YOUR CONGREGATION OR PARISH

1. How long have you been attending worship services at your congregation?

   o Less than 1 year   o 6–10 years
   o 1–2 years   o 11–20 years
   o 3–5 years   o Over 20 years

2. Does your congregation have serious financial needs?

   o Yes, very serious needs
   o Yes, somewhat serious needs
   o No, only routine needs
   o No, it is financially well-off
   o I don't know

3. Do you feel you have enough information about the handling and allocation of funds by the leaders of your congregation?

   o Yes, enough
   o No, not enough
   o No opinion

4. Do you feel that typical members of your congregation have enough influence in decisions about the use of church money?

   o Yes, enough
   o No, not enough
   o No opinion

5. How much do you trust the handling and allocation of funds by the leaders of your congregation?

   o High level of trust
   o Medium level of trust
   o Low level of trust
   o No opinion

6. How much enthusiasm do you feel, in general, about the work and programs of your congregation?
    o Very high enthusiasm
    o Moderately high enthusiasm
    o Moderately low enthusiasm
    o Very low enthusiasm
    o I am generally opposed to them
    o No opinion

7. In the last year did you, or another adult in your family, fill out a pledge card or commitment card regarding church giving for the year?
    o Yes
    o No
    o Don't know

8. Do you approve or disapprove of the practice of asking lay members of the congregation to fill out annual pledge cards or commitment cards regarding church giving for the year?
    o Approve
    o Disapprove
    o Don't know

9. Do you prefer that clergy (priests or ministers) or lay leaders handle financial matters in your congregation?
    o I prefer clergy (priests or ministers).
    o I prefer a combination of clergy and lay leaders.
    o I prefer lay leaders.
    o I have no preference.

10. Has your congregation actively promoted a "stewardship approach" to the giving of time, talent, and money—which teaches the spiritual meaning of how we use God's gifts?
    o Yes, and therefore I am likely to give more.
    o Yes, but it has no effect on my giving.
    o Yes, and therefore I am likely to give less.
    o No, my congregation has not promoted a stewardship approach.
    o I don't know.

11. How do you make decisions about how much money to contribute to your congregation? (Remember to choose only ONE.)
    o I give 10% or more of my income.
    o I decide on a percent of my income annually.

○ I decide on an annual dollar amount.

○ I decide on a weekly dollar amount.

○ I give what I can afford each week.

II. YOUR DENOMINATION

12. Do you feel that lay members have sufficient influence on the decision-making in your denomination?

   ○ Yes, enough

   ○ No, not enough

   ○ No opinion

13. Does your denomination as a whole (nationwide or worldwide) have serious financial needs?

   ○ Yes, very serious needs

   ○ Yes, somewhat serious needs

   ○ No, only routine needs

   ○ No, it is financially well-off

   ○ Don't know

14. Do you feel you have enough information about the handling and allocation of funds by the leaders of your denomination?

   ○ Yes, enough

   ○ No, not enough

   ○ No opinion

15. How much do you trust the handling and allocation of funds by the leaders of your denomination?

   ○ High level of trust

   ○ Medium level of trust

   ○ Low level of trust

   ○ No opinion

16. For supporting mission projects of your denomination, either overseas or in this country, do you prefer that the denomination select and fund the mission projects or do you prefer that you select the mission projects to which to give?

   ○ I prefer that the denomination select the projects.

   ○ I prefer giving to missionaries and projects which I select.

   ○ I prefer a combination of both.

   ○ I have no opinion.

17. Do you read any magazines, newspapers, or newsletters published by your denomination or a denomination-related group (e.g., diocese, synod, association, or convention)?
    - o Yes, regularly   o Yes, but rarely
    - o Yes, occasionally   o No

18. How much enthusiasm do you feel, in general, about the work and programs of your denomination?
    - o Very high enthusiasm
    - o Moderately high enthusiasm
    - o Moderately low enthusiasm
    - o Very low enthusiasm
    - o I am generally opposed to them
    - o No opinion

19. Would you prefer that *congregations* make more decisions about funding programs, such as missions, outreach, and social service, rather than having *denominational* leaders decide?
    - o I would prefer more local decision-making.
    - o I like the situation now.
    - o I would prefer more denominational decision-making.
    - o I have no opinion.

For the next set of items, indicate how much you agree or disagree with each statement.

Choose one of the following options:

	Strongly agree	Moderately agree	Neither agree nor disagree	Moderately disagree	Strongly disagree	I don't know
20. Only followers of Jesus Christ can be saved.	o	o	o	o	o	o
21. If I had to change the congregation I attend, I would feel a great sense of loss.	o	o	o	o	o	o
22. Opportunities to serve in lay leadership in my congregation are available if one is willing to make the commitment.	o	o	o	o	o	o
23. Important decisions about the life of my congregation are made with open discussion by church leaders and members.	o	o	o	o	o	o

	Strongly agree	Moderately agree	Neither agree nor disagree	Moderately disagree	Strongly disagree	I don't know
24. The budget priorities of my congregation are appropriate.	o	o	o	o	o	o
25. My whole approach to life is based on my religion.	o	o	o	o	o	o
26. What religion offers me most is comfort in times of trouble and sorrow.	o	o	o	o	o	o
27. The leaders of my *congregation* are sufficiently accountable to members regarding how church contributions are used.	o	o	o	o	o	o
28. The leaders of my *denomination* are sufficiently accountable to members regarding how church contributions are used.	o	o	o	o	o	o
29. Overall, the pastor of my *congregation* is doing a good job.	o	o	o	o	o	o
30. Overall, the leadership of my *denomination* is doing a good job.	o	o	o	o	o	o
31. Overall, I approve of the decision-making processes in my *congregation*.	o	o	o	o	o	o
32. Overall, I approve of the decision-making processes in my *denomination*.	o	o	o	o	o	o

33. What do you believe the *primary* duty of Christians is? Mark **ONE** statement which comes closest to your belief.
    - o Helping others to commit their lives to Christ.
    - o Helping to change unjust social structures.
    - o Following the teachings of Jesus as the basis for spiritual growth.
    - o Faithfully participating in the tradition and sacraments of the Church.
    - o Cannot choose or don't know.

34. How often do you attend worship services at your church?
    - o Never

○ A few times a year
○ About once a month
○ Two or three times a month
○ About once a week
○ More than once a week

35. How many hours, if any, during the last month have you attended programs or events at your church other than worship services? (If you attended Sunday school, include those hours here.)

○ 0 hours   ○ 6–10 hours
○ 1–2 hours   ○ 11–20 hours
○ 3–5 hours   ○ More than 20 hours

36. How many hours, if any, during the last month have you given volunteer time at your church to teach, lead, serve on a committee, or help with some program, event, or task?

○ 0 hours   ○ 6–10 hours
○ 1–2 hours   ○ 11–20 hours
○ 3–5 hours   ○ More than 20 hours

During the last year, approximately how much money did your household contribute to each of the following? Write your best estimate on the lines provided. Use only whole dollar amounts; *do not use* "cents."

37. To your church, in regular giving (not including school tuition or contributions to a capital campaign). Include the value of material goods as well as monetary gifts. $_____

38. To your church, in giving to a special capital campaign for a new building or a new program. $_____

39. During the last year, approximately how much money did your household contribute to groups or causes in your denomination other than those described in questions 37 and 38? (Include material goods.)

○ $0   ○ $501–$1000
○ $1–$50   ○ $1001–$2000
○ $51–$100   ○ More than $2000
○ $101–$500

40. During the last year, approximately how much money did your household contribute to all religious groups or causes outside your denomination? (Include material goods.)

○ $0   ○ $501–$1000
○ $1–$50   ○ $1001–$2000
○ $51–$100   ○ More than $2000
○ $101–$500

41. During the last year, approximately how much much money did your household contribute to non-religious charities, community organizations, or social causes? (Include material goods.)
    - o $0
    - o $1–$50
    - o $51–$100
    - o $101–$500
    - o $501–$1000
    - o $1001–$2000
    - o More than $2000

Are there situations under which you might consider donating more money to your congregation?

I would give more money to my congregation if . . .

	Yes	No	Don't know
42. it were more spiritually nourishing	o	o	o
43. the preaching were more meaningful	o	o	o
44. it paid more attention to social issues	o	o	o
45. it paid less attention to social issues	o	o	o
46. the worship services were more traditional	o	o	o
47. the worship services were more modern	o	o	o

III. ABOUT YOURSELF

48. What is your sex?
    - o Female
    - o Male

49. What is your age?
    - o Under 18
    - o 18–25
    - o 26–30
    - o 31–35
    - o 36–40
    - o 41–45
    - o 46–50
    - o 51–55
    - o 56–60
    - o 61–65
    - o 66–75
    - o 76 or older

50. How would you describe yourself?
    - o Asian or Pacific Islander
    - o Black or African-American

o Hispanic
o White
o American Indian
o Bi-racial or bi-cultural

51. Which of the following best applies to you currently?
o Single
o Single, but living in a committed relationship
o Married
o Separated
o Divorced
o Widowed

52. If you are currently married or living in a committed relationship, does your partner attend the same congregation you do?
o This does not apply to me.
o Yes
o No

53. What is your highest level of education?
o High school graduate or less
o Some college or technical training
o College graduate
o Graduate degree (graduate or professional)

54. About how much income did your family or household receive last year from all sources, before taxes? (If you do not know, please estimate by marking the category that seems to be closest to your family's income.)

o Less than $10,000   o $50,000–$59,999
o $10,000–$14,999   o $60,000–$69,999
o $15,000–$19,999   o $70,000–$79,999
o $20,000–$29,999   o $80,000–$99,999
o $30,000–$39,999   o $100,000–$149,999
o $40,000–$49,999   o $150,000 and above

55. How many dependent children (under 18 years of age) do you have living with you?
o 0
o 1
o 2
o 3
o 4 or more

56. How many dependent children (under 18 years of age) in your household attend religiously affiliated grammar school or high school
(Catholic, Lutheran, etc.) five days a week?
    o 0
    o 1
    o 2
    o 3
    o 4 or more

THANK YOU FOR YOUR PARTICIPATION!
PLEASE RETURN THE QUESTIONNAIRE IN THE
ENVELOPE PROVIDED.

Notes

INTRODUCTION

1. Lilly Endowment Annual Report (1994): 2
2. The largest association of professional fund-raisers is the National Society for Fund-Raising Executives, with a membership of thirteen thousand. Another important society is the American Association of Fund-Raising Counsel. The three main journals are *The Chronicle of Philanthropy, Non-Profit Times,* and *Fund-Raising Management.*
3. William I. Thomas and Dorothy S. Thomas, *The Child in America: Behavior Problems and Programs* (New York: Alfred A. Knopf, 1928), 572.

CHAPTER 1:
AN OVERVIEW OF CHURCH GIVING

1. Virginia A. Hodgkinson and Murray S. Weitzman, *Giving and Volunteering in the United States* (Washington, D.C.: Independent Sector, 1992), 38. Other estimates vary widely, depending on whether they are based on nationwide polls or on compilations of data from nonprofit organizations. For example, *Giving USA,* an annual report based on nonprofit organizations, estimated religious giving in 1995 at $58.8 billion, or 45 percent of all giving by individuals and organizations in 1994. See *Giving USA* (1995): 85.
2. John L. Ronsvalle and Sylvia Ronsvalle, *The State of Church Giving through 1992* (Champaign, Ill.: empty tomb, 1994). Also see John L. Ronsvalle and Sylvia Ronsvalle, "The State of Church Giving through 1991," in *Yearbook of American and Canadian Churches 1994,* ed. by Kenneth B. Bedell (New York: National Council of Churches, 1994), 12–15.
3. The figures here are approximations. The best research on the question is by Roger Nemeth and Donald Luidens and by D. Scott Cormode. See Roger J. Nemeth and Donald A. Luidens, "Congregational vs. Denominational Giving: An Analysis of Giving Patterns in the Presbyterian Church in the United States and the Reformed Church in America," *Review of Religious Research* 36, 2 (December 1994): 111–22; D. Scott Cormode, "A Financial History of Presbyterian Congregations since World War II," chap. 7 in *The Organizational Revolution: Presbyterians and American Denominationalism,* ed. Milton J. Coalter, John M.

Mulder, and Louis B. Weeks (Louisville, Ky.: Westminster John Knox Press, 1992), 171–98.

4. For a recent analysis of these trends, see Ronald E. Vallet and Charles E. Zech, *The Mainline Church's Funding Crisis: Issues and Possibilities* (Grand Rapids: Wm. B. Eerdmans Publishing Co., 1995).

5. See Tony Campolo, *Can Mainline Denominations Make a Comeback?* (Valley Forge, Pa.: Judson Press, 1995). The most discussed essay on the future of denominations is probably Craig Dykstra and James Hudnut-Beumler, "The National Organizational Structures of Protestant Denominations: An Invitation to a Conversation," in Coalter, Mulder, and Weeks, eds., *Organizational Revolution,* 307–31.

6. For information on the history of American religious giving, see Robert Wuthnow and Virginia A. Hodgkinson, eds., *Faith and Philanthropy in America* (San Francisco: Jossey-Bass, 1990); Loyde H. Hartley, *Understanding Church Finances: The Economics of the Local Church* (New York: Pilgrim Press, 1984); Robert Wuthnow, *The Restructuring of American Religion* (Princeton, N.J.: Princeton University Press, 1988); and Mary J. Oates, *The Catholic Philanthropic Tradition in America* (Bloomington: Indiana University Press, 1995). On Jewish philanthropic giving, see Barry A. Kosmin and Paul Ritterband, eds., *Contemporary Jewish Philanthropy in America* (Savage, Md.: Rowman & Littlefield, 1991). Robert Lynn Wood is now at work on a book tracing the history of American church finances.

7. Two recent books describe the Assemblies of God. See Margaret M. Poloma, *The Assemblies of God at the Crossroads* (Knoxville: University of Tennessee Press, 1989); Edith L. Blumhofer, *Restoring the Faith: The Assemblies of God, Pentecostalism, and American Culture* (Urbana: University of Illinois Press, 1993). Also see Paul B. Tinlin and Edith L. Blumhofer, "Decade of Decline or Harvest? Dilemmas of the Assemblies of God," *Christian Century* 108, 21 (July 10, 1991): 684–87. The estimate that Hispanics comprise 15 percent of the membership is by Blumhofer, *Restoring the Faith,* 2.

8. We thank Sherri Doty of the Assemblies of God Foundation for compiling statistical data.

9. Poloma, *Assemblies of God,* 143.

10. Ibid., 197.

11. *Annual Church Profile* (Nashville: Corporate Planning and Research Department, Southern Baptist Convention Sunday School Board, 1994).

12. Ibid.

13. Jim Castelli and Joseph Gremillion, *The Emerging Parish: The Notre Dame Study of Catholic Life since Vatican II* (San Francisco: Harper & Row, 1987), 53.

14. See Thomas P. Sweetser and Patricia M. Forster, *Transforming the Parish: Models for the Future* (Kansas City, Mo.: Sheed & Ward, 1993), 169. Their estimate of baptized Catholics on the lists is 72 percent. Joseph Claude Harris, on the basis of earlier research, estimated 77 percent. See Joseph Claude Harris, *The Cost of Catholic Parishes and Schools* (Kansas City, Mo.: Sheed & Ward, 1996); Barry A. Kosmin and Seymour P. Lachmann, *One Nation under God: Religion in Contemporary American Society* (New York: Harmony Books, 1993).

15. Jay P. Dolan, ed., *The American Catholic Parish: A History from 1850 to the Present*, 2 vols. (Mahwah, N.J.: Paulist Press, 1987).

16. Data were provided to us by Joseph Claude Harris, who is currently at work on a book on Catholic school finances.

17. Andrew Greeley and William McManus, *Catholic Contributions: Sociology and Policy* (Chicago: Thomas More Press, 1987).

18. Ibid., 70–71.

19. Joseph Claude Harris, "U.S. Catholic Contributions—Up or Down?" *America* (May 21, 1994): 14–16, esp. 15.

20. Ibid., 15.

21. Joseph Claude Harris, *An Estimate of Catholic Household Contributions to the Sunday Offertory Collection during 1991* (Washington, D.C.: Life Cycle Institute, Catholic University of America, 1992), 52. Also see Francis Kelly Scheets, O.S.C., and Joseph Claude Harris, "Is the Sunday Collection in Trouble?" *America* (July 15, 1995): 18–20; they found that total Catholic contributions to parishes increased 3.7 percent from 1991 to 1993.

22. Ibid., 62.

23. Peter A. Zaleski and Charles E. Zech, "Economic and Attitudinal Factors in Catholic and Protestant Religious Giving," *Review of Religious Research* 36, 2 (December 1994): 165.

24. Jeff Rexhausen and Michael J. Cieslak, "Relationship of Parish Characteristics to Sunday Giving among Catholics in the Archdiocese of Cincinnati," *Review of Religious Research* 36, 2 (December 1994): 218–29.

25. See Thomas P. Sweetser, "The Money Crunch: Why Don't Catholics Give More?" *Chicago Studies* 30, 1 (April 1991): 99–111; Sweetser and Forster, *Transforming the Parish*, chap. 11.

26. See examples reported in David Scott, "Where are Catholics When the Collection Basket Is Passed?" *St. Anthony Messenger* (November 1991): 37–41.

27. This paragraph is based on Kenneth W. Inskeep, "Giving Trends in the Evangelical Lutheran Church in America," *Review of Religious Research* 36, 2 (December 1994): 238–44.

28. 1993 CWA Pre-Assembly Report, vol. 2, part 2, "Reports and Records: Financial Stewardship Strategy" (Chicago: ELCA Department of Research and Evaluation, 1993).

29. *Comparative Statistics 1994* (Louisville, Ky.: Research Services, Presbyterian Church (U.S.A.), 1994), 3–4.

30. Milton J. Coalter, John M. Mulder, and Louis B. Weeks, eds., *The Reforming Tradition: Presbyterians and Mainstream Protestantism* (Louisville, Ky.: Westminster John Knox Press, 1992), 236–37.

CHAPTER 2:
CONGREGATIONS AND LAITY: PROFILES

1. The numbers in Table 2–3 are the result of averaging across the congregations. We first calculated the giving per member, household, and attendee within each

congregation, then averaged within the denomination. This is the most defensible method, and the results are slightly different than those obtained by simply dividing average contributions by average membership for entire denominations.

2. Lyle Schaller has noted that most mainline churches operate with a budget of about $15 to $22 per week per worship attender (*Parish Paper* 2, 3 [September 1994]: 1). This coincides with our data. The average contributions per weekly attender were Assemblies of God, $16.87; Baptists, $18.31; Lutherans, $15.85; and Presbyterians, $21.27. Catholic parishes operate at a much lower cost: $5.44 per week per attender. Knowledge of these lower costs among Catholics may be a factor in the lower level of Catholic giving.

3. Two of the theorists are Dean Kelley and Laurence Iannaccone. See Dean M. Kelley, *Why Conservative Churches Are Growing: A Study in the Sociology of Religion*, 2d ed. (New York: Harper & Row, 1977); Laurence R. Iannaccone, "Why Strict Churches Are Strong," *American Journal of Sociology* 99, 5 (March 1994): 1180–1211.

4. The General Social Survey, an annual nationwide poll conducted by the National Opinion Research Center, inquired into self-reported contributions "to your religion" in 1987, 1988, and 1989. The means were $927 for Assemblies of God, $729 for Southern Baptists, $289 for Catholics, $467 for the Evangelical Lutheran Church in America, and $522 for Presbyterians. Even allowing for the effects of inflation, our survey respondents reported higher giving. See Dean R. Hoge and Fenggang Yang, "Determinants of Religious Giving in American Denominations: Data from Two Nationwide Surveys," *Review of Religious Research* 36, 2 (December 1994): 123–48. A 1992 nationwide survey by Independent Sector charted self-reported *total* contributions—not just contributions to churches—by people of different denominations who reported that they had contributed to religion among other causes. For Baptists, the total contributions averaged $1,215; for Catholics, they averaged $859; for Lutherans, they averaged $1,120; and for Presbyterians, they averaged $1,267. Contributions by these persons to their churches would be lower than these total amounts. See Virginia A. Hodgkinson and Murray S. Weitzman, *Giving and Volunteering in the United States* (Washington, D.C.: Independent Sector, 1992), 110–11. In a 1987 survey of Catholics, self-reported contributions were somewhere between $482 and $502 per family. See William D'Antonio, James Davidson, Dean Hoge, and Ruth Wallace, *American Catholic Laity in a Changing Church* (Kansas City, Mo.: Sheed & Ward, 1989), 152.

5. We can estimate the bias in our lay survey by comparison with the Gallup poll. It had identical questions and a maximally similar sample in three denominations—Baptist, Catholic, and Lutheran. Our lay questionnaires came from persons in each denomination who are older, slightly more educated, and more affluent than the Gallup poll respondents. They also attend church more often. In our lay questionnaire, the reported levels of giving to one's congregation (total of regular giving and giving to special campaigns) were $2,810 for Baptists, $1,032 for Catholics, and $1,471 for Lutherans. In the Gallup poll, these amounts were $1,994 for Baptists, $678 for Catholics, and $1,107 for Lutherans.

6. These figures are consistent with the results of the Notre Dame Study of Catholic Parishes in 1983. It included a survey of registered parishioners in a rep-

resentative sample of parishes. The average self-reported giving to the parish was $559 per household, and the average giving to all Catholic causes outside the parish was $274 per household. See Dean R. Hoge and Douglas L. Griffin, *Research on Factors Influencing Giving to Religious Bodies* (Indianapolis: Ecumenical Center for Stewardship Studies, 1992), 48.

CHAPTER 3:
INDIVIDUAL FACTORS INFLUENCING GIVING

1. We remind the reader that our hypotheses are solely about giving to one's church, not about other forms of religious giving or giving to other, nonlocal religious causes. The determinants of these forms of giving will be investigated elsewhere. A recent study in the United Church of Canada looked separately at giving to the local church and giving to the denominational Mission and Service Fund, and it found that giving to the denominational programs was influenced by attitudes toward the national program and satisfaction with the United Church of Canada as a whole, whereas giving to the local church was not. See Reginald W. Bibby, *Unitrends: A Summary Report Prepared for the Department of Stewardship Services* (Toronto: Department of Stewardship Services, United Church of Canada, 1994). The distinction between local and mission giving was not made in the present analysis.

2. All research studies of churches have found that a small number of members contribute a disproportionate amount—that is, distributions are skewed, and about 20 percent of the members typically give about 80 percent of the money. For reviews of research, see Dean R. Hoge and Douglas L. Griffin, *Research on Factors Influencing Giving to Religious Bodies* (Indianapolis: Ecumenical Center for Stewardship Studies, 1992). Also see the special issue of the *Review of Religious Research* (36, 2 [December 1994]) on financial contributions to churches, which contains reviews of past research.

3. A 1994 study of Catholic parishes by the Educational Testing Service (ETS) found that the average regular household contribution in parishes with schools was $281. It was highest in the Plains states ($357), followed by the Great Lakes states ($327). It was lowest in New England ($199). In all Catholic parishes, with or without schools, the average regular household contribution was $254. See Educational Testing Service, *Toward Shaping the Agenda: A Study of Catholic Religious Education/Catechesis* (Washington, D.C.: Washington Office of Educational Testing Service, 1994). Further analysis of the ETS data was done and shared with us by Joseph Claude Harris of Seattle, Washington. See Francis Kelly Scheets, O.S.C., and Joseph Claude Harris, "Is the Sunday Collection in Trouble?" *America* (July 15, 1995): 18–20; Joseph Claude Harris, *The Cost of Catholic Parishes and Schools* (Kansas City, Mo.: Sheed & Ward, 1996).

Southern Baptist giving reported by the denominational research office in 1991 was highest in the eastern seaboard states and lowest in the southern part of the Midwest (from Oklahoma eastward to Tennessee and Kentucky). See *Southern*

Baptist Handbook 1992 (Nashville: Southern Baptist Convention Sunday School Board, 1992), 51.

4. As a reminder to nonstatistical readers, a correlation is a statistic measuring how strongly two variables are related to each other. Correlations vary from -1 to $+1$, and correlations near to 0 indicate that the two variables in question are not related at all. As a rule of thumb, correlations between $-.18$ and $+.18$ are too weak to have practical importance. Correlations of .25 or more, either plus or minus, are called "moderately strong" in the text. Correlations do not prove anything about causation; they merely tell us how strongly one variable is associated with another. Inferences about causation must be based on other information. A negative sign on a correlation indicates that one variable tends to be high when the other is low and vice versa. See Hubert M. Blalock, Jr., *Social Statistics,* 2d ed. (New York: McGraw-Hill Book Co., 1972).

CHAPTER 4:
CONGREGATIONAL FACTORS
AND COMBINED FACTORS INFLUENCING GIVING

1. Other research has looked at Catholic parish size with inconsistent findings. Cieslak found that per-household giving was higher in smaller parishes in the diocese of Rockford, Illinois. However, Rexhausen and Cieslak failed to find this pattern in the Archdiocese of Cincinnati. In a nationwide study, Michael Welch found the opposite—larger parishes had higher per-household giving. See Michael J. Cieslak, "Parish Responsiveness and Parishioner Commitment," *Review of Religious Research* 26, 2 (December 1984): 132–47; Jeff Rexhausen and Michael J. Cieslak, "Relationship of Parish Characteristics to Sunday Giving among Catholics in the Archdiocese of Cincinnati," *Review of Religious Research* 36, 2 (December 1994): 218–29; Michael R. Welch, "Participation and Commitment among American Catholic Parishioners," chap. 16 in *Church and Denominational Growth,* ed. David A. Roozen and C. Kirk Hadaway (Nashville: Abingdon Press, 1993), 324–45.

2. This theory is stated in economic models such as the club model. See Peter A. Zaleski and Charles E. Zech, "Determinants of Contributions to Religious Organizations," *American Journal of Economics and Sociology* 51 (1992): 459–72; Dennis H. Sullivan, "Simultaneous Determination of Church Contributions and Church Attendance," *Economic Inquiry* 23 (1985): 309–20.

3. See Dean M. Kelley, *Why Conservative Churches Are Growing: A Study in the Sociology of Religion,* 2d ed. (New York: Harper & Row, 1977); Laurence R. Iannaccone, "Why Strict Churches Are Strong," *American Journal of Sociology* 99, 5 (March 1994): 1180–1211.

4. Several statistical clarifications are needed here. In preliminary analysis, we tested regressions at both the congregational level and the individual level. The former came out clearest and are depicted here. Researchers interested in other outcomes will find them in the *Research Report on the American Congregational Giving Study.* See Appendix A on how to acquire the report.

All congregations that returned fewer than ten lay questionnaires were deleted from the analysis. The average number of questionnaires in the remaining churches was 18.5. We experimented with several dependent variables and selected the mean of self-reported household giving (square root) in each church. Apparently, the measures of giving derived from the Congregational Profile Booklet contained excessive errors, thus reducing their analytical usefulness. Multicollinearity was avoided by removing several predictor variables closely associated with others. We tested for heteroskedasticity and adjusted the regressions where it was found to exist.

5. A good catalog of theories about differences between Protestants and Catholics is given by Thomas P. Sweetser, "The Money Crunch: Why Don't Catholics Give More?" *Chicago Studies* 30, 1 (April 1991): 99–111; Thomas P. Sweetser and Patricia M. Forster, *Transforming the Parish: Models for the Future* (Kansas City, Mo.: Sheed & Ward, 1993), chap. 11. Also see Andrew Greeley and William McManus, *Catholic Contributions: Sociology and Policy* (Chicago: Thomas More Press, 1987); Tim Unsworth, "Parish Finances: Are Catholics Reluctant to Pay Their Own Way?" *U.S. Catholic* (September 1987): 32–38. On trends in Catholic giving, see Francis Kelly Scheets, O.S.C., and Joseph C. Harris, "Is the Sunday Collection in Trouble?" *America* (July 15, 1995): 18–20.

CHAPTER 5: TITHING, PLEDGING, AND OFFERING CHURCHES: CASE STUDIES

1. Max Weber, *The Protestant Ethic and the Spirit of Capitalism* (1905; reprint, New York: Charles Scribner's Sons, 1958).

2. See Teresa Odendahl, *Charity Begins at Home: Generosity and Self-Interest among the Philanthropic Elite* (New York: Basic Books, 1990); Joseph R. Mixer, *Principles of Professional Fundraising* (San Francisco: Jossey-Bass, 1993); Russ Alan Prince and Karen Maru File, *The Seven Faces of Philanthropy* (San Francisco: Jossey-Bass, 1994).

CHAPTER 6: MOTIVATION AND THEOLOGY

1. The classic statement of this is Kenneth E. Boulding, *The Economy of Love and Fear: A Preface to Grants Economics* (Belmont, Calif.: Wadsworth Publishing Co., 1973). Boulding argues that a gift is one instance of the larger class of one-way payments of money, a class including robbery and payment of protection money. We agree that gift giving should not be seen as different from other one-way payments of money.

2. See Max Weber, *The Theory of Social and Economic Organization*, introduction by Talcott Parsons (Glencoe, Ill.: Free Press, 1947), 115–16.

3. See Douglas W. Johnson, *The Tithe: Challenge or Legalism?* (Nashville: Abingdon Press, 1984); John Reumann, *Stewardship and the Economy of God* (Grand Rapids: Wm. B. Eerdmans Publishing Co., 1992); Douglas John Hall, *The Steward: A Biblical Symbol Come of Age*, rev. ed. (Grand Rapids: Wm. B. Eerdmans Publishing Co.,

1990); Ronald E. Vallet, *Stepping Stones of the Steward* (Grand Rapids: Wm. B. Eerd-
mans Publishing Co., 1989); C. H. Dodd, *The Parables of the Kingdom*, rev. ed. (New
York: Charles Scribner's Sons, 1961); Bruce C. Birch and Larry L. Rasmussen, *The
Predicament of the Prosperous* (Philadelphia: Westminster Press, 1978).

4. The conception that giving tithes is like paying an insurance premium came
up in some interviews but always was attributed to someone else. No pastors
taught it. Yet the comparison undoubtedly exists among laity. It was uncovered in
a sociological study of factory workers in the Eastern United States: "When asked
why, given their skepticism about . . . many aspects of Christian theology, workers still attend church, the commonest explanation is insurance. Many are doubt-
ful about the official view of heaven and hell, but why take a chance? A couple of
hours a week and couple of dollars for the collection are a small price to pay
should the church's account of life after death prove correct" (David Halle, *America's Working Man* [Chicago: University of Chicago Press, 1984], 269).

5. John Wesley, as quoted in William Warren Sweet, *Methodism in American
History* (Nashville: Methodist Book Concern, 1954), 159.

6. See Teresa Odendahl, *Charity Begins at Home: Generosity and Self-Interest
among the Philanthropic Elite* (New York: Basic Books, 1990); Susan A. Ostrander
and Paul G. Schervish, "Giving and Getting: Philanthropy as a Social Relation," in
Critical Issues in American Philanthropy, ed. Jon Van Til and associates (San
Francisco: Jossey-Bass, 1990), 67–98.

7. Jewish synagogues in the United States differ from Christian churches in
that a majority of the synagogues sell annual memberships to families or individuals. Then, on the High Holy Days, when synagogues are filled, only membership
holders are assured of seats. (Theoretically, only membership holders are admitted, although in practice this is not always enforced.) Also, membership holders
may enroll their children in the school or language program at a lower tuition
rate. Annual membership is usually on a sliding cost scale, depending on age and
income. For a businessman in his fifties, a yearly family membership would typically cost between $600 and $1,200. For younger persons, single persons, and
lower-income persons, membership would cost less. The concepts of an annual
membership fee and annual dues are rejected by Protestants and Catholics. The
theological and traditional norms undergirding this difference between synagogues and Christian churches need to be studied. See Barry A. Kosmin and Paul
Ritterband, eds., *Contemporary Jewish Philanthropy in America* (Savage, Md.: Rowman & Littlefield, 1991).

8. See John Ronsvalle and Sylvia Ronsvalle, *Behind the Stained Glass Window:
Money Dynamics in the Church* (Grand Rapids: Baker Book House, 1996).

9. The work of William James is basic to research on the extent of the self. See
his *Psychology: The Briefer Course* (New York: Henry Holt, 1910), 177–205. Excerpts
are given in William James, "The Self," chap. 3 in *The Self in Social Interaction*, ed.
C. Gordon and K. Gergen, (New York: John Wiley & Sons, 1968), 41–49.

10. Garrett Hardin, "Discriminating Altruisms," *Zygon: Journal of Religion and
Science* 17 (1982): 163–86. Also see Howard Margolis, *Selfishness, Altruism, and
Rationality* (New York: Cambridge University Press, 1982); and Roger A.

Lohmann, *The Commons: New Perspectives on Nonprofit Organizations and Voluntary Action* (San Francisco: Jossey-Bass, 1992).

11. Jane A. Piliavin and Hong-Wen Chang, "Altruism: A Review of Recent Theory and Research," *Annual Review of Sociology* 16 (1990): 27–65. Also see E. Gil Clary and Mark Snyder, "A Functional Analysis of Altruism and Prosocial Behavior," in *Review of Personality and Social Psychology*, ed. M. S. Clark, (Newbury Park, Calif.: Sage Publications, 1991), 12:3–15.

12. We expect that motives for religious giving develop during childhood and adolescence, much as Lawrence Kohlberg has found moral thinking to develop. See Lawrence Kohlberg, "Moral Stages and Moralization: The Cognitive-Developmental Approach," chap. 2 in *Moral Development and Behavior*, ed. Thomas Lickona (New York: Holt, Rinehart & Winston, 1976), 31–53. The relationship between moral development and giving is an important topic that needs study.

13. Hall, *The Steward*.

14. For a review of research on the effect of these programs, see Dean R. Hoge and Douglas L. Griffin, *Research on Factors Influencing Giving to Religious Bodies* (Indianapolis: Ecumenical Center for Stewardship Studies, 1992), 137ff. For additional, Catholic research showing the effect of stewardship programs, see Joseph C. Harris, "An Analysis of Catholic Sacrificial Giving Programs in Seattle, Washington," *Review of Religious Research* 36, 2 (December 1994): 230–37; and Jeff Rexhausen and Michael J. Cieslak, "Relationship of Parish Characteristics to Sunday Giving among Catholics in the Archdiocese of Cincinnati," *Review of Religious Research* 36, 2 (December 1994): 218–29. In addition, we have seen unpublished reports evaluating Catholic stewardship programs that show a modest positive effect on giving.

15. See Thomas W. Gornick, *Stewardship: Faith or Money? Survey of Roman Catholic Dioceses*, printed report (Dublin, Ohio: Thomas W. Gornick Co., 1995).

CHAPTER 7:
CONCLUSIONS

1. As our study progressed, we were sometimes asked whether recent sexual scandals within the Catholic priesthood affected levels of Catholic giving. We have no information. Our survey instrument was completed before these scandals became national news and hence did not include questions about them. All we can say is that denominational issues outside the local congregation or parish *generally* are not the foremost factors influencing what people give to their churches.

2. See Douglas W. Johnson and George W. Cornell, *Punctured Preconceptions: What North American Christians Think about the Church* (New York: Friendship Press, 1972). For further analysis of the data, see Dean R. Hoge and David T. Polk, "A Test of Theories of Protestant Church Participation and Commitment," *Review of Religious Research* 21, 3 (summer 1980): 315–29.

3. See Laurence R. Iannaccone, "Why Strict Churches Are Strong," *American Journal of Sociology* 99, 5 (March 1994): 1180–1211, esp. 1188.

4. For research on Catholic attitude trends regarding church leadership, see

William V. D'Antonio, James D. Davidson, Dean R. Hoge, and Ruth A. Wallace, *Laity American and Catholic: Transforming the Church* (Kansas City, Mo.: Sheed & Ward, 1995).

5. Lyle Schaller's main works on stewardship are *Activating the Passive Church: Diagnosis and Treatment* (Nashville: Abingdon Press, 1981) and *Forty-four Ways to Expand the Financial Base of Your Congregation* (Nashville: Abingdon Press, 1989). Several works by other consultants should also be mentioned: Kennon L. Callahan, *Giving and Stewardship in an Effective Church* (San Francisco: Harper Collins, 1992); Kennon L. Callahan, *Effective Church Finances* (San Francisco: Harper-Collins, 1992); Richard B. Cunningham, *Creative Stewardship* (Nashville: Abingdon Press, 1979); Douglas W. Johnson, *Finance in Your Church* (Nashville: Abingdon Press, 1986); Loren B. Mead, *Transforming Congregations for the Future* (Washington, D.C.: Alban Institute, 1994); Herb Miller, *Consecration Sunday Stewardship Program* (Lubbock, Tex.: Net Press, 1988). Catholic works include Patricia M. Forster and Thomas P. Sweetser, *Transforming the Parish: Models for the Future* (Kansas City, Mo.: Sheed & Ward, 1993); Patrick J. Brennan, *Re-Imagining the Parish* (New York: Crossroad, 1990); Patrick J. Brennan, *Parishes That Excel: Models of Excellence in Education, Ministry, and Evangelization* (New York: Crossroad, 1992).

6. Schaller, *Forty-four Ways to Expand*, 35. Both of these statements agree with our findings reported in chapter 2: The less evangelical the denomination, the higher the percentage of members' giving that will go outside the church; the more affluent the family, the higher the percentage of the family's giving that will go outside the church.

7. Schaller, *Forty-four Ways to Expand*, 47.

8. Kennon Callahan, for example, insists that stewardship education is a long-term, not an annual, effort. He recommends that stewardship education and annual drives be planned four years at a time, not year by year, so as to have continuity and to include all the necessary elements. Each annual stewardship campaign should be seen in the context of years to come. According to Callahan, if a church hires a professional fund-raising consultant, it should be for four years, not one (See Callahan, *Effective Church Finances*, chap. 2). We agree with him in criticizing promoters of stewardship programs that have a one-year, in-and-out philosophy.

9. In Harris polls, the average decline in confidence for nine institutions (television news, medicine, the military, the press, organized religion, major companies, Congress, the executive branch of government, and organized labor) was twenty percentage points from 1966 to 1979, and the trend has continued since (See the magazine *Public Opinion* [January 1980]: 42). Another series of polls on confidence in institutions, running from 1973 to 1989, found a similar decline (See Richard G. Niemi, John Mueller, and Tom W. Smith, *Trends in Public Opinion* [New York: Greenwood Press, 1989]). The *Washington Post* compiled survey trend data on trust in government and other American institutions and found a massive fifty-one-point decline between 1964 and 1995 in favorable responses to the question "How much of the time do you trust the government in Washington to do the right thing?" (See Richard Morin and Dan Balz, "Americans Losing Trust in Each Other and Institutions," *Washington Post*, January 28, 1996, A1, A6, A7).

Index of Names and Subjects

Note: Page numbers followed by *t* represent tables; those followed by *f* represent figures.